BAKHTIN AND GENRE THEORY
IN BIBLICAL STUDIES

Society of Biblical Literature

Semeia Studies

Gale A. Yee, General Editor

Number 63

BAKHTIN AND GENRE THEORY
IN BIBLICAL STUDIES

BAKHTIN AND GENRE THEORY IN BIBLICAL STUDIES

Edited by

Roland Boer

Society of Biblical Literature
Atlanta

BAKHTIN AND GENRE THEORY
IN BIBLICAL STUDIES

Copyright © 2007 by the Society of Biblical Literature

Library of Congress Cataloging-in-Publication Data

Bakhtin and genre theory in biblical studies / edited by Roland Boer.
     p. cm. — (Society of Biblical Literature Semeia studies ; no. 63)
    Includes bibliographical references and indexes.
    ISBN: 978-1-58983-276-3 (pbk. : alk. paper)
    1. Bible—Study and teaching—Congresses. 2. Bakhtin, M. M. (Mikhail Mikhailovich), 1895–1975—Congresses. I. Boer, Roland, 1961–. II. Society of Biblical Literature. Meeting (2004 : San Antonio, Tex.).
    BS600.3.B35 2007
    220.6'6092—dc22
                                           2007035329

15 14 13 12 11 10 09 08 07   5 4 3 2 1
Printed in the United States of America on acid-free, recycled paper conforming to ANSI/NISO Z39.48-1992 (R1997) and ISO 9706:1994 standards for paper permanence.

CONTENTS

RESPONSES

ABBREVIATIONS

AB	Anchor Bible
AB	Anchor Bible Reference Library
ABD	*Anchor Bible Dictionary.* Edited by David Noel Freedman. 6 vols. New York: Doubleday, 1992.
AOAT	Alter Orient und Altes Testament
AS	*Aramaic Studies*
Bib	*Biblica*
BibInt	*Biblical Interpretation*
BIS	Biblical Interpretation Series
BibOr	Biblica et orientalia
BTB	*Biblical Theology Bulletin*
BZAW	Beihefte zur Zeitschrift für die alttestamentliche Wissenschaft
BZNW	Beihefte zur Zeitschrift für die neutestamentliche Wissenschaft
CBQ	*Catholic Biblical Quarterly*
CCSL	Corpus Christianorum: Series latina
FOTL	Forms of the Old Testament Literature
HBT	*Horizons in Biblical Theology*
HUCA	*Hebrew Union College Annual*
IBC	Interpretation: A Bible Commentary for Teaching and Preaching
ICC	International Critical Commentary
IDB	*The Interpreter's Dictionary of the Bible.* Edited by George A. Buttrick. 4 vols. Nashville: Abingdon, 1962.
JAAR	*Journal of the American Academy of Religion*
JANESCU	*Journal of the Ancient Near Eastern Society of Columbia University*
JBL	*Journal of Biblical Literature*
JCS	*Journal of Cuneiform Studies*
JNSL	*Journal of Northwest Semitic Languages*
JR	*Journal of Religion*

JSJSup	Supplements to Journal for the Study of Judaism
JSNTSup	Journal for the Study of the New Testament Supplement Series
JSOT	*Journal for the Study of the Old Testament*
JSOTSup	Journal for the Study of the Old Testament Supplement Series
NCB	New Century Bible
NIB	*The New Interpreter's Bible*
NovTSup	Supplements to Novum Testamentum
OBO	Orbis biblicus et orientalis
OTL	Old Testament Library
PMLA	*Proceedings of the Modern Language Association*
PRSt	*Perspectives in Religious Studies*
REJ	*Revue des études juives*
RevExp	*Review and Expositor*
SBLAcBib	Society of Biblical Literature Academia Biblica
SBLDS	Society of Biblical Literature Dissertation Series
SBLSymS	Society of Biblical Literature Symposium Series
SBT	Studies in Biblical Theology
SemeiaSt	Semeia Studies
SJOT	*Scandinavian Journal of the Old Testament*
SNTSMS	Society for New Testament Studies Monograph Series
SP	Sacra pagina
TTS	Theologische Texte und Studien
WBC	Word Biblical Commentary
WUNT	Wissenschaftliche Untersuchungen zum Neuen Testament

Introduction: Bakhtin, Genre and Biblical Studies

Roland Boer

This volume seeks to bring about a rather gentle meeting between genre theory in biblical studies and the work of Mikhail Bakhtin, the great Soviet-era Russian literary critic. The collection grew initially out of a session at the Society of Biblical Literature's Annual Meeting in San Antonio (2004) entitled "Bakhtin and Genre." It has since grown beyond this base with a number of additional essays. As the title suggests, it brings the insights of Mikhail Bakhtin to bear on the question of genre in biblical texts.

In many respects, Bakhtin needs little introduction. His personal story is integral to his theory and practice of literary criticism. The fact that he had to write covertly beneath the hot blanket of Stalinist censorship only added to his appeal in a West hungry for dissidents in the Soviet Union. One path was of course to write under the pseudonyms of his friends, most notably Valentin Voloshinov, and the debate has gone to and fro as to how much of the more explicitly heterodox Marxist works that appeared under Voloshinov's name were in fact Bakhtin's, especially the book written in the 1920s, *Marxism and the Philosophy of Language* (2006). By comparison, *Rabelais and His World* (1984a), *Problems of Dostoyevsky's Poetics* (1984b) and *The Dialogic Imagination* (1982) seem much more tame, at least on the surface. Many critics opt for the double-headed "Bakhtin and Voloshinov" when referring to their ideas, preferring to leave what is murky murky, whereas others prefer the less overtly Marxist side, although it hovers quietly in the background.

Before I proceed, however, some definitions of key concepts from Bakhtin are in order, some of which will appear in the essays. We may distinguish roughly between three groups of such terms: those that identify specific features of narrative; the ones that develop a theory of language out of literature; and the overtly political terms. As for the literary features, the first is the contrast between *monologic* and *dialogic* narrative. As the words suggest, whereas monologic narrative (and indeed truth) proceeds as though there were one dominant voice, dialogic narrative has at least two. He refers not merely to the explicit dialogue between characters but more to the quietly insistent "voice" or indeed "voices" that pick at and undermine the dominant one in a text. This distinction between monologic and dialogic narrative has been used most thoroughly in biblical studies by Robert Polzin's three studies of the Deuteronomistic History (1989; 1990; 1993). Bakhtin, however, goes further, arguing that meaning itself is generated through dialogism.

The second literary feature that appears at a number of points in this collection of essays is the *chronotope*. The word means "time space," defined by Bakhtin as "the intrinsic connectedness of temporal and spatial relationships that are artistically expressed in literature" (Bakhtin 1982: 84). The chronotope comes into play when an author creates new fictional worlds. Yet those worlds must relate in some way to the actual world in which the author happens to live. The intersection between actual and fictional worlds happens by means of the chronotope.

The second group of terms focus on the question of language. To begin with, there is *polyphony*, which marks the multiplicity of voices that one finds in any one text. This multiplicity may be identified in terms of characters, but more often than not polyphony cuts across characters. The reason for such crossing over is due to the *unfinalizability* of any character, or indeed any human being. He or she always remains partially hidden, never fully revealed or complete—a position that he unwittingly shares with Ernst Bloch's idea of the *homo absconditus*. Of course, the unfinalizability of characters and persons is one factor in the polyphony of a text. Later on, in his perpetual effort to redefine and clarify his thought, Bakhtin would introduce the term *heteroglossia* into his theory of language and literary criticism. *Heteroglossia*, literally "other tongues," designates the common but extralinguistic features of all languages, features such as ideology, assessment and perspective. Always in a state of flux, language perpetually escapes the efforts of grammarians, politicians and educationalists to define and contain language. All of these terms—unfinalizability, polyphony, dialogism, and heteroglossia—are part of an effort not merely to produce a theory and practice of the interpretation of texts, but also a philosophy of language. Only as words bounce, ricochet and rebound in utterance, transmission and reception does meaning begin to take place.

All these definitions begin with the individual and then move on to the problem of how they interact. Yet Bakhtin is not a theoretician of liberalism and its sacrosanct individual with her or his rights. He is also a distinctly political writer, as the third group of terms shows. It is with his category of the *carnivalesque* that we see an explicit collective focus that is more implicit with the terms I have discussed above. The carnivalesque comes to the fore in

Rabelais and His World (1984a) and the last part of *Problems of Dostoyevsky's Poetics* (1984b). In his study of the passing medieval carnival, he points out that the crowd is not merely a gathering of individuals; rather, the carnival becomes a different entity, a whole, with a subversive political and social organization. Apart from the slippery territory of *Marxism and the Philosophy of Language* (2006), the Rabelais book is Bakhtin's most overtly political book. In the carnival we also find the *grotesque*, for here we find a concern with eating, pissing, shitting, sex and death; in short with bodies as pulsating, heaving and living entities—the body of the carnival crowd as well as the individuals that are created out of this collective.

Bakhtin continues to be immensely influential in literary criticism. Apart from interest in his writings directly, his thought is also one of the influences on postcolonial criticism, and increasingly on biblical criticism, as this volume attests. While such influence on biblical studies thus far has taken place under the banner of "literary approaches," or indeed "postmodern approaches," what has not been explored are the ways in which Bakhtin's thought and critical practice intersect with longer traditions within biblical studies such as form criticism. The meeting point between Bakhtin's thought and form criticism is that of genre.

Form criticism initially sought to connect the question of genre with the settings in life (context) of those genres, but it seems as though both foci have been traveling different paths. *Sitz im Leben* has been released from Gunkel's original straightjacket and applied to a whole range of biblical phenomena, finding its most natural applications in studies of a text's production rather than being linked to the context of the genre in question. In contrast, the study of genre has been carried on independently, taken up by reception theorists, narrative and reader-response critics. In New Testament studies, the work of Vernon Robbins is synonymous with the newer explorations of questions of genre from a sociorhetorical perspective (1990; 1996).

Bakhtinian theory and biblical form criticism may easily be viewed as academic siblings: long lost to one another, and raised in different worlds, yet the similarities are striking. This volume then offers an opportunity for them to meet. Readers will be thankful that the volume contains none of the massive chunks of theory that they are usually—at least in collections such as this—expected to ingest before proceeding: rather, it is an exploration of the way Bakhtin's work might enliven, leaven even, contemporary work on genre in biblical studies. Thus, this collection eases into Bakhtin by means of setting the scene of contemporary debates over genre in literary criticism and biblical criticism before moving into Bakhtin's work more directly. Subsequent essays practically engage Bakhtin in unique readings of specific biblical texts, exploring the possibilities of Bakhtinian theory by practical example.

The opening essays focus on genre theory, setting the scene within both biblical studies and Bakhtinian theory. This task is carried out by both Martin Buss and Carol Newsom, and, while there are significant agreements between them, they carve out different paths in their discussions of genre. Buss proposes his own model of genre classification in the Hebrew Bible. Contra Gunkel, he discusses how an understanding of Bakhtinian speech types may enliven genre studies of the Hebrew Bible. By first identifying who speaks to whom—God to human, human to human, and so forth—Buss aims to explore each speech type, its commonalities and differences and to explore the implications for such classification across the Hebrew Bible. His classification is however far from static. In proposing a dialogue *between* speech types Buss opens up the potential for genre classification to enliven rather than ossify the debate.

Carol Newsom offers an introductory overview of both form criticism and Bakhtinian theory. She clearly maps the history of genre studies within biblical scholarship, beginning with classic form criticism (that of Gunkel, Dibelius, and Bultmann) through to the "literary turn" of the 1970s Genres Project of the Society of Biblical Literature. In particular, she examines "apocalypse," being interested in how a rigid classificatory system holds up in light of more recent developments and options in genology, such as poststructuralist, neopragmatist, and family-resemblance theorists, intertextuality, prototype theory, and cognitive science. More historically oriented approaches are also considered. The essay concludes with a consideration of the Bakhtin circle and their contribution to this field. The essay provides an excellent introduction to the other contributions, each of which takes up her call to explore the potential of conversations between Bakhtin's ideas and biblical texts.

There follow five Hebrew Bible pieces (Mitchell, Green, Fentress-Williams, Mandolfo, and Valeta), a crossover piece discussing the genre of apocalypse in the tradition of John Collins (Vines), and two New Testament essays (Fuller and Anderson). These are then rounded out by a final essay (Maddison) that explores the appropriation of biblical allusion in a contemporary text.

Taking direction from Bakhtin's well known distrust of formalism, Christine Mitchell seeks to detach the study of biblical genres from form criticism. Drawing on Bakhtin's notions of chronotope and heteroglossia, she develops these concepts further to argue that all genre is dialogically constructed, becoming a site for politics constructed by the operation of power (Foucault) and eros (Deleuze). Thus the paper inevitably moves beyond Bakhtin and goes on to explore the perspectives of Foucault, Deleuze, Hegel, and Lacan. This detailed theoretical exploration is supported by exegetical examples drawn from Chronicles.

Barbara Green aims to use Bakhtin's reading strategies to examine the development of Jonathan in 1 Sam 20. Here Jonathan's attitudes to both David and Saul shift considerably by chapter's end; Green aims to explore how. Her focus here is squarely upon the utterances of the characters within the narrative, notably, David, Jonathan, and Saul. By tracking the course of these exchanges, she is able to clarify Jonathan's role in the story. In tracing the "educational" construction of Jonathan, Green focuses on language, genre, and readerly presuppositions.

Using Bakhtin's notions of dialogue and chronotope, Judy Fentress-Williams explores Gen 38 not as an interruption in the narrative but as an interpretive lens that provides a key for understanding the larger narrative. Because of the thematic links between the Tamar story and the surrounding material, Gen 38 functions as a "play within a play" that is in dialogue with the surrounding story in Genesis. Moreover, the dialogue in the narrative, terminology, and wordplay in Tamar's story forms a rubric that functions as a reader's guide for Joseph's story.

Carleen Mandolfo introduces Gunkel and Bakhtin to one another, drawing our attention to a fundamental difference in their respective understandings of form (genre). For Gunkel this definition is rigid, as those of us who spent time in undergraduate theological schools will well appreciate. For example, his distinctions between complaint, thanksgiving, royal, eschatological psalms, and others still stand as benchmarks. For Bakhtin, genre is more fluid. Her reading of Lam 1–2 focuses on the oscillations and slips. She identifies first the distinct voices of a "female supplicant" and another "didactic voice" that usually speaks in defense of YHWH. Mandolfo goes on to identify a point at which this "didactic" voice appears to switch sides.

David Valeta offers a study of the Aramaic text in Daniel, arguing that the language used is a deliberate tool to express the narrator's view and to offer a satirical critique of the king, court, and empire. Engaging extensively with Bakhtin, in particular his concept of polyglossia, Valeta is able to read the book of Daniel both synchronically and as a text of resistance.

In the transitional essay to the New Testament, Michael Vines revisits John Collins's famous discussion of "apocalyptic." He finds Collins's definition too formalistic, and, given Bakhtin's resistance to formalism, Vines draws on the notion of Bakhtin's chronotope to show how we might define the genre of apocalyptic in terms of its use of narrative time and space.

Bringing a Bakhtinian flavor to traditional form-critical studies of Matthew's Gospel, Christopher Fuller shifts us into the New Testament and pursues a chronotopic reading of the genealogy, with a distinct focus on its rogue women (Tamar, Rahab, Ruth, and Bathsheba). In making use of the idea of the chronotope, Fuller argues that we should read the text as "eschatological satire." His concern is with the spatial allusions, the temporal rhythm, the structure, all of which contribute, with the women, to the undermining of primogeniture.

Paul Anderson seeks to uncover the function of the Johannine misunderstanding dialogues. He begins with Bakhtin's assertion that devices such as misunderstanding are always rhetorical and polemical. He further explores the "polyphonic" nature of the text, its utterance, transmission, and reception, inferring a number of acute crises in the Johannine context. However, Anderson councils against finite readings of this text, finishing with further discussion of Bakhtin's writing, notably, that "there is neither a first word nor a last."

The final essay, by Bula Maddison, is of a different order than those that precede it, for it seeks the intersections between the Bible and contemporary literature. In a sparkling use of language, Maddison is concerned with Toni Morrison's *Beloved* and its use of biblical allusion. Extending Bakhtin's theory of dialogization, she examines the intersection between biblical apocalypse and African cosmology within the cosmology of the novel. Maddison suggests that a number of language-worlds intersect in the novel—historical slave narrative, African spirit-world, and the Bible—and with such intersections we end up with what she calls a hybrid chronotope, specifically as the intersection of biblical apocalypse and the "rememory" of African cosmology.

While this collection is the first gathering in an edited volume of essays on Bakhtin and biblical criticism, there is a genealogy, of you like, of individual studies that lies behind this volume. While there have been some theological studies, such as those by Coates (1998), Bruce (1990), Cartwright (1992), Classens (2003), Olson (1998), and Ward (1997), most have concerned the Bible, usually specific texts (Reed [1993] is the exception here). Robert Polzin, as I indicated earlier, blazed a trail with the three studies that move through Deuteronomy (1980) and the books of Samuel (1989; 1993). Kenneth Craig read the book of Esther in terms of the carnivalesque (1995), Barbara Green gave us two studies, one a general introduction to Bakhtin (2000) and the second a study of 1 Samuel (2003b), favored ground for literary critics. The sole monograph on the New Testament comes from Barnet's study of Matthew (2003). As for the articles, the vast bulk have focused on the Hebrew Bible, covering Deuteronomy (Bergen 1999), the Psalms (Levine 1992; Mandolfo 2002b; Tull 2005), Lamentations (Miller 2001), Job (Newsom 1996; 2002; 2003b), and then a couple of the essays from the 1993 *Semeia* volume on characterization (Malbon 1993; McCracken 1993). Finally, there is but one solitary essay on Bakhtin and the New Testament, notably, Knowles on the "Good Samaritan" (2004). This collection, then, continues the discussion but also seeks to move it to a new level.

A final word of thanks is due, first to Fiona Marantelli, who helped immensely with the earlier stages of the volume, and to Ibrahim Abraham, who ably assisted with the last stages.

Dialogue in and among Genres

Martin J. Buss

One of the most prominent features of biblical literature is dialogue, especially if this is taken to include speech by one person to another even if no immediate response by the addressee is recorded. To what extent biblical dialogue is different in character or frequency from that of other traditions is an interesting question, but one that will be touched on here only briefly. The primary present focus is on the phenomenon of dialogue within the Hebrew Bible.

The first point to be made is that *address form is a basis on which a genre, or speech type, can be identified.* Since the word "genre" is used in this statement, a word is in order about what I mean by "genre." Negatively (contra Gunkel), I reject the notion that genres have "essences," that is, the idea that there are right or wrong ways to categorize genres. Instead, together with other relational theorists, I accept the view that genres are more or less useful ways of treating similar literary phenomena together. In positive terms, I adopt Gunkel's three criteria for the identification of a genre: life situation (I prefer to say "process"), ideational content, and verbal form.[1] Any one of these three criteria can be sufficient to constitute a genre. For instance, if greeting someone is a life process, then "greeting" represents a genre, no matter what content appears and no matter what form of expression is used. Furthermore, one can group together discussions of a certain kind of content, such as theology or conversation about the weather, despite differences in formulation or role. In fact, as a survey of German genres found again, most speech classifications (such as recipe, weather report, or death notice) are based on content, although each have characteristic styles. Third, narratives—that is, temporally sequenced accounts—are often treated as a genre on the basis of their literary

---

1. Gunkel always listed content before verbal form and came to list *Sitz im Leben* first in terms of importance; however, verbal form provided for him a convenient entrée (see Buss 1999:247).

form, although they may have various kinds of content and can play different roles in life.

The three criteria mentioned—life process, content, and verbal form—correlate with each other to a certain extent, but not as rigidly as Gunkel implied. The correlations are not simply arbitrary but make a certain sense. For instance, in a condition of distress, it is understandable that the content of an expression is a complaint and that the verbal form for this employs the first person. Yet other content and another verbal form are possible and may be preferred in another culture.[2]

In the present context, I will deal with patterns as they appear in the sphere of the Hebrew Bible. In doing so, I will begin with verbal structure, specifically with address form, but I will move from verbal patterning to a view of its correlation with content and life process.

My first example will be a type of speech that in biblical studies is often called "law." Laws are formulated as pronouncements by an authoritative source that are directed to a generalized public. Within this large category, several variations can be regarded as subtypes, which themselves have further subdivisions.

In one subtype, the public is addressed in the second person in the individual laws (not merely in their introductory frame). Although no response may be recorded, this style represents an implied dialogue, in that speaker and addressee are involved in an ongoing relationship.

In a subdivision of this form that appears in the Decalogue, God speaks to Israel in the first person, although Moses is indicated as God's mouthpiece (Exod 20:1–14; Deut 5:4–5). In the biblical text, these commandments—most of which employ second-person address, although the positive ones among them use the infinitive absolute—are called God's "words" (*debarim*). In regard to how their style correlates with content and process, Philo pointed out that it highlights the personal character of biblical law as one that involves a relation between people and God and not merely a mechanical obedience to a set of rules (*Dec.* 36–39). In fact, the decalogic "words" are quite general and leave much open in regard to specific application. One

---

2. My conception of genre (or speech type), with which I have operated from 1969:1 on, is as follows: (1) Genres can be usefully identified on the basis of different criteria, so that they cut across, and can be combined with, each other. (2) Genres are probabilistic, not rigid structures. (3) The life situation of genres is best treated in terms of human processes rather than in terms of organizational arrangements, although attention to these add an element of concreteness as long as they are not taken rigidly. (4) Generic patterns are neither strictly necessary (contra essentialism) nor purely arbitrary (contra one-sided particularism) but are to some degree appropriate and to some degree contingent.

can ask: What does it mean to have no other god "before" me? Are images permitted if one does not "worship" them? What constitutes "work" that is prohibited on the Sabbath? How does one "honor" parents? Furthermore, murder, theft, adultery, and false witness are wrong by definition. They constitute unjustified killing, unjustified taking, etc., without spelling out what makes an act unjustified (for instance, in both Jewish and Catholic traditions, a hungry person's taking needed bread is not theft). Thus, attention is drawn to several aspects of social life, while details are left to other contexts. The tenth commandment forbids property accumulation and competitive bidding for employees, but it does not specify a maximum for permitted holdings and centers instead on attitude.

In another subtype of second-person directive, God addresses Moses, who is to speak either to the people in general or to Aaron as the representative of the priests. The directives thus formulated are fairly specific. Quite a few of them do not use second-person address in the laws themselves and can thus be treated as a separate subgenre of law (see further Buss 1977).

In Deuteronomy, the immediate verbal source of regulations is not God but Moses, who speaks to the people on behalf of God. Moses can quote the Ten Commandments as God's direct words to Israel, but otherwise he gives instructions that often have an expository and hortatory character, like that of a sermon.[3] Many of the exhortations are humanitarian in their character, but Moses also directs the Israelites to exterminate the Canaanites (Deut 7:1–5). Thus, in being more expansive than strictly divine words, this kind of speech, too, shows some correlation of style with content and process.[4]

We can now turn from address patterns in law to those in nonlegal genres, which differ in ways that are appropriate for their specific type of speech. To give just a few examples: Proverbs sometimes address an individual person. When they do so, they use the so-called "imperative" form of the verb, which in generalized directives has the flavor of strong advice. At other times, proverbs are worded impersonally, especially in order to describe consequences of behavior which should be taken into account by the hearer. Both forms appeal primarily to an individual's material or idealistic well-being, including self-respect, just as ancient and modern philosophy often do. They do not inculcate a sense of one's having a place within a large-scale divine movement or employ gratitude as a motive. When the speaker of a proverb is identified, it is a parent, who is represented either by Solomon (1:1) or by a king's

---

3. See the convenient summary of this phenomenon in von Rad: 835.
4. Within the book of Hosea, similarly, speech by God is less specific than speech not so identified (see Buss 1969:60–69).

mother (31:1). Nevertheless, personified wisdom, perhaps as a daughter of God, is cited (8:4–36). Thus there is indeed a connection with deity, although it is less pronounced than in laws.

In contrast to Proverbs, Qoheleth emphasizes the reflective first-person "I," with its experience. This "I" is probably not simply that of an individual writer but represents a certain way of looking at reality.[5] It is indeed misleading to compare Qoheleth with Proverbs in a way that assumes that they have a common purpose. Proverbs often gives direction that is moral or useful for operation in society. In content and purpose, as well as in address form, Qoheleth represents a different genre, one that is also observable worldwide in both written and oral cultures.[6] Occasionally Qoheleth gives advice, but that advice is a recommendation that one enjoy life, in contrast to seeking ephemeral or meaningless achievements (2:24, etc.). Basic moral standards and a belief in some degree of divine justice are accepted (see Fox:121–131), but the reader or hearer is advised that adherence to righteousness should be moderate (7:16–18; 8:11–14; 11:9). In regard to the question of how Qoheleth fits into the Hebrew Bible as a whole, it should be recognized that although the Hebrew Bible generally is quite strongly ethical in its orientation, it leaves a good part of human life open for the pursuit of happiness. Such a pursuit is part of the design of the Creator implied in Genesis 1 and 2 and in Qoheleth (12:1). Furthermore, Qoheleth's advice to enjoy life as it is is a complement to the Tenth Commandment against accumulating wealth (2:26), so that, in this respect at least, Qoheleth does not contradict the legal structure of the Hebrew Bible. More definitely moral, to be sure, is the ending of the book, which stands outside of Qoheleth's first-person speech (12:13–14). In other words, Qoheleth is not strongly other-centered but rather I-centered, as its style indicates. Yet is seems to represent a legitimate aspect of life.

Differently again, the Song of Songs, like much of love poetry cross-culturally, features a dialogue between lovers, who enjoy each other. The book is similar to Qoheleth in that no divine revelation is assumed. In fact, God is not even spoken of in the third person. In content and thrust, the Song resembles Qoheleth in that its interest lies in enjoyment, not ethics. However,

---

5. This point is supported by the fact that "I" refers to a "king" in 1:12 (thus, rightly, Schellenberg: 165). According to Mills (107), the "I" presented "offers a mode for readers to explore their selfhood."

6. Cf. Radin. That Qoheleth's genre may indeed be old also within Israel can perhaps be supported by the echoes of its themes in Pss 39:5–7, 12; 62:10; 73:2–12; 90:5–6; 94:11; 144:4; Prov 5:18, within a more religious/moral frame (although these texts are hard to date), and by the observation that a number of Qoheleth's forms are similar to those of the "old" Israelite wisdom (Fischer: 37–39).

it reaches this point via a positive rather than a negative route. In terms of an implied setting, the Song presupposes youth and perhaps ordinary people (with the "king" taken in a metaphoric sense), while Qoheleth represents a mature urban intelligentsia (with a heritage that goes back to pre-Israelite Jerusalem).[7] Yet, despite this difference, scribes may have been trained to work with both of these genres, under a wisdom umbrella that is symbolized by Solomon.[8]

The rest of the Hebrew Bible can be analyzed similarly in terms of address structures. In connection with such a view, it is important to note that a given genre, with its peculiar conversational structure, can incorporate other genres. Such an incorporation is true especially for narratives. These third-person accounts include various kinds of interactive dialogue or first-person statements which either represent thoughts by a character or presuppose a real or fictive diary.

To repeat my first point, then, address form is a basis on which a genre can be identified, at least in part.

My second point is that *the Hebrew Bible is largely arranged according to what appear to be culturally significant genres, which each represent a dimension of life and which engage metaphorically in a dialogue with each other.* Indeed, the organization of the Hebrew Bible gives an indication of how Israelite culture categorized texts, for the fact that certain texts are placed together probably reflects their being viewed as similar to each other. For instance, most of what we call "hymns" or "psalms of lament" stand together in one book. Similarly, all authoritative directives stand together in one place. Proverbs, critical reflections, and ordinary love songs are each grouped together. Stories about the origin of the world, of humanity, and of Israel's immediate antecedents (one can call them "narratives of orientation") are almost completely limited to Genesis and Exodus.

The consequence of this arrangement is that every biblical book, or sometimes group of books, deals with a specific aspect of Israelite life. In observing this phenomenon, one should recognize that human life requires, or at least makes possible, a variety of processes. Almost every human being participates in all of them, although most individuals will not emphasize them equally. In societies that are sufficiently large, different aspects of life come to be assigned to specialists for their cultivation on behalf of others. Thus, different biblical

---

7. The phrase "all who were before me" was a stock phrase for kings (Seow: 124), but it is likely that a reference to pre-Israelite "Jerusalem," expressly mentioned, is partly in view (cf. Gen 14:18–20).

8. Abraham ibn Ezra later produced both synagogal and drinking poetry, with an even greater divergence in assumptions.

genres were cultivated respectively by singers, priests, prophets, and so-called "wise"—religiously "lay"—persons, although the "wise" probably included many who were not highly specialized. The organization of the canon reflects such a division of tasks, so that several priestly genres stand together in one part, several prophetic genres appear in another, and a variety of genres belonging to the spheres of either laity or lower clergy (specifically, singers) in a third one, with lesser sanctity.[9]

To some extent, the various processes of life compete with one another, since they cannot all be carried out simultaneously. For instance, I recently heard someone who is heavily involved in idealistic pursuits say that each day he faces the question to what extent he will pursue his idealism and to what extent he will simply enjoy life. To be sure, some processes can be combined. Nevertheless, one can think of human life as metaphorically embodying a huge dialogue between these different aspects of life and thus between the genres in which they are expressed. Such a dialogue does not have to be altogether harmonious, of course.

One way in which this dialogue between genres appears in the Hebrew Bible is that words from God to human beings, highlighted in some parts of the Bible, find a complement in words directed toward God in other parts. God and human beings, so-to-say, converse with each other. Neither of these two sides of the conversation is necessarily prior to the other, although the organization of the canon privileges divine revelation.[10] In fact, each of the major literary structures includes within it instances of what is typical of another structure. Specifically, the Pentateuch, devoted primarily to revelation, includes some arguments with God and prayers—including the perhaps unspoken cry of the Hebrews in Egypt—and the book of Psalms includes some oracles.

An important question now is whether it is possible to date these dialogue structures and the aspects of life they represent. At a very basic level, the different life processes are well-nigh universally human. However, the specific dialogical formulations that appear in each aspect may well vary from culture to culture. One can then ask how old the biblical patterns within Israel are. For better or worse, we do not know the answer to this question, since it is hard to date biblical writings. Even if it is true that these writings were not constructed in roughly their current form until after the destruction

---

9. The placement of the book of Daniel in the third division can be due to either (or both) of two reasons: (1) the prophetic canon was already closed; (2) dream interpretation and angelic revelation have a status lower than direct divine revelation.

10. For earlier discussions of this issue by Israel Abrahams, H. W. Robinson, Walther Zimmerli, Claus Westermann, and Gerhard von Rad, see Buss 1999:375–79.

of the First Temple, it is possible and even likely that their generic patterns are older. It would be nice to know the history of these genres, but our inability to be certain about their micro-history virtually forces us to pay attention to the sociopsychological processes that entered into them irrespective of their precise circumstances.

Among these processes is a duality of receptivity and assertive activity. In order to recognize this dual dynamic, it is helpful to see that speech is a kind of action. If A speaks to B, A acts on B. In contrast, listening to someone represents a kind of receptivity. This is not a purely passive process, of course, for there is the important phenomenon of "active listening," of giving attention to, and even prodding, the other.

Stated in terms of a human process, divine words in the Pentateuch, the Prophets, and elsewhere presuppose and express receptivity on the part of humans. Again, this does not involve pure passivity; rather, laws and prophecies present spurs to activity, such as to engage in ethical action or ritual. However—in my judgment and in that of quite a few others—the first step and even the heart of ethics involves being open, metaphorically listening to the other.

In contrast, prayers and reflections represent a kind of human activity, specifically, efforts to obtain welfare and to grasp the meaning of life even without extensive divine revelation. Yet the three books in which such efforts appear—Psalms, Job, and Qoheleth—also express a sense of dependence on God. Psalms seek and applaud God's aid. Job and Qoheleth give voice to a sense of being exposed to divine capriciousness, as they declare the limits of human efforts to understand or to achieve success. Thus, receptivity and activity are interwoven in virtually all biblical books, although in different ways.[11]

One book, the Song of Songs, contains a dialogue that comes close to full mutuality between partners. The woman's voice is somewhat more extensive than the man's. It also both opens and concludes the Song, so that the intervening portions may even represent a dream or fantasy by the woman. Yet Solomon's name appears in the opening verse, and the man's voice is almost equal in extent to the woman's.[12] Especially important, perhaps, is the fact that the approaches of the two to each other are comparable. In fact, it appears that a high degree of mutuality and even of equality is characteristic—although, to

---

11. Most purely oriented toward human action is the story of Esther, in which the word "God" does not even appear in the third person, although God presumably stands in the background.

12. In one example of partial balance, the male is placed in the role of king but crowned by his mother (3:11).

be sure, not universally true—of love poetry. This phenomenon would indicate that the love relation tends toward equality or at least mutuality, even when societal patterns are hierarchical.

We have thus seen that one can speak of a dialogue between genres. Furthermore—this is my third point—one can say that *dialogues exist metaphorically within genres*, for genres are not internally homogeneous.

This way of looking at the biblical text has an important practical implication for exegesis. In recent decades, there have been many efforts to treat individual books of the Bible or certain parts within these books as coherent unities. In my opinion, these efforts are largely misplaced. When we look at a book or passage, we can indeed take it as it is, without attempting to reconstruct sources that lie behind this book or that passage. In this sense, one can engage in "final-form" exegesis. Yet, it is doubtful that it is regularly useful to treat a book or extended passage as a coherent whole. It is usually more appropriate to recognize divergences within the text and to place the divergent parts into a dialogue with each other. That is, we should view a given body of material as one that furnishes examples of a certain genre and then see that different perspectives can be expressed within that genre.

The prophetic book of Hosea can illustrate this situation. It has been recognized for some time that chapters 1–3 constitute a complex that is somewhat different from chapters 4–14. One can explain this phenomenon in at least three different ways: (1) two major authors are involved; (2) the two parts emanate from different periods in Hosea's life; (3) the two parts were transmitted by different circles. However, even if we were able to determine which of these alternatives—or perhaps still another one—is correct, such knowledge would not add much to our understanding of the book, except by removing a temptation to view one part in terms of the other. Furthermore, perhaps more importantly, neither of the two major complexes appears to be internally homogeneous. To impose a rigid unity on them would probably mean that one fails to grasp the nuances of various parts. The same situation appears to me to be true in the book of Job taken as a whole including the Elihu speeches.

Did editors of such texts have in mind a unified vision that brought the divergent elements together? I rather doubt it. I suspect that they were too respectful of the materials they received to disturb them sharply, although they did make some adjustments. In other words, biblical texts lack coherence since their antecedents were already semicanonical. After all, in theory the canon was to preserve old revelations and insights. A canonical qua canonical approach should thus envision partial incoherence instead of strict unity, just as we would not expect an anthology of high-quality poetry to be unified.

This analysis may stand close to Mikhail Bakhtin's carnival-like interpretation in *Rabelais and His World* (1984b).[13] It does not, however, imply
sheer chaos. Rather, the structure of genres presents a pattern that furnishes
a degree of order, together with which there can be a degree of disorder. The
genres can do this since they represent a kind of "speech act" in which people
can be engaged in their various involvements of life.

I have, then, set forth three propositions. (1) Address form, which may
be at least implicitly dialogical, is a basis on which a genre can be identified,
at least in part. (2) The Hebrew Bible is largely arranged according to genres,
which can be said to enter into dialogue with each other. (3) Within each
genre, there are divergences that, in effect, constitute a dialogue.

A fourth point that I want to set forth briefly is as follows: *the Hebrew
Bible enters or can enter into a dialogue with other literary complexes.* This dialogue is meaningful primarily if it proceeds by genres. When such a dialogue
is carried out, it will be seen that the list of genres that appear in the Hebrew
Bible is close to, but not quite identical with, the list of genres that are prominent in other traditions. In addition to the comparisons that have already
been made for understanding Qoheleth and the Song of Songs, let me give
just one example.

The Hindu canon shares with the Jewish Bible most of the major genres
and also a gradation of sacredness. However, the Hindu canon privileges
hymns over laws by placing hymns in the more strongly revelatory part of
the canon, while the reverse is true in the Jewish canon. This fact may well
reflect the greater importance that Hinduism assigns to mystical devotion.
Thus, there is difference along with similarity.

In making such comparisons, it is often tempting to downgrade another
tradition precisely because it differs from one's own. A difference, however,
does not in itself indicate which is to be preferred. Rather, one can listen to
a tradition other than one's own in order to see whether there is something
to be learned. Alternatively, one might simply grant legitimacy to both variations. Furthermore, if a comparison—shall we say, dialogue—is carried out
with sensitivity, one often learns to understand better one's own orientation.

Indeed, the comparison of the genres of the Hebrew Bible with those
of other ancient cultures is only part of a transhistorical approach. Biblical
genres can also be placed in conversation with present-day life and speech.
Undoubtedly, a major reason why Gunkel's analysis of biblical genres became

---

13. See Newsom 2000:26. A dialogue in my view is more open still than a polyphony;
the latter does create a certain kind of "unity," according to Bakhtin 1984a:6 and Newsom
2003:261.

widely popular is that he described the genres in a way that highlighted processes that resonate with our own existence.

In short, we have seen four ways in which the notions of dialogue and genre can be usefully joined for an understanding of the Hebrew Bible. Together, they show relations between dialogue and genres on a large scale. Barbara Green (2003a:141–59) has, in a very interesting way, provided a fine-grained analysis of relations between genre and dialogue in 1 and 2 Samuel. Perhaps, through cooperation, a dialogic analysis of genres—or a generic analysis of dialogue—can be extended in detail to the whole of the Hebrew Bible.

Spying Out the Land: A Report from Genology[*]

Carol A. Newsom

Biblical studies has a natural affinity with genology, the study of genres, but has had a strangely on and off again relationship with that discipline. For biblical studies the investigation of genres largely took shape as part of the development of form criticism. Although Gunkel was in conversation with several disciplines (e.g., classics, Germanics) that were concerned with the nature of genres, he did not apparently read literary theory.[1] Despite this, or more likely because of it, early form criticism included some elements that made it among the most progressive developments in genre criticism of the time. Form criticism, of course, was not primarily interested in literary genres but in the oral *Gattungen* that came to be recorded in written texts. In this regard form criticism might be seen as an early investigation of issues similar to those that intrigued Mikhail Bakhtin (1986) in his reflections on "speech genres" and their function in discourse, though form criticism's focus was primarily on the reconstruction of these oral *Gattungen*. More significantly, form criticism's attention to the *Sitz im Leben* of speech forms was a significant contribution to the sociology of genres. Indeed, this contribution was acknowledged in the work of Robert Jauss (1982), a leading figure of the Konstanz school of "reception aesthetics," which emphasizes the function and reception of literary genres in their historical and social contexts. Jauss contrasts the relative neglect of attention to these aspects of genre in many strands of literary studies at the turn of the century with the development within biblical studies of "a concept of genre that is structural as well as sociological," describing briefly the work of Gunkel, Dibelius, and Bultmann. Despite its accomplishments, however, early form criticism was marked by a tendency toward rigidity in its assumption that oral forms were "pure forms," with a tight connection between their life settings and their structures (Buss 1999: 251, 255, 259).

---

[*] Reprint of Newsom 2005.
1. See Buss 1999:227–28 for a discussion of influences upon Gunkel.

A new interest in the potential of genre theory for biblical studies was part of the "literary turn" of biblical studies in the 1970s and was reflected in the SBL Genres Project, initiated by Robert Funk. Groups were established to investigate the genres of parable, pronouncement story, miracle story, letter, and apocalypse. Results from some of the groups were published in various issues of *Semeia* and have been quite influential in shaping the discussion of these ancient genres.[2] Since that time, of course, various individual scholars have utilized genre theory in their research (e.g., Burridge 1992; Collins 1995), but the conversation between biblical studies and genre studies continues to be sporadic.

In this essay I wish to make a brief and selective review of some of the trends in genre theory and their possible usefulness in biblical studies. In order to organize this discussion I will examine the approach and findings of the Apocalypse Group of the SBL as published in *Semeia* 14, *Apocalypse: The Morphology of a Genre* (1979), noting how more recent developments in genre theory might change the assumptions, approaches, and questions to be posed in a study of the genre of apocalypse. My comments are in no sense a criticism of the work of the Apocalypse Group. To the contrary, even some twenty-five years later, the quality of the analysis of this deservedly influential work remains impressive and its results valuable. But not surprisingly, the framework of genre studies has changed significantly, so that now one would probably approach the issues somewhat differently.

Characteristic of genre studies of the time, the Apocalypse Group frames the task primarily as one of definition and classification, so that the authors describe their purpose as that of identifying "a group of written texts marked by distinctive recurring characteristics which constitute a recognizable and coherent type of writing" (Collins 1979a:1). The metaphors and images that appear in the description refer to the "members" of the genre, to texts "belonging" to the genre, and to the genre's "boundaries." In several of the chapters grids are presented that list the various features of form and content on one axis and the names of the apocalypses on the other axis. Each feature attested in the apocalypse is marked with an "x." Over the past quarter century, however, genre theorists have become increasingly dissatisfied with an approach that defines genres by means of lists of features. The objections are of several sorts. Definitional and classificatory approaches are now seen as not representing well the functions of genre in human communication. As Alastair Fowler remarks, genre primarily has to do with communication. "It is an instrument not of classification or prescription, but of meaning" (Fowler

---

2. See *Semeia* 11 (1978), 20 (1981), 22 (1981), 29 (1983), 36 (1986).

1982:22). Moreover, classificatory schemes are by their very nature static, whereas genres are dynamic. Thus Fowler memorably objects that the classification approach tends to treat genres as though they were pigeonholes, when in fact genres are more like pigeons (36). "Mere" classification obscures the way in which every text—however it relates to similar texts—whether "by conformity, variation, innovation, or antagonism" will change the nature of the genre and indeed give rise to new genres (23).

The objections from poststructuralists such as Derrida are, not surprisingly, even stronger. In characteristically paradoxical fashion Derrida claims that while "a text cannot belong to no genre" he would rather "speak of a sort of participation without belonging—a taking part in without being part of, without having membership in a set" (Derrida 2000:224, 230). In my opinion, there is much to be said for following Derrida's lead and thinking of genre in relation to a text's rhetorical orientation so that rather than referring to texts as belonging to genres one might think of texts as participating in them, invoking them, gesturing to them, playing in and out of them, and in so doing, continually changing them. With respect to apocalypses, this shift in how one thinks about texts and genres accommodates better not only the multigeneric nature of many apocalypses but also their irreducible particularity. It also allows one to think more flexibly about apocalypses and the penumbra of related kinds of texts.

Classification continues to have its defenders in genre theory, but often in a way that quite changes the nature and purposes of classification from a descriptive enterprise to that of a critical category devised by the critic for the purposes of the critic. Thus Adena Rosmarin, in *The Power of Genre*, argues that genre can be seen as a kind of intentional category error in which two things that are not the same are brought together "as if" they were the same. Drawing on art historian E. H. Gombrich's dictum that "all thinking is sorting, classifying," she argues that it is the critic who draws together different texts for productive purposes. This is how we

> can explain texts that are different—"Composed upon Westminster Bridge" and "The Windhover"—as if they were the same kind of thing, namely, a sonnet.... We can always choose, correct, invent, or define a class wide enough to make the desired [category] mistake possible.... The initial thesis of a rhetorical and pragmatic theory of explanation, then, is that the inevitability of making mistakes is not the bane of criticism but, rather, its enabling condition. It makes classification possible, and classification enables criticism to begin. (Rosmarin 1985:21–22).[3]

---

3. For a similar approach, see Cohen 1986: 203–18.

Thus for the neopragmatist genre critic such as Rosmarin, the "validity" of a genre category has to do with its potential for creating new critical insight rather than with its correspondence to the author's own sense of genre.

The authors of *Semeia* 14 initially appear to have some sympathy for such a pragmatic approach to genre, since they observe that the use of the term *apokalypsis* in ancient manuscripts is "not a reliable guide to the genre." Rather "an 'apocalypse' is simply that which scholars can agree to call an 'apocalypse' " (Collins 1979a:2). If that is the case, then there would be little objection to a classificatory approach that defines the genre of apocalypse in terms of a clustering of features of form and content. Nevertheless, it does not seem to me that the authors of *Semeia* 14 intended their clarification of the genre apocalypse simply to function as a convenience for critics but in some sense to make explicit the tacit assumptions held by ancient writers about how one composes an apocalypse. That is to say, I judge that their critical act was not intended so much as a constructive act as a reconstructive one. If that is the case, then the limitations of the classificatory approach have to be addressed.

Even if one wishes to move beyond classification, however, the fact remains that genre recognition involves some sort of mental grouping of texts on the basis of perceived similarity. Many of the recent discussions have struggled to find more apt ways of describing this process. One of the most popular of these explanations is developed from Wittgenstein's notion of family resemblance. In *Philosophical Investigations* Wittgenstein posed the question of what is common to the various things we call games:

> board games, card games, ball games, Olympic games, and so on. What is common to them all? ... If you look at them you will not see something that is common to *all,* but similarities, relationships, and a whole series of them at that.... We see a complicated network of similarities overlapping and criss-crossing: sometimes overall similarities, sometimes similarities of detail.—And I shall say: "games" form a family. (Wittgenstein 1958:31–32)

Adapted and popularized by Fowler (41–42) as a means of thinking about genre, the notion of family resemblance does seem to get at aspects of the perceptual processes by which the mind sorts things that belong together from those that seem not to belong together. One might, of course, argue that classification by means of features is simply the systematic and self-conscious application of a model of family resemblance, but that is not usually the way in which genre theorists invoke the model. Fowler insists that it is neither "as an inferior substitute for a class" nor "a mere preliminary to definition" (41). It rather makes the "blurred edges" of genres of the essence. Indeed, among its more radical proponents, the family resemblance model appears to dissolve category boundaries in a fairly decisive manner. But for that very reason the approach runs into problems of its own. For example, texts in group A might exhibit features a, b, c, group B might exhibit features b, c, d, and group C might exhibit features c, d, e, and so forth. One is left with the uncomfortable conclusion that the family resemblance model could produce a genre in which two exemplars in fact shared no traits in common! As John Swales (1990:51) remarks, "family resemblance theory can make anything resemble anything."[4]

Another attempt to describe how genre recognition and genre competence takes place invokes the notion of intertextuality. Jonathan Culler (1975:139) describes the way in which readers make sense of texts as follows: "A work can only be read in connection with or against other texts, which provide a grid through which it is read and structured by establishing expectations which enable one to pick out salient features and give them a structure." One of the appealing aspects of this account is that it suggests the tacit and unselfconscious way in which people acquire a sense of genre by reading many texts. Culler's account also attends to the communicative function of genre as establishing "a contract between writer and reader so as to make certain relevant expectations operative and thus to permit both compliance with and deviation from accepted modes of intelligibility" (147). In many respects the practice of the Apocalypse Group could be described as a highly intentional form of intertextuality, as they read texts closely in relation to one another in order to cultivate a disciplined sense of genre recognition. But they did so with a much more limited purpose than that which Culler ascribes to intertextuality. Culler's model is not only about genre recognition but also about the dynamics of genre deviation as part of the text's communicative purpose. Culler does not, however, draw the implications for the history of genres, as Fowler does in his reference to an author's practice of "conformity, variation, innovation, or antagonism," by means of which the very body of intertexts is changed with each new instance, so that ultimately the very genre itself may be transmuted into something else (Fowler: 23). While the Apocalypse Group did not include an attempt to establish a diachronic map of the changing nature of the apocalypses, the intertextual approach described by Culler and Fowler could well be adapted for such purposes.

As helpful as the invocation of intertextuality can be, it is based on a hypothetical sense rather than an empirical finding of how readers actually acquire a sense of genre, and in fact it is in some ways mistaken about the

---

4. See also the extended examination of the family resemblance model by David Fishelov 1993:53–68.

nature of this process. One of the most promising recent developments in exploring how people do recognize and engage genres emerges from cognitive science and its radical overturning of our understanding of how mental categories are formed and function. Since genres are categories of speech or literature, they function in much the same way as other mental categories. The key insight of the cognitive theory of categories is that conceptual categories are not best thought of as defined by distinctive features possessed by every member of the group but rather by a recognition of prototypical examples which serve as templates against which other possible instances are viewed. In a series of experiments in the 1970s Eleanor Rosch (1975) showed that this is how categorical structures function. For instance, even though robins, ostriches, swallows, eagles, and penguins are all birds, people tend to treat robins and sparrows as "typical" members of the category birds and ostriches and penguins as "atypical." Thus robins and sparrows are the prototypes for the category "bird." The category can be extended to cover other birds that do not conform to the prototype (e.g., those that are large or do not fly or do not sing), but those that do not closely resemble the prototypes have a marginal status. Categories are thus structured with central and peripheral members. Indeed membership in a category may be a matter of degree (Sinding 2002:186).

One of the advantages of prototype theory is that it provides a way for bringing together what seems so commonsensical in classificatory approaches while avoiding its rigidity. At the same time it gives more discipline to the family resemblance approach, since not every resemblance or deviation is of equal significance (Swales: 52). As applied to genre categories, prototype theory would require an identification of exemplars that are prototypical and an analysis of the privileged properties that establish the sense of typicality.

How would this approach compare with the project of the Apocalypse Group? In fact, it appears that they intuitively worked with something like a prototype model. Consider the following statement:

> There is a general consensus among modern scholars that there is a phenomenon which may be called "apocalyptic" and that it is expressed in an ill-defined list of writings which includes (on any reckoning) the Jewish works Daniel (chaps. 7–12), 1 Enoch, 4 Ezra and 2 Baruch and the Christian book of Revelation. The list is generally agreed to be more extensive than this but its precise extent is a matter of dispute. (Collins 1979a:3)

The apocalypses named are clearly recognized as "prototypical," though a prototype theory of genre would find the dispute about the extent of the genre category not to be a problem that requires solving by recourse to a strict definition. Also similar to prototype theory is the distinction made by the Apocalypse Group between "a few elements [that] are constant in every work," a larger number that may or may not be present, as well elements distinctive to particular works (9–10). Thus there is a distinction between central or privileged properties and those that are more peripheral.

To this point prototype theory may sound as though it is not much different than a slightly chastened form of definition by features. But there are other aspects of prototype theory that differentiate it from traditional forms of category definition. Categories are not simply collections of features but also involve cognitive models or background framework schemata. The difference between the two approaches can be illustrated by a classic example (Sinding 2002:193–94). By definition, the concept "bachelor" means "an unmarried adult male." But no one really thinks of the Pope, Tarzan, or a Muslim with three wives as a bachelor. The category is implicitly related to a script-like semantic frame that understands the course of a typical man's life as beginning with childhood, progressing to a period of sexual maturity, and involving (or not) marriage to one woman. Only in relation to that "idealized cognitive model" does the category "bachelor" make sense.[5]

The significance of this analysis of cognitive models for genre is that "elements" alone are not what triggers recognition of a genre but rather the way in which they are related to one another in a *Gestalt* structure that serves as an idealized cognitive model. Thus the elements only make sense in relation to a whole. Since the *Gestalt* structure contains default and optional components, as well as necessary ones, individual exemplars can depart from the prototypical exemplars with respect to default and optional elements and still be recognizable as an extended case of "that sort of text" (Sinding 2002:196).

The members of the Apocalypse Group seem to have anticipated something like the Gestalt notion as essential to genre recognition in their discussion of what they called "the inner coherence of the genre." As they noted, "the different elements which make up our comprehensive definition of the genre are not associated at random but are integrally related by their common implications" (Collins 1979a:10). Specifically, they note "transcendence" as the key to the relationships, linking the manner of revelation, the existence of a heavenly world, the nature of its beings, and the function of apocalyptic eschatology. "There is, then, an intrinsic relation between the revelation which is expressed in the apocalypse as a whole and the eschatological salvation promised in that revelation" (11). Thus an element like pseudepigraphy, which is surely a central category for the genre apocalypse, may nevertheless be absent even from one of the prototypical exemplars (the

---

5. The term "idealized cognitive model" is from Lakoff 1987:68.

book of Revelation). Certain "default" features characteristic of prototypical apocalypses (e.g., resurrection of the dead) do not, however, appear in all of the Jewish apocalypses (e.g., the Apocalypse of Weeks and Testament of Levi 2–5) and may be represented by different content in others (e.g., the way in which revealed knowledge conveys present salvation in gnostic apocalypses). The *Gestalt* structure (or idealized cognitive model) organizes and authorizes the extension from the prototypical cases to those that are atypical.

Prototype theory, however, challenges the classificatory approach in a more fundamental way. Classification, no matter how nuanced, tends toward a binary logic. Does a text belong or not belong? Does it belong to this genre or to that one? Thinking in terms of prototype exemplars and a graded continuum challenges this artificial manner of assigning texts to generic categories (Sinding 2002:192). In a witty analogy Marie-Laurie Ryan (1981:118) describes the existence of both "highly typical" and the "less typical" texts of a genre as encouraging one "to think of genres as clubs imposing a certain number of conditions for membership, but tolerating as quasi-members those individuals who can fulfill only some of the requirements, and who do not seem to fit into any other club." Though it may seem to be a mere quibbling over metaphors, metaphors are quite important in how we think. Thus the prototype and family resemblance approach to genre seems to me to offer advantages for how one would think about Jubilees or the Temple Scroll or revelatory discourses in relationship to the genre apocalypse in contrast to a classificatory approach that talks of the boundaries of the genre and the problem of borderline cases.

One final aspect of prototype theory remains to be noted, and it is one that raises the issue of the limits of this approach. Michael Sinding, one of the strong advocates of prototype theory, argues that, in contrast to the historically oriented family resemblance approach as developed by Fowler, prototype theory operates ahistorically. That is to say one can read the prototypical exemplars out of historical order and thus without a sense of how one text influences or imitates another "and still have a good a grasp of the genre, *as a genre,* as anyone" (Sinding 2002:193).[6] Here, too, the Apocalypse Group works with a similar perspective in that they define their concern as that of "phenomenological similarity, not historical derivation" (Collins 1979a:1). For the purposes of genre recognition, this ahistorical approach can certainly be justified. But developing a sense of the genre is not the only matter to be pursued. Some of the most interesting issues in genology are precisely those of genealogy.

---

6. Sinding argues against Fishelov and Fowler, who stress the role of literary tradition.

The recognition of the historical nature of genres was a surprisingly late development in genre theory. Until the emergence of Romanticism most genre criticism treated genres as transcendent or "natural" forms that were valid, descriptively and prescriptively, across historical periods (see Duff 2000). This explains various attempts to identify biblical compositions in terms of classical genres, as, for instance, Theodore Beza's comparison of Job to classical tragedy. Romanticism's new recognition of genres as dynamic entities historically and culturally conditioned was given its classic expression in Hegel's lectures on aesthetics. Not surprisingly, this new historicist understanding of genres soon found an intriguing model in Darwin's theory of evolution, developed most fully in Ferdinand Brunetière's *L'évolution des genres,* published in 1890. Although the evolutionary model has been criticized, it has received a recent defender in David Fishelov, who argues that a more careful use of Darwinian analogies can be of significant use in understanding why some genres are productive at particular periods and then become extinct or "sterile," as Fishelov would prefer to describe it (35–52).

For reasons that should be evident, this is an extremely important issue for understanding the genre of apocalypse, since it is possible to date the emergence of apocalypses (sometime in the third century B.C.E.) and to date their demise within Judaism (in the aftermath of the Bar Kokhba revolt), though they continued to be composed in Christian circles, including the gnostics. Moreover, most of the Jewish apocalypses and many of the Christian ones can be dated with reasonable certainty, and patterns of influence often can be traced. The relationships among these documents have frequently been explored with respect to ideas, motifs, or theological perspectives, but rarely has the focus been on describing the evolution of the genre as such.

Another aspect of the historicist perspective on genre has to do with the relationship of different genres to one another in succeeding historical periods. The Russian Formalists, in particular, took up the question of the evolution of genres not as isolated developments but in relation to the genre system as a whole.[7] Whether or not one could describe a hierarchy of genres within the Second Temple period, as the Russian Formalists proposed for various epochs in Western literature, is a difficult question. But it is worth asking how one might describe the relationships among the narrative, historiographical, poetic, paraenetic, apocalyptic, halakic, and other genres that flourished during the Second Temple period. Were some more dominant than others? Are certain genres absorbed into others? And how might one describe the radical restructuring of the genre system in the period after the destruction

---

7. These ideas are developed by Shklovsky and Tynyanov.

of the Temple and especially after the failure of the Bar Kokhba revolt? Shklovsky drew attention to the fact that genre change is not simply continuous development but often discontinuous, or, as one might say, that it requires not only evolutionary but revolutionary models (Duff: 7).

Even though Shklovsky rightly challenged the simple linearity of the nature of genre change, his own metaphors—the knight's move in chess or an inheritance that proceeds from uncle to nephew rather than from father to son—suggest a rather schematic sense of motivated directionality. While this may be adequate for an investigation of large scale changes in genre systems, the change that takes place in particular genres is generally much less tidy. Fowler describes a process of continuous metamorphosis in which "every literary work changes the genres it relates to. This is true not only of radical innovations and productions of genius. The most imitative work, even as it kowtows slavishly to generic conventions, nevertheless affects them, if only minutely or indirectly" (Fowler: 23). Fowler's observation might be recast in terms of Mikhail Bakhtin's (1981:281) notion of texts as utterances in dialogical relationship to one another. Not only is every utterance unique but also must be conceived of as a reply to what has gone before. Thus every instance of a genre can be understood as a reply to other instances of that genre and as a reply to other genres, whether or not self-consciously conceived of as such. The dialogical relationship carries forward the ever changing configuration of the genre.

Bakhtin, however, recognized not only the continuous transformation of genres but also their profound conservatism. In a paradoxical formulation he asserted that "a genre is always the same and yet not the same, always old and new simultaneously" (Bakhtin 1984a:106). This paradox was contained in what he referred to as genre memory, the fact that new iterations of a genre always contained archaic elements. "A genre lives in the present, but always *remembers* its past, its beginning. Genre is a representative of creative memory in the process of literary development." Bakhtin's formulation thus brings together the synchronic and diachronic elements of genre (Thompson 1984:35).

With respect to the problem of the genre of apocalypse this perspective might be of particular use for understanding the internal dynamics of late Christian and gnostic apocalypses, which stand chronologically far from the beginnings of apocalyptic. But it might also be a fruitful approach to the issue of the multi-generic nature of apocalypses. Many apocalypses contain paraenesis, historical resumes, dream reports, and a variety of other small genres. These, too, have genre memory and retain archaic elements even as they are newly contextualized and transformed by being incorporated into apocalypses.

As so often, Bakhtin is more suggestive than systematic. To understand better the issues posed by the origin of the genre of apocalypse, its multigeneric quality, and its relation to what the Apocalypse Group terms "related texts" one might turn again to the intersection of cognitive theory and genre theory. Cognitive theory has concerned itself extensively with the mechanisms of mental creativity, most particularly in the notion of "conceptual blending" in the work of Gilles Fauconnier and Mark Turner (2002). Although this is a highly complex and subtle theory, to which I cannot begin to do justice in this short essay, it understands certain forms of creative thinking as occurring as two or more mental schemata are brought together and integrated in networks of "mental spaces." This is, in essence, how we think by means of metaphors or the way we integrate a figural scenario and a political scenario in political cartoons. The extension of this theory to genre is only in its initial stages, and its usefulness remains to be demonstrated (Sinding 2004). Nevertheless, it might well provide a more rigorous way in which to investigate, for instance, how late prophetic vision accounts, parabiblical narrative, historical resumes, and other such forms are creatively blended to produce what we recognize as apocalypses. Or, one might use such an approach to understand the way in which apocalypses and testaments are brought together to create novel types of texts that occupy the periphery between genres.

A final perspective on genres that holds particular promise for the investigation of apocalyptic literature comes from the work of the Bakhtin circle. For Bakhtin and his colleagues genre is not simply a literary form but a mode of cognition. The metaphor invoked by Pavel Medvedev was that of genre as a means of seeing: "Every genre has its methods and means of seeing and conceptualizing reality, which are accessible to it alone....The process of seeing and conceptualizing reality must not be severed from the process of embodying it in the forms of a particular genre.... The artist must learn to see reality with the eyes of the genre" (Medvedev 1978:133). Medvedev compares the different ways of conceptualizing reality that are accessible to a graph as opposed to a painting, or to a lyric poem as opposed to a drama or a novel. Genres are thus ideological instruments in that they are the expressions of mental structures or worldviews. Thus the exploration of the genre apocalypse needs to include the question of what kind of *thinking* is performed by the genre *qua* genre.

But how might one approach that question? Bakhtin's own work on the genre of the novel led him to privilege the particular configurations of space and time, the chronotope, as he called it, as that which defines and distinguishes different genres (Bakhtin 1981:85). Thus the adventure novel of ordeal has a repertoire of characteristic physical settings (journeys, voyages, exotic locales, marketplaces, etc.) as well as a repertoire of characteristic ways of handling time (abrupt meetings and partings, coincidental arrivals, a series of episodes that are largely interchangeable in sequence, etc.). By contrast, the *Bildungsroman* has a quite different repertoire of privileged places and constructions of temporality. These differences have implications for the kind of characters who can inhabit these different worlds. Indeed, they are very different ways of construing reality itself.

Although the chronotope has mostly been explored in relation to narrative structures, there is no reason why it would not be fruitful for other types of literature. Apocalypses, in particular, are deeply concerned with the nature and significance of time and with the relation of certain privileged spaces to one another and to time. The distinctive character of the apocalyptic seer and the privileging of apocalyptic knowledge as a moral and religious virtue are integrally related to the chronotope characteristic of apocalypses. To go beyond superficial observations would require considerable detailed work, but the aptness of Bakhtin's conception of the chronotope for research on apocalypses should be evident.

One could, of course, go on and on, but I hope in this short article to have shown ways in which the conversation between biblical studies and genology can continue to be highly productive. Although it is always hazardous to attempt to predict the future of an intellectual inquiry, I suspect that the most creative work in genology in the next decade will take place at the intersection of the Bakhtinian understanding of genre and that which is developing in conversation with cognitive theory. Not only can cognitive theory help refine the intuitive insights of Bakhtin and Medvedev concerning the cognitive force of genre, but the Bakhtin circle's emphasis on the social and historical dimensions of genres can also prevent cognitive theories from becoming too abstract. Given the rich tradition of the study of oral and written forms in biblical studies, there is every reason to think that this discipline can play an important role in the developing discourse concerning genre.

POWER, *EROS*, AND BIBLICAL GENRES

Christine Mitchell

WHAT IS GENRE?

> But something created is always created out of something given.... What is
> given is completely transformed in what is created. (Bakhtin 1986:119–20).

Biblical form criticism supposes that genres are givens: they are forms
that give the key to content. This is the reason there is such concern for tracing, say, the development of apocalyptic literature as a genre. Genre simply
exists as a set form. This particular kind of deductive genre theory, seen in literary studies most clearly in the work of Northrop Frye (247–48), is implicit
in almost all work on biblical genres. We may consider, with Thomas Beebee,
that genre theory has moved through four phases: (1) ancient-through-
Renaissance "production-oriented" theory, that is, "genre as rules"; (2) early
modern classification theory, looking at the growth and change in genre, that
is, "genre as species"; (3) early twentieth-century theory, looking at the textual
forms and features that indicate genre, that is, "genre as patterns of textual
features"; and (4) late twentieth-century theory, locating the meaning of genre
not in the intention of the author or in literary history or in the features of
the text, but in the reader/s of the text, that is, "genre as reader conventions"
(2–3). In this broad scheme, biblical genre theory is located roughly in the
third phase, although the concern with tracing the development of a genre
(like apocalyptic from prophecy) is located squarely in the second phase. But
before biblical scholars start jumping on the fourth-stage bandwagon (i.e.,
genre as reader-created), it should be noted that with a revived interest in
genre theory in literary studies, most contemporary genre theory has moved
into a new phase, one that locates genre both in text and in reader, in text and
in context, and in the combination and recombination of genres and fragments with each other (Cohen 2003). In a volume dedicated to examining

genre from a Bakhtinian perspective, it is useful to note that Bakhtin's influence on contemporary genre theory is greater than ever.

Thus I would like to suggest that our entry point and first answer to the
question "what is genre" is a negative one: genre is not form. Or it is not form
alone. The ancient preoccupation with generic rules that is the basis for all
later Western theories of genre should give us pause anyway; those rules
are Greek and Roman, retroactively applied to the non-Western texts of the
Hebrew Bible. If a classical, deductive, theory of genre is being applied universally and so improperly, then perhaps we should be looking at finding or
developing an inductive theory of genre. However, this is difficult to do, as
Adena Rosmarin has shown: inductive theories of genre tend to be based on
deductive models of genre; we only realize genre inductively because of certain preconceived ideas about genre (26–33); or, the genre theorist feels "guilt
for always being deductive while trying to appear inductive" (Snyder: 203).
It may not be possible, therefore, to derive a theory of genre for the Hebrew
Bible inductively. Until it is attempted, we cannot know. In this essay I will
attempt to develop a theory of genre inductively. Although I think that I am
operating inductively, in that the theory I am about to present derives from
my reading of texts, in many ways I am also operating deductively, by working
with (imposing?) concepts from elsewhere that are suggested by my reading.

To return to the schema of genre theory presented by Beebee (above), the
goal of this project is to look for a way into genre that is neither concerned
solely with text or its sociohistorical situation or with how readers construct
genre. In terms of the text, any theory of genre has to make sense in the terms
of the text and the text's generic markers and conventions (cf. Hirsch:73–74,
93; Hirsch argues that authorial intention is crucial for making generic assessments, which I do not agree is necessarily the case). In terms of the reader,
any theory of genre also has to make sense in terms of the reader—and not
necessarily any "ideal" or "implied" reader of the text (cf. Iser). I would like
to suggest, following John Snyder, that one way into an in-between notion of
genre is to conceive of genre as operation, "historically generated and modi-
fied" (204), and to do so, I will draw on the work of M. M. Bakhtin and his
interpreters. Although Bakhtin's work is very congenial to Snyder's, Snyder
does not draw very much on Bakhtin's work. Instead, Snyder develops his
theory of genre from classical (largely Platonic) models, using a Jamesonian
dialectic, in order to see genre as a mediator, "between history and cultural
artifact, avoiding both empty abstractions and trivial empiricism" (17).

In his earlier work, *Problems of Dostoevsky's Poetics*, Bakhtin commented,

A literary genre, by its very nature, reflects the most stable, "eternal" tendencies in literature's development. Always preserved in a genre are undying

elements of the *archaic*. True, these archaic elements are preserved in it only thanks to their constant *renewal*, which is to say, their contemporization. A genre is always the same and yet not the same, always old and new simultaneously.... A genre lives in the present, but always *remembers* its past, its beginning. (1984:106; emphasis original)

This quotation spells out in some detail what is more generally summarized in the quotation at the beginning of this paper. The location of the genre in history and in social situation is crucial to a Bakhtinian analysis of genre. Bakhtin continued by saying, "For the correct understanding of a genre, therefore, it is necessary to return to its sources" (1984:106). But by the time of "Discourse in the Novel," he was more interested in demonstrating how the various speech types interact in a novel than in tracing their origins in sources (cf. 1981:263–65).

Already very early in Bakhtin's thought we can see the detachment of the form of the artistic work from its content. Content is seen as something to be tamed by form, but content does not determine form; nor does form determine content. Instead content can be liberated from its form when the *reader* stops enacting the form (1990:305). "[F]orm is the expression of the active, axiological relationship of the author-creator and of the recipient (who co-creates the form) to content" (1990:306). In other words, for Bakhtin even at an early period, form is the means by which the author and reader can interact with the content of an utterance. However, form is not identical with content, although it is related to it. In "Discourse in the Novel," Bakhtin explicitly set out to link form and content through the understanding of discourse as a social event (1981:259).

Even though Bakhtin detached form from an external referent, there is still a connection between style and genre even in Bakhtin's later work. In "The Problem of Speech Genres," he stated that, "[S]tyle is inseparably related to the utterance and to typical forms of utterances" (1986a:63): there is an "organic, inseparable link between style and genre.... each sphere has and applies its own genres that correspond to its own specific conditions" (64). He also stated, "Where there is style there is genre. The transfer of style from one genre to another not only alters the way a style sounds, under conditions of a genre unnatural to it, but also violates or renews the given genre" (66). Each utterance's style has an impact on the interaction of the utterances in a particular text and in the genres that make up the polyglot text.

Genre, for Bakhtin, also meant social construction and social context: "The meaning of a text does not lie in the particular combination of devices but in the ways in which the text is produced and interpreted, transmitted and used" (Cobley: 326). Social context alone is not enough to form genre;

it is the combination of style, content and social context that form a generic meaning (Branham 2002:163–64). Indeed, as Francis Dunn has remarked, for Bakhtin, "literary genres are neither collections of works nor formal attributes shared by those works but ways of understanding the world" (188). Similarly, according to Gary Saul Morson, Bakhtin's view on genre was that genre is inextricably bound up with worldview: a genre expresses a certain worldview. Genre is all about perspective, and to read a work within a genre is to "learn to think in the genre's terms" (410–11). If that is so, if genre, as giving meaning to utterance, is socially situated, then it is part of the discourse-network that constructs and constrains all social discourse. And if that is so, then genre must be operative in both space and time (Bakhtin's chronotope). Genre is not just a given: it has an effect.

To return to the quotation of Bakhtin's that I used at the beginning of this essay, the genre effect is to create out of the given and to transform the given in the creation. This is why each example of a genre is irreducible to a set form: each example is unique—each utterance is its own. Yet, "if speech genres did not exist and we had not mastered them, if we had to originate them during the speech process and construct each utterance at will for the first time, speech communication would be almost impossible" (Bakhtin 1986:79). In genre theory, there is always the conundrum of the generic and the specific: Bakhtin did not, I think, resolve it, nor did he intend to. It is one of the great unfinalizabilities of literature and of being.

As a brief example, I would like to look at an example from Chronicles, 2 Chr 13:23–15:15, the beginning of the reign of Asa (this section is unparalleled in Kings). The first thing we are told about Asa is that "In his days the land had rest for ten years" (2 Chr 13:23); Jacob Myers pointed out that this formula is very similar to the formula used of the judges (81; cf. Williamson: 259; Japhet: 719), as found in Judg 3:11, 30; 5:31; 8:28. The speech of the prophet Azariah in 2 Chr 15:3–6 also seems to recall the period of the judges, "For a long time Israel had … no law.… In those times there was no peace [שלום] for anyone to go or come.… they were beaten in pieces [וכתתו], nation against nation and city against city." This describes quite accurately the situation in Judges, particularly Judg 17–21; one does not need to follow Peter Ackroyd's argument that the language might be referring to events contemporary to the Chronicler (138). This language of the period of the judges might well be part of the unprecedented appearance of the altars, *asherim*, and so on in 2 Chr 14:2—there had been no such places earlier in Chronicles, but they appear many times in Judges (especially in Judg 6)—that are removed by Asa (15:8) following Azariah's speech. Sara Japhet suggests that the sudden appearance of the altars, idols and so on were the result of "a lack of full integration between history and theology" on the part of the Chronicler, so that

Asa's reforms contradict the story given so far in Chronicles but make sense in the context of the story in Kings (707). The use of כתת "to beat in pieces" evokes images both of idols being smashed (2 Kgs 18:4; 2 Chr 34:7) and of swords beaten into ploughshares/ploughshares into swords (Isa 2:4; Mic 4:3; Joel 4:10); images both of idolatry and peace/war. I would suggest, rather, that the Chronicler is deliberately reflecting on the book of Judges and the prophetic texts and trying to draw parallels between the reign of Asa and the period of the judges (perhaps Asa as a new Gideon?). Azariah also reminds Asa and the people in his speech that when the people of old "turned in their distress to YHWH, the God of Israel, and sought him, he was found by them" (15:4); this is language reminiscent of David's charge to Solomon in 1 Chr 28:9 and of Judg 10:10–16 (the unique yet key piece of the Deuteronomist's/s' framework [Polzin 1980:176–77]).

The language of Judges, in particular, informs Azariah's speech in 2 Chr 15. By using this language, the folktales and Deuteronomic framework texts are renewed in Chronicles. From this one example it is perhaps premature to suggest that the generic renewal is also a generic shift, but this is precisely what I do suggest. Through the heteroglossic text of Chronicles, the genre of Judges (the larger Deuteronomic History as well?) is shifted into something else: perhaps theology? This is the *effect* of genre.

However, a Bakhtinian theory of genre does not entirely address the question of what motivates uses of genres or generic innovation or the genre effect. If social context and situation is taken as the only motivating factor for the interplay of style and content, then we run the risk of a certain kind of social determinism. In order to extend and refine a Bakhtinian theory of genre, I would like to examine the role of power in genre theory. If genre is an operation, then a study of the power dynamics in the operation may lead to a greater understanding of genre effect.

WHAT IS POWER?

[P]ower is tolerable only on condition that it mask a substantial part of itself. Its success is proportional to its ability to hide its own mechanisms. (Foucault 1978:86)

Biblical scholars are used to seeing a lot of overt power. The word כֹּחַ appears many times, used of human beings and of God. People have power, God has power. This is what Michel Foucault called "*le Pouvoir*," the thing that he emphatically said that power was not: "I do not mean 'Power' as a group of institutions and mechanisms that ensure the subservience of the citizens to a given state ... [or] a mode of subjugation which, in contrast to violence, has the form of the rule … [or] a general system of domination exerted by one group over another, a system whose effects, through successive derivations, pervade the entire social body" (1978:92). Rather, power is "the multiplic-ity of force relations immanent in the sphere in which they operate … as the strategies in which they take effect" (92–93). So power, too, is not a given, but rather an effect.

The power effect is to operate, which is why we can trace how it works, through the networks of power relations, of domination and resistance. Because every circumstance is different, every part of the network open to influence, power also is not reducible to form: it does operate in a multitude of ways and means. But, as commentators on Foucault have noted, defining power in this way also runs into difficulty, specifically with respect to the problem of the theory and the examples; Foucault's examples are something less than his theoretical formulation (Beer: 85–90). That is, the examples can easily be seen as examples of dominating or repressive power, rather than the flow of power between individuals. Foucault's defense against this charge was to suggest that power and its correlative freedom is only possible between free subjects (1983:221–22) (a problematic defense). But again, perhaps this is a problem that cannot be resolved—another part of the unfinalizability of being.

The link between power and genre comes when we see both as an effect, when we see both as operative. If genre is an effect, coming not from form but from how it operates, then it is a short step to see that genre is a power-effect. Although Foucault explicitly tried to detach power (*le pouvoir*) from the exclusive purview of the politico-legal sphere, if we understand politics as one of the places where power operates, then genre as a power-effect is also political. Genre is a site of politics, a site where power operates. Taking the given of a genre and transforming it into what is created is a manifestation of the power-effect. I would like to briefly examine the source citations from Chronicles as a manifestation of the power-effect.

The Chronicler's source citation formula is different from the formula of Kings. The standard source citation formula in Kings is: הלא־הם כתבים על־… "Are they not written in…?" (1 Kgs 11:41; 14:29; 15:7; 23, 31; 16:5, 14, 20, 27; 22:39, 46; 2 Kgs 1:18; 8:23; 10:34; 12:20; 13:8, 12; 14:15, 18, 28; 15:6, 21, 36; 16:19; 20:20; 21:25; 23:28; 24:5; this form is also found in 2 Chr 9:29; 12:15). The standard source citation formula in Chronicles is: הנם כתובים על־… "Behold, they are written in…." (1 Chr 9:1; 29:29; 2 Chr 9:29; 16:11; 20:34; 24:27; 25:26; 27:7; 28:26; 32:32; 33:18, 19; 35:25, 27; 36:8; this form is also found in 1 Kgs 14:19; 2 Kgs 15:11, 15, 26, 31; all of these passages are non-synoptic with Chronicles). In addition, the subject of the clause, the "they," is described using a different formula in Kings and Chronicles. In Kings, the standard formula is: ויתר דברי−(וכל־)אשר עשה "And the rest of the affairs of X and (all) that he did" (1 Kgs 11:41; 14:29; 15:7, 23, 31; 16:5, 14, 27; 22:39, 46; 2 Kgs 1:18; 8:23; 10:34; 12:20; 13:8, 12; 14:15, 28; 15:6, 21, 26, 31, 36; 16:19; 20:20; 21:25; 23:28; 24:5). There is considerable variation in the next part of the formula, but the pattern is usually clear: an elaboration of some of these deeds or affairs. In Chronicles, the standard formula is: (ויתר) דברי־הראשנים והאחרנים "And (the rest of) the affairs of X, first through last" (1 Chr 29:29; 2 Chr 9:29; 12:15; 16:11; 20:34; 25:26; 26:22; 28:26; 35:27). Again, there is some variation in this next part of the formula. Considering the two parts of the formula in both Kings and Chronicles, there are some textual variants in all four of these formulae. The LXX is not tremendously consistent in the form of these formulae; methodologically, it is preferable to heed James Barr's caution on using the versions and in particular the LXX to reconstruct the MT from a grammatical/syntactical stance (265–72). In the MT, however, the overall pattern is clear. I am more tempted toward thinking that the exceptions prove the rule than I am towards thinking that each exception says something profound about the creation and/or evolution of the text.

The consensus has been that the Chronicler had access to other sources beyond Samuel-Kings for the period of time covered in the text. But the consensus also says that whenever the Chronicler cited a source, it is a fictitious source, and that whenever the Chronicler used a real source, it is left uncited (so, e.g., Knoppers: 126). What is interesting is that the rhetorical implications of this hypothesis have not been fully explored. What does it mean to cite a source that does not exist? How does it bolster the authority of the Chronicler (which is a commonly asserted reason; cf. Duke: 119) to cite a source that does not exist? Why would one cite a nonexistent source and then not cite a very-existent source? Why would one not cite the very-existent source of Samuel-Kings when the omissions from the source are sometimes glaringly evident (e.g., the emergence of Jeroboam in 2 Chr 10)? I believe the answers to these questions are most evident once the genre analysis has been performed.

I would argue that the difference in the formulae is actually a generic innovation. It is a deployment of power within the genre. The power effect of a declarative, presentative statement like הנם כתובים "behold they are written" (Waltke and O'Connor:40.2.1) is different from a rhetorical question like הלא־הם כתובים "are they not written?" (Waltke and O'Connor: 40.3). A rhetorical question has the possibility of being answered with a negative: "Are they not written in the Book of the Kings of Israel and Judah?" has the possible (if highly unlikely) answer of: "No, in fact, they are not." But there is no answer to the statement: "Look, they are written in the Book of the Kings of Israel and Judah." The statement demands acceptance. Similarly, the phrase "the rest of the affairs of X and all that he did" as used by Kings may imply that some of that king's deeds are described in the book of Kings, and some of his deeds are described elsewhere. This may be, in fact, the kind of canonical loophole that even permits the existence of Chronicles: the things left out. But Chronicles makes a different claim; it is "the rest of the affairs of X, first through last" that are recorded elsewhere; thus it is not only the king's deeds that are recorded, but also all of the affairs that took place during that king's reign. The Chronicler can, through this means, imply that only a certain selection of material has been presented in Chronicles. Within the genre that includes both Samuel-Kings and Chronicles, the Chronicler has taken the genre and made an innovation: it is not bits and pieces of everything that are included in his work, but a clearly made selection. This, I would argue, is a power play. The answer to the questions about citation of nonexistent sources when existent sources are not cited may be made along the same lines: the Kings formula says, "If you do not believe me, then you can look in this other source;" the Chronicles formula says, "If you do believe me, then you can look in this other source," but if the reader does believe the Chronicler, then there is no need to look at another text! This too is a use of the power of the genre by the Chronicler.

What Is *Eros*?

"For eros is not, Socrates," she said, "of the beautiful, as you believe." "Well, what then?" "It is of engendering and bringing to birth in the beautiful." (Plato, *Symp.* 206e, trans. Benardete)

Platonic *eros* is closely linked if not identical with desire (Plato, *Phaedr.* 237d). Often it is taken to mean sexual desire, but *eros* goes beyond that to describe all kinds of desire (see the discussion in the *Republic* on the tyrannical man). As Paul Ludwig has put it, though, it is important to distinguish between "any banal desire, such as the wish for a second helping at the dinner table," and *eros* (12). He suggests that in platonic thought, *eros* is something beyond basic needs, and that it has something of a compulsion or obsession about it; the subject of *eros* will pursue it as far as possible (13). Ultimately, all discussions of desire in the Western tradition are based on the discussion of *eros* in Plato, and especially the discussions in the *Symposium* and the *Phaedrus*—and the *Republic* is also a text to attend to. In the *Symposium*, there are two basic definitions of *eros*: that *eros* is motivated by a lack—that we seek what we do not have, especially beauty; and that *eros* is motivated by generation—that we seek to create the beautiful—and it is this definition that I have quoted. *Eros*, then, is either a lack, or it is a productive act, or it is both.

Eros as a lack is very common in the Western philosophical tradition: it is found in Hegel, in Nietzsche, in Freud and Lacan and Irigaray, and in Foucault. However, what is much more interesting to me is the conception of *eros* as productive, and this has found its most recent expression in the work of Gilles Deleuze. In a note written after Foucault's death, Deleuze wrote: "The last time we saw each other, Michel told me, with much kindness and affection, something like, I cannot bear the word *desire*; even if you use it differently, I cannot keep myself from thinking or living that desire = lack, or that desire is repressed.... For me [Deleuze], desire implies no lack; neither is it a natural given" (189, emphasis original). In this view of *eros*, it is also an operation: it is an arrangement, it leads to creation; it motivates creation. In addition, I would argue, it would also act as the motivation behind power (with Deleuze: 186: "power is an affection of desire."). And it is this link that is most forcefully made in the *Republic*. Once we have made the link between *eros* and power, where *eros* is the creative motivator of power—when power is understood as the network of embedded discourses—then we can also link *eros* to genre. *Eros* motivates the power effect; *eros* motivates the genre effect. So the effect of genre, the operation of genre, is motivated by *eros*, and especially *eros* as a productive act. Taking the given of the genre and transforming it into something created is both a manifestation of the power-effect and also a manifestation of *eros*, intense desire for creation. And, I would argue, the intense desire for creation is a motivator for the deployment of power.

In order to use this completed model to explore a biblical text, we need to recognize that it is only in a series of examples that its usefulness will become clear or not. In fact, in order to be most useful, the theoretical model needs to be derived from the reading of the biblical texts; it needs to be arrived at inductively (as I noted above). In this way, I take issue with those who have taken literary-critical methods from other fields of study and simply applied them to the biblical text. Although I have used the insights of literary criticism and philosophy to describe my theoretical model, it is not a simple matter of finding a method from literary studies and using it on the biblical text.[1] I have

---

1. In the spirit of Bakhtin (if not his practice; cf. Holquist: 188), there are the voices of two of my teachers, Fernando de Toro and Robert Polzin in the Comparative Literary Studies program at Carleton University, who speak through me here. In a doctoral seminar in the mid-1990s, when one student spoke of "applying" a method to a literary text, de Toro snapped back, "You do not apply a method to a text. The method grows out of your reading of the text." And Polzin once told me that while his generation had fruitfully used the methods and theories of literary criticism to read the biblical text, it was up to my generation to develop our own theories from our readings of the texts rather than to continue to mine literary studies for our theory and method. I am reminded of Stephen D. Moore's

abstracted the theoretical model from the text, but now I would like to demonstrate briefly where the model has come from. My previous example dealt with the aspect of Foucauldian power, now this example shows how all the threads come together; the threads of Bakhtinian genre, Foucauldian power, and Deleuzian desire.

The final particular example is one verse, 2 Chr 32:19, which reads: "And they spoke about the god of Jerusalem as about the gods of the peoples of the lands, the work of human hands." This particular verse is unique in its use of the term אלהי־ירושלם, "god of Jerusalem." The verse comes at the end of the Chronicler's version of the story of Sennacherib's invasion of Judah, which differs not inconsiderably from the version in Kings. The verse as a whole draws on the language of the passages in 2 Kgs 18–19 and Isa 36–37, language that is placed in the mouths of the Assyrians in those passages, and that is picked up in the language of the Assyrians in 2 Chr 32. It is in these Assyrian speeches that YHWH is compared with the gods of other nations and other cities. However, 2 Chr 32:19 is not a quotation of the Assyrians but a narratorial aside about their speech. It may be a parody of their speech: a sneering narratorial rebuttal of their theology. But in this sneering rebuttal, the language of the particularity of YHWH, YHWH as patron of Jerusalem the city (rather than Israel the *ethnos*) is maintained from the Assyrians' speeches of 2 Kings and Isaiah. This slip, this ungrammaticality (cf. Riffaterre), reveals both the aspect of parody, and the aspect of desire. The Chronicler, despite protestations to the contrary (1 Chr 16), desires a particular, patron, visible god, like the gods of the nations. Here, then, we see an example of *eros* in the text. It may be that this example of *eros* has to do with a lack or a repression, as Foucault, Hegel, et al. would have it. But Deleuze argues that desire is social and collective; any desire that is "deterritorialized" wants "a transcendental signified such as happiness, God, wealth, fame" and is "reterritorialized" as a "negative will to power [that] aims to encompass the whole world in its interpretations" (Goodchild: 196–97). What, then, does this example of *eros* have to do with genre?

This particular episode, Sennacherib's invasion of Jerusalem, is an excellent place to make a study of genre, since it appears in both Kings and Chronicles, which many would consider "historiography," as well as in Isaiah, which most would consider "prophecy." Yet while 2 Kings and Isaiah have almost identical versions of the story, so much so that it is common

---

comment, "The arrival in biblical studies of a fledgeling literary-critical methodology … generally signals its geriatric status, or utter exhaustion, if not its outright demise, in literary studies" (289).

for commentaries on Isaiah to refer readers to the literature on Kings, especially for the "historical issues," (e.g., Blenkinsopp: 461)—and in the case of Isaiah, where for the most part scholars consider the passage to have been borrowed from 2 Kings, Yuri Lotman's notion of the inserted text (377–84), which is close to Bakhtin's idea of heteroglossia, is particularly helpful—it is Chronicles that has the different version. More to the point, Chronicles has transformed the "given" of Kings and Isaiah in its creation of another text. What is the effect of this transformation? It is to simplify the story, to create a very clear chain of cause and effect. What does this have to do with genre? One of the clearest areas of agreement among scholars on the text of 2 Kgs 18–19 is that there are two stories combined into the text: the text is messy (Childs: 69–103; Cogan and Tadmor: 240–44). This seems to be a feature of much of Samuel and Kings (so, e.g., the three stories of the death of Goliath in 1–2 Samuel, two of which are combined in 1 Sam 17; the other is in 2 Sam 21), and it has the effect of positing that there may well be more than one story about a particular event and the author has decided to provide both: it is a feature of the genre with a particular effect. This genre-effect of messiness in Samuel and Kings is transformed into the simplifying genre-effect of tidiness and order in Chronicles. The power of the transformation is easily seen: possibilities and meanings are shut down or repressed, although occasionally they break out, as in the Chronicler's story of the division of the kingdom in 2 Chr 10, when Jeroboam pops up after having been excised from the account of Solomon in 2 Chr 1–9. Chronicles is operating within the same genre as Kings, but uses the power of the genre in such a way that certain conclusions must be drawn by the reader of the text rather than leaving the reader to puzzle it out on his or her own. Yet the power is hidden: the story told seems to be the same one as told in 2 Kings and Isaiah. What motivates the use of this power? It is intense desire, *eros*, in this case going mostly hidden, implied, and unspoken until it erupts in 2 Chr 32:19: an *eros* for YHWH, one, particularist, and local. This *eros* for YHWH motivates the use of genre-power to reshape the story to show his ultimate power (a negative will to power, in Deleuzian terms). This *eros*, therefore, looks like it may indicate a lack or a repression (and it does, in a way), but it also leads to a singularly productive act, the productive use of genre-power to create a new text.

If we return to Bakhtin, who insisted upon the social-situatedness of all genre and utterance, then we must seek out the context for such a generic transformation, from rambling and compendious to narrowly focused. As with all biblical literature, this is a difficult and delicate task, tending toward the circular in its argument. As such, this is not an argument that can be fully made in the space here, but if we locate the writing of Chronicles in a fifth-to-third century B.C.E. context, then it is not difficult to see an intense desire for a powerful, particular and local YHWH as a strong motivator for using the power inherent in the genre to transform the genre.

Genre, then, is an effect, an operation. Power operates on genre in order to achieve the genre effect; that power is motivated by *eros*. In many cases, this use of power is a political use of power; the motivating *eros* is a political kind of *eros*. Genres can be transformed through this operation of power and *eros*, and that operation can have a political outcome. By situating the genre change in a social context, by observing how power and *eros* are delineated, we can discover something about that genre and about the use of biblical genres generally.

EXPERIENTIAL LEARNING: THE CONSTRUCTION OF JONATHAN IN THE NARRATIVE OF SAUL AND DAVID

Barbara Green

The *questions* driving this study are able to be subsumed under the issue of Jonathan's construction: How will I read him and offer him to you? How will I suggest that he has been drawn by the story's author, handled by its narrator? How might he have been plausibly interpreted by intended readers and rereaders? How is Jonathan read and dealt with by other characters in the story, notably by Saul and by David?[1]

My *thesis* is that Jonathan initially articulates one stance but ends up with quite another, an education which is available to us in careful linguistic detail. In between our meeting him abruptly in 1 Sam 14 and hearing him eulogized after his death in 1 Sam 31 and 2 Sam 1, we have two short moments and one lengthy scene with him. In the first short moment (1 Sam 19:1–7), Jonathan urges his father to desist from suspecting any threat from and thus opposing David; much later (1 Sam 23:17), Jonathan has acceded to the reality of David's ascendancy over Saul. The key chapter for present purposes is 1 Sam 20: there Jonathan begins with one point of view about Saul's intent on his lips (20:2) but has changed his position substantially by the end of that long chapter (20:41–42). Thus Jonathan's education, managed primarily by David but also by Saul, is accomplished as he makes his way through a long narrative comprising fifteen pairs of utterances, interacting with "brother" or father. Careful attention to language, genre and readerly presuppositions will show us the process.

An initial point to raise is the *sociohistorical context* of the narrative. Given the impacted state of questions regarding date, composition and context of the Deuteronomistic History and its components, I will simply stipulate that a moment of great relevance for the production and proclamation of the long

---

1. This piece on Saul's son Jonathan is a sort of companion to a short study of his daughter Michal. See Green 2003a.

narrative seems the early postexilic period, when issues of leadership in Persian-sponsored Yehud were fraught. Ehud Ben Zvi reminds us how thoroughly the Deuteronomistic History features the topic of leadership, specifically as failing. If dynastic leaders failed repeatedly and dismally in the past, what sort of governance holds better promise? If dynastic kings were implicated in the loss of land in the early sixth century, how will a new such catastrophe be avoided once the land has been re-entered and the community has a fresh chance to live there fruitfully (Ben Zvi: 32–35)? My conviction is that the story of Saul and his "sons" (Jonathan and David in the present story) was recomposed to be meaningful in the moment when the prospect of postexilic royal leadership was possible but not ultimately chosen.[2]

RELEVANT CONCEPTS FROM BAKHTIN

The *theory* to be utilized is provided by Mikhail Bakhtin (1895–1975) and nuanced by various contemporary scholars. Bakhtin's most basic concept is *"dialogism"*: the conviction that all reality is fundamentally engaged with and embedded tensively within other reality. Though the word was coined by scholars rather than by Bakhtin himself, in some of his last writings he alluded briefly and impressionistically to "dialogical relations" (Bakhtin 1986:104–6, 117, 125). The concept is specifically modern, arising in the twentieth century's discovery of alterity, its turn to language, and its science. Dialogism is thus actually a set of ostensibly diverse concepts unified by the insight that encountering the other is crucial for the construction of our consciousness and being, and of course for every other's as well. Two Bakhtin scholars who occasionally publish excerpts from what they call a "heteroglossary" offer the useful insight that there are several levels of the dialogic, among which Bakhtin moves without signaling, perhaps confusingly for us (Morson and Emerson 1997:264–66). The concept of dialogism becomes useful beyond a general situation of mere alternation of interlocutors in life or literature or of simple disagreement or contradiction. In a technical sense, every exchange is dialogic, assuming two participants shaped foundationally by their interaction. In a more factored sense, we can think of such discourse as either monologic or dialogic—located along a spectrum from one of those ideal points to the other. In monologic discourse, each speaker retains his or her own point of view with virtually no spillage from what the partner is saying beyond reinforcement of the original view. In dialogic discourse there is a reverberating shaping of one viewpoint

---

2. See Green 2003b:1–19 for a fuller (though still roughly sketched) treatment of these circumstances.

under the influence of another. Gaps and differences are crucial, while bridges and continuities are stressed as well, perhaps more. The genuinely dialogic requires two or more distinct speakers, each with a voice, a set of experiences, distinct placement, attitudes and outlooks on the world. For language to be dialogic in this sense, the two voices and their relationships must both register with hearer/readers. A yet more intense level of dialogism opens out on the polyphony that Bakhtin found most clearly in Dostoyevsky, which is beyond the scope of this particular reading.

Why is dialogism helpful, and what proceeds differently for us as a consequence of attending to it and incorporating its wisdom among our strategies? First, it counts foundationally on the ignorance of all of us, the necessary presence of gaps in all our fondest schemes and most elaborate systems and our need for an other to contribute. Second, it challenges us to a revised concept of the self: Though we may look like tidy little units, bounded by our own skin and quite able to tell where one of us ends and another begins, in fact dialogism shifts "the differential relation between a center and all that is not that center" (Holquist 1990:18). We need to be aware of the limits of our apparent autonomy and of the importance of our own particularity and that of the other. To commit consciously to construct meaning as pervasively as possible in relation to others alters most things considerably. Third, voices in life but also in literature will need to undergo a repositioning. Characters and narrator alike will achieve their positions and make their meaning while contending with each other; the readerly task will involve our discerning a way amid the cacophony, claiming our own path forward as we construe speech in our particular way. The reliable and omniscient narrator is displaced from an erstwhile natural authority.

A second most useful insight of Bakhtin's is his conviction that the basic unit of discourse is the *utterance*. Katerina Clark and Michael Holquist name it as the basic building block of Bakhtin's dialogism, and Ken Hirschkop goes so far as to say it is co-pivotal with dialogism in Bakhtin's language theory (Clark and Holquist: 10; Hirschkop: 209). "Bakhtin defines utterance as the simultaneity of what is actually said and what is assumed but not spoken" (Clark and Holquist: 207). Bakhtin develops the discussion about utterance somewhat polemically in relation to formalist thinking about language.[3] Hence we can usefully see what utterance is not: a syntactic, linguistically

---

3. For more information, consult Morson and Emerson 1990:123–39. Bakhtin's essay "Speech Genres" is also shaped in conversation with criticism he holds to be inadequate; he mentions alternative ways of conceiving language (1986:61–75 but sporadically elsewhere in the essay as well). Though he touches on the concept of utterance in earlier work as well, the "Speech Genres" essay is quite complete in itself.

marked unit like the sentence. An utterance can take sentence form, but not every sentence is an utterance. An utterance is identifiable by a pause, a relinquishing of the floor, a change of speaker; that the first speaker stops indicates that the utterance is, temporarily, complete and awaits, invites, a response. Bakhtin specifies various aspects that an utterance rolls together: grammar and syntax, certain compositional structures, style (at various levels, including that of the language or dialect used, the genre, the individual speaker's patterns), intonation (Bakhtin 1986:60–102). He stresses that the utterance is simply a small part of a much broader flow of communication: "The utterance proves to be a very complex and multiplanar phenomenon if considered not in isolation and with respect to its author (the speaker) only, but as a link in the chain of speech communication and with respect to other, related utterances" (Bakhtin 1986:93; Hirschkop: 210). The enthymemic character of the utterance invites and even compels us to work out its logic creatively if we are to take advantage of all that is on offer. Part of participating well in language and literature is taking joyful advantage of the fact that all goods are secondhand, with the patina of associations available from some of the many places our language has already been.

Vital to understand in this concept of utterance is its relational and malleable nature. As a speaker shapes an utterance, he or she is already taking into account the responses of the listener; the listener is also authoring the utterance and the speaker is simultaneously a listener. An utterance is shaped *for* someone, is addressed *to* a particular recipient (not necessarily a named individual but to a receiving and co-shaping party) (Bakhtin 1986:95–99). And as the elements compose the utterance, they bring with them associations they have had previously, which are likely to be in contention with each other. Utterances have their own internal politics, say Morson and Emerson (1990:130). These features of the utterance explain why Bakhtin classifies it as a "border phenomenon," living its life at the crossroads of many users and usages, its "fated in-betweenness" making it thoroughly social (Holquist 1990:60–61). To understand an utterance is to commit actively to construe as many of the circumstances of its production that we are able; passive decoding will fall short. Such reading must also be relational; understanding is an effect of interaction. And part of what must be queried is the evaluative aspect of the utterance, which is inevitably present and anticipates both the speaker's angle and that of the intended hearer, who will reevaluate it while construing it.

Germane here are two caveats: First, our reading of ancient literature is typically disabled from access to the social context so vitally necessary in Bakhtin's thought. To stipulate a historical-social context as I have done is scarcely adequate to what really needs to be explored for discourse to be understandable. Second is that with Bakhtin, we need to make the sometimes difficult distinction between character psychology (which is *not* our concern, not available to us) and the language that we as interpreters manage in our own centers of consciousness (which *is* of urgent concern). In a word, the Jonathan, Saul, and David that we—you and I—are reading is primarily our own and needs to be owned as such. We have "the same" text before us, the same discourse, but how we construe it will vary as we each take it up. We likely will not agree, a situation that roots less in our explicit procedures than in our more implicit and possibly unrecognized assumptions and ideologies as we work with the text.

Finally, the *plan* here is to make central to our study the galvanizing experience of Jonathan represented in 1 Sam 20. With its impact made clear, the other four scenes involving Jonathan will be commented upon more briefly and in terms of the longer piece.

THE EXPERIENTIAL EDUCATION OF JONATHAN: 1 SAMUEL 20

Robert Polzin contributes to the present reading several general observations. He notes the apparently anomalous characterizations of Jonathan, Saul, and David, who all may seem to be acting against expectation here. Jonathan seems naïve beyond belief, Saul unrealistically oblivious of recent events, David foolish to wager that Saul might change. Polzin finds coherence in a careful rereading: Jonathan consistently views matters in a straightforward and uncomplicated way, unless carrying out another's plan. Saul's outbursts are credible, given David's provocation and the stakes involved. Polzin finds David hardest to recharacterize, a result of the narrator's tendency to withhold David's inner view, leaving me a path for making him intent on provoking Saul to chase him (187–90). Polzin's second helpful point: the double-voicing of the covenant language is obvious, its emotional tone, vehement urgency, and participation in political and personal realms carrying those involved (our reading selves included) into multiple pools and their deep waters. David induces Jonathan to use duplicitously this language which pledges mutual fidelity; can such contradictory assertions be relied upon? Polzin asks (third) who is set up to learn new information about Saul? Jonathan may seem to be helping David gain clarity, but Polzin prefers that David is assisting Jonathan to see a reality about his father that the son has heretofore resisted to accept (190–94). The drama we are about to witness is staged tactically for Jonathan, if more strategically for Saul.

The event of chapter 20 unfolds in great detail.[4] It seems simple at first:

---

4. Fokkelman gives many excellent insights and offers several charts that are visually

Saul reinforces his opposition to David, such that David must flee the court definitively. But it is also possible to characterize the chapter as detailing a manipulation of Saul by David and Jonathan (or of both king and prince by David), such that by the conclusion Saul himself must go more decisively on the defensive in order to survive as king. Jonathan will not again intervene to dissuade Saul for all that he remains at his father's side to death. Utterance language—direct discourse in all its complexity—is the means used to draw this scenario. Especially in the front part of the story there is only the minimum narrator intervention needed for the clear arranging of the scene. We hear the characters struggle to engage each other: to set traps and spring them, alternatively to detect danger and escape it. Of fifteen pairs of utterances, some are very simple (even nonverbal), others more complex: four of David (to Jonathan, who responds); two of Jonathan (to David who responds); four of Saul (to himself and to Jonathan, who counters); and finally five apparently very one-sided ones between Jonathan and "the boy" in the field (which are actually as response-shaped as any of the others).

DAVID AND JONATHAN'S FIRST SIX UTTERANCE PAIRS: 20:1–23

All flows from David's initial question, "What is my guilt … my sin against your father that he is seeking to take my life [נפשׁ]?" David's question both hides and reveals a quick pair of his answers: Saul's unprovoked assault on David is either malicious or irrational. In either case, the king is at fault. A question may be pursued independent of the intent which we may presume underlies it. So David's asking what he has done prompts me, at least, to review from the angle of Saul what in fact David *has* done that makes Saul wish him dead or disabled (e.g., 18:10–12, 29; 19:2, 10, 11). There are two levels to the question, which we can scrutinize in terms of David. The first is the problem of the old king's alienation from YHWH's favor, made tangible by YHWH's spirit leaving Saul and resting with David (16:13–14; 18:10–29; 19:9–10, 20–24). Mixed right in with that language of God's spirit is something more "horizontal": the pattern that persistently evokes Saul's hostility to David is his registering (rightly or wrongly) other people being drawn to the young man: Saul's people in general (18:12–16, 29), the women (18:6–9), Saul's younger daughter (18:20–29, 19:11–18), Jonathan (18:1–4; 19:1–7), perhaps even Saul's prophet (19:18–24). In the six utterance rounds here, David will in fact set up the same entrapping dynamic to which Saul has already reacted and use it to reshape Jonathan's viewpoint.

---

clarifying (295ff.) Edelman has good observations of the ways in which language echoes what has been said earlier (153–91).

In the first exchange (round 1, 20:1–2), each young man sketches his sense of the king. David assays most obviously that Saul is mistaken in his pursuit of David and that he himself is unaware of his own guilt or sin, hence the similarity of his claim to Jonathan's assertion of 19:2. The alternative, also subtly proffered, is that Saul hunts David without rational cause, perhaps with malicious intent. And yet Saul has turned back from the project of David's death at Jonathan's intervention (19:6) and apparently abandoned pursuit of David when thrown into prophetic behavior (as ch. 19 ends). So Saul seeks David's life intermittently at most. David has also hinted that Saul seeks to kill Jonathan as well, since their lives are intertwined (18:3). That point is not made explicit by David but remains available to any interpreter who picks up on the doubled speech. Whether David's self-portrait (innocence) is specious is not relevant here; that his sketch of Saul is partly right (seeking characterizes Saul, and the life of the sons is his objective), but also off the mark is to some extent evident. Saul is reactive to many impulses, not excluding David's actions (whether guilt or sin) but not limited to David's qualities. That Saul has dismissed such concerns verbally to Jonathan in 19:1–7 does not mean he banished them, as the rest of chapter 19 has shown. David has begun to undermine Jonathan's confidence, prompting him first to defend it.

Still within this utterance Jonathan makes five rebuttals to David's initial three questions, his view of his father differing from David's in a number of particulars. Jonathan verbalizes Saul as confiding all his purposes and plans to his son, from great to small. That Jonathan does not know of a plan to kill David, he reasons, means it cannot be so. But Jonathan's portrait of Saul, which he urges on David, overlooks a lot to draw this unity between them and reactivates the question of the singleness of life shared between David and Jonathan. Though a reader may catalogue times and places where Saul has hurled a spear or urged his people to kill David or sent messengers to take him, nonetheless Jonathan is committed to the sense that such are not Saul's current thoughts. That Jonathan can overlook these moments suggests that his father may be able, driven, to do so too. Toward the end of his strong denial Jonathan poses to David's lead question the query that moves the whole chapter forward: Why might Saul hide such a thing from his son? By asking that question, Jonathan admits the possibility that David's charge may be true. Saul may be seeking David's life without David's deserving it and without Jonathan's knowing it. Though there is a push on the part of commentators to resolve the complexity of Saul's intent in favor of single-minded pursuit of David by Saul, in fact that is not quite so simply the case. Jonathan's defense of Saul, though it will be overrun, is not wholly without merit.

In 20:3–4 (round 2) David responds less to Jonathan's denials of his father's deeds than to his question of his father's motive and mode of secrecy. He explains away that portrait of Saul who confides in his son by suggesting that Saul is unwilling to split Jonathan's feelings by making him choose between his father and "brother": "Do not let Jonathan know this, or he will be grieved," David explains, is Saul's inner process (hypothetical quoted direct discourse). David offers Jonathan and intensified sense of the closeness of the father and son but denies it simultaneously, draws a different conclusion from that bond than had Jonathan.

Jonathan seems convinced by what David has said, shifting his picture of Saul who would not hide plans from a son for what David has urged, a sketch which draws the father concerned for his son. Jonathan consequently offers David a blank check: "Whatever you say, I will do for you." The phrasing is key: "What you(rself) [נפש] say(s), I will do for you." Thus begins Jonathan's direct and doubled discourse on the topic of his bond with David (for which the narrator primed us at the start of chapter 18). The language here picks up as well on the exchange between Jonathan and his armorbearer (14:7), a pregnant allusion in terms of the exchange with the weapon-bearing boy at the end of this chapter. There is a series of minor, unnamed and untextured figures throughout this book, attracting our notice in their consistency and homology. Jonathan's armorbearer accompanied him obediently and faithfully, assisting him in his victory over the Philistines (14:1–15). David begins as armorbearer to Saul (16:21), then accepts the weapons of Jonathan (18:4). From this moment Jonathan acts for his friend rather than for his father and to some extent acts against his father, thus tripping, trapping, Saul into the murderous pursuit of David. Who is the hunter here, and who the quarry?

The next lineaments of the royal portrait (round 3, found in 20:5–9) are supplied by David, though they shrewdly capitalize both on Jonathan's claims to intimacy with his father's plans and on the closeness between the two "sons." He first sketches the king's festal table on the morrow, situating himself in hiding rather than at table—a summary sketch, in fact, of the whole scenario to follow. Picking up on a technique utilized by Saul and servants in chapter 18, David hands his own words to Jonathan for him to recite at the proper time. David proposes a small drama that will scrutinize the issue that is most fraught between himself and Saul: sonship. Whose son is David: Saul's or Jesse's? Whose servant: Saul's or Jonathan's? David is now altering the father-son bond shared by Saul and Jonathan. We note also that the plan presumes that Saul expects David at his table (their rift being not total yet) and makes diagnostic Saul's reaction when he learns David has gone to Bethlehem with Jonathan's permission. David calls Saul both "the king" and "your father." He avoids referencing his own father clearly, saying rather "his city," "the family."

David similarly crafts for Saul two utterances: either "good," which will approve David's return to his father; or a wordless anger, which will signify the opposite.[5] David again draws Saul clearly either able to approve or to grow angry, yet it seems that Jonathan's very presence in the experiment will affect how his father responds, a Heisenbergian factor that seems to surprise Jonathan when it happens. David delicately does not articulate to Jonathan what Saul might say besides "good." The plan implicates Jonathan, since he will have known and approved David's plan, whether Saul likes it or does not. Though David's moves seem reactive to Saul's earlier ones, it is also patent that David is closing in on Saul here, closing down his options to two, from which the king will select one. The positive response—owned by all its speakers, "Good!" (טוב)—is a loaded word in this narrative, tasting bitterly of the occasion when Saul was fired from kingship and a better man appointed in his place (15:28). Though it has been made obvious to the reader who that man is, Saul's information on the identity is less unequivocal. The word "good" has hovered around David in the appraisal and even in the words of Jonathan about David. Is it likely that Saul will be able to use this word wholeheartedly of his protégé? David seems certain of his quarry, and indeed he is not wrong in his plottings. We can hear David reminding Saul as well as Jonathan (and ourselves) that the two "sons" are one and that they deal with each other apart from him. David is also making that bond one strand thicker by his plan here. More than a test of Saul—though framed as showing what is set or established (כלה) this is an experiment precipitating new outcomes as well as reinforcing old ones, since it implicates Jonathan and forces awareness of collusion onto Saul. And more than a test, it is arguably an entrapment, whether that awareness is shown as David's or not. David also prescribes for Jonathan a conclusion and an implicative order: if I am to be killed, you do it; why let your father do it? A rhetorical question? Is David relatively safe in asking Jonathan to kill him? Jonathan's response is to deny the possibility of filial complicity, with strong language and with a loaded question anticipating David's assent: "If I knew that evil was decided by my father to come upon you, would I not tell you?" David has extracted a choice from Jonathan now.

In 20:10–11 (round 4) the conversation moves from what will happen to how the king's response can be communicated. David asks that detail, prompting Jonathan to propose a change of venue. They go out to the field, the site where the rest of their planning and communication will take place.

---

5. Polzin queries (188) why the two (or either of them) should continue to trust Saul's expressions of goodwill toward David. He thinks (192) that Jonathan rather consistently misses the negative undertow of persons and situations, despite David's direction that he be more duplicitous or at least suspicious.

It is, perhaps, a reminder that the court is unsafe for David (to some extent a fugitive), or that the court is unsafe for the conversation the two are holding. It also prompts the question of why their talk is dangerous for them. Is the court dangerous for Saul?

Jonathan takes the initiative in 20:12–17 (round 5) in the field, rehearsing the communication of the information,[6] making three complicated, condition- and oath-laden assertions: the first sentence involves the reconnaissance and communication of each alternative Saul may take, depending on Saul's dispositions; a second voices an oath that Jonathan will send David away safely if Saul is not well-disposed toward him; the third pronounces a blessing for David with proviso for David's reciprocal commitment to survivors of Jonathan's house. The detail of the king's possible anger is elaborated ominously. Jonathan's emotional reaction can scarcely be missed within this very strong utterance. Jonathan binds David to himself and his own life to David again, recommitting them to the matters begun—granted one-sidedly and nonverbally—in 18:1–5. Jonathan's language locks all three principals— God as well—in the roles just evolved in the exchanges set up here by David. Jonathan will assist David, who is, in turn and in time, to reciprocate to Jonathan or his seed. David does not utter, but the narrator implies (by verb form), that David completes his own oath as urged by Jonathan and reminds us of the significance of what we have just heard: Jonathan loves David as himself. Whether Jonathan sketches his own father as the opponent so dangerous to David whom YHWH is to cut off is unclear but not impossible, at least to a reader. Part of the trap here is this strong language of Jonathan about David's enemies, one of whom, the narrator has told us (18:29), is Saul. Jonathan's words intensify the enmity, anticipated as they are before Saul has had his chance to choose an option. We are again reminded of the language between Jonathan and his armorbearer in 14, where Saul is again the eventual if unintended fall guy of his son's speech. His own awareness of the import of his words is uncertain. Does Jonathan intend to set his father up here by oath? Jonathan aligns himself against those who see David as enemy and curses them.

The final planning utterance (round 6, 20:18–23) opens with Jonathan now echoing antiphonally David's speech of 20:5–8, envisioning both the

---

6. Fokkelman calls the field the antipole of the court (308–9)—and a different place as well from the field in which David hid when Jonathan successfully urged reconciliation to his father; Saul's court Fokkelman names as the intersection of all the quests of this whole unit (294). Pleins suggests (34) that the field (and David's other venues) take him outside the circle of Saul's realm. See Campbell (209–12) for a thorough review of the apparent inconsistencies as well as a solution to them.

king's table and the missing David, whose position Jonathan specifies in detail, sending David as the two rehearsed, though not to Bethlehem but to the field nearby. Jonathan reiterates the particulars of the table, never quite filling in the moment of denouement, and promises information. He then responds more specifically to the question David proposed in 20:10: Who will communicate the bad news and how? Presumably the difficulty will not arise if the king turns out to say, "Good"! The plan he crafts seems perhaps overly complex, but for our purposes it can be classed as another doubled speech, in that it is rehearsed here for a later use and will be directed to a boy with one ostensible referent and to the hidden man with another.[7] The heft of the communication of the arrows is on the "flee danger" option, as before. That the system will break down in the event does not mean it is not sensible when set up.

To sum up: if I am correct to construct David as ultimately tracking Saul (Green 2003b:367–410), then to reassign Jonathan from placating the king is key. And insofar as Saul has been shown particularly reactive to collaboration between David and Saul's own intimates, David has chosen an apt curriculum. Splitting Jonathan from his father, David has shown to Jonathan a side of his father whom—as enemy to David—Jonathan must oppose. Notably, Jonathan does not explicitly envision what actually is about to happen, which is to say he does not acknowledge except hypothetically Saul as a danger to either himself or David; but the possibility reverberates in his utterance, given his resolves. Saul has been made near-incorrigible, at least by David and Jonathan whose oaths have asked God's participation as well.

SAUL AND JONATHAN'S FOUR UTTERANCE PAIRS: 20:24–34

The narrator intrudes in 20:24–26 (round 7) suddenly, but still primarily to position us for viewing, to cue us to what Saul is about to note. The time is the feast of which David and Jonathan have just spoken, and the place is the king's table. Saul is seated, Jonathan and Abner present, David's place noticeably empty, since the narrator situates him in terms of language used of him recently: hiding, hidden—David, hiding *from* Saul or—and—David hidden as a lure *for* the king. Saul speaks once to himself, in relation with Jonathan, as he and we know. His answer reveals his question, the reason for David's absence from the table: "he is not clean, surely he is not clean." The dialogical quality of the rumination suggests the intensity of the soliloquy, though in terms of utterances, Saul is engaged, for us, with David and Jonathan. Saul

---

7. Fokkelman discusses the level of the communication at great length (intermittently, 319–51), hiding some good insight amid a great deal of other detail.

accounts for David's absence, pictures David as present except for a disqualifying technicality.

The next moment (20:27–29, round 8) repeats "the same" query. But time has moved on, though the place repeats: It is the next day, and Saul cannot contain his speech within him any longer and poses his question to his son Jonathan—the narrator's tag again reminding us of the paternal/filial agenda. Calling David (three times) Jesse's son, Saul requests, demands, to know where he is. His question now, flushed from the underbrush of his self-talk, reveals the inadequacy of his own previous effort to convince himself that it must be temporary uncleanness, since he backs up to the absence of the previous day. That he is correct to doubt the excuse offered does not alter much the portrait of the king, chased by his own fears into the thicket of testing woven by David and Jonathan. Saul's calling David by his patronym (disparagingly in the view of most commentators) underlines his failure to make David his own son, retraces the pattern of Saul's unhappiness when any third party engages David—even his natural father. The language brings forward the verbal struggles of this pair of protagonists from just after the Goliath slaying (17:55–58), from the two betrothals, which also redirect us to the Goliath contest, which put the boy and the king into competition (N.B. 17:25–27 as well as 18:18 and 23).

Jonathan's response to his father, echoing David's words (20:6) but ringing some crucial changes, starts in a sort of reporting mode: "David urgently asked leave of me to go to Bethlehem"; then switching into direct discourse, Jonathan amplifies: "He said, 'Send me, please, for there is a family sacrifice for us in the city, and he has summoned me—my brother. If I have found favor in your eyes, I would slip away [מלט], please, so I may see my brother'" (my translation). Jonathan then drops his quasi-direct quoting and resumes the more indirect mode, rounding out the explanation: "For this reason he has not come to the king's table." Jonathan first mixes his own language with David's and David's with his, making prominent their collaboration in this matter. His changes, whether deliberate or not—and discernible only to ourselves and him, not to David or Saul, each of whom misses either the rehearsal or the performance—highlight some issues to which Saul has been already shown sensitive: the father/son bond triangulating David, Saul, and Jesse as well as David, Saul, and Jonathan; the favor that David finds in the eyes of diverse appraisers; the escape of David at the hands of Michal; and now also the matter of brothers, which Saul picks up on shortly.[8] Jonathan places

---

8. Fokkelman (332–33) catches them carefully; his reading assumptions demand the question of Jonathan's intent, which in Bakhtin's mode does not arise.

around Saul the scenario he and David have co-authored. Saul is preforming as anticipated and scripted, has responded as prodded to do.

In 20:30–34 (round 9) we come to the heart of this section, the place where Saul is most explicit about his understanding of himself and this son. Saul's anger, directed not unsuitably against Jonathan, slurs him and indirectly his birth.[9] In one of his most candid reflections, Saul tells Jonathan that he knows that the son is choosing Jesse's son over against his own lineage (and his mother's nakedness). Avoiding, for the most part, to make explicit his own interest, Saul charges Jonathan with acting for David to the hurt of his own (i.e., Jonathan's) kingship. Of course, from another angle, the reference to "Jonathan's kingdom" denies the information Saul was given so unequivocally by Samuel in 13:13–14 and 15:26. There will be no kingdom for Jonathan, no matter the efforts of any. So Saul's candor here, even if we take it as sincere, is nonetheless unreal. Then, as if his blunt detailing of realities might convince his son, Saul once again demands that Jonathan send David—not to his father's table (20:29)—but to Saul to be killed. Jonathan's response to the paternal outburst defies that fatherly expectation and echoes both his own and David's earlier language (19:4; 20:1): "Why should he be killed? What has he done?" If previously (19:4–7), this intervention of Jonathan dissuaded Saul from pursuit of David, now the effect seems the opposite.

Saul's response, a nonverbal utterance (round 10), is to confirm what he hates, the conflation of the two "sons," as he hurls the spear formerly aimed at David now at Jonathan. Saul's action belies his own verbal utterance and makes manifest his frustration and irrationality on the matter of his son and the kingdom. The narrator ties off the scene with, having showed us the basis on which Jonathan seems now convinced that Saul is intent on David's death. Now not one but two sons are conspicuously missing from the table, as Jonathan leaves, grieving for David, according to words of David in 20:3; the narrator, with clever ambiguity, says his father had shamed him.[10]

---

9. Alter (127) translates "perverse and wayward." Fokkelman suggests the slur is not directed against Jonathan's mother per se but conveys the notion that the son is congenitally flawed (334); that may be so, though contemporary feminist theory will not so easily overlook the manner of derogation, nor will a Bakhtinian reader miss the positioning of the old conflict of sons and their parentage. For a more gender-sensitive interpretation, consult Jobling (178). The disparaging expression also breathes life into the suggestion of Jon Levenson that the Ahinoam who becomes David's wife in 25:43 may be the same as Saul's wife (11–28). See also Gary Stansell: 59–61.

10. Stansell (59–61) brings to bear categories of Mediterranean honor and shame and makes the case that it is Jonathan, not David, who has been shamed (David has been threatened, not shamed). That may be so, but the larger issue of the confusion of "sons" and the king's disparate hopes for each of them makes the ambiguity of phrasing effective.

A summary is once again in order. Saul has been assessed accurately, to some extent, by David. He acts as anticipated, as programmed, calling once again for the death of David. It is a formidable, if not quite definitive, move. Capable of forbearance with David when handled appropriately, Saul will not kill David even when later positioned to do so. It is difficult to make the case that Jonathan anticipated the outcome of the scenes just completed and in any case moot. Saul has clearly now stated his priority, which is to leave his son Jonathan to rule, a goal unable to be accomplished while David survives; it is a subset of Saul's main drive, which is to remain king. To throw a spear at his son is to admit, by gesture, that the quest is hopeless. It is a startling moment in the story of Saul, a moment of great vulnerability for him. Saul the king overrules Saul the father. Jonathan's education at the hand of his friend and his father is now complete.

JONATHAN'S UTTERANCES TO "THE BOY": 20:35–42

The last five verbal utterances are Jonathan's, spoken both to his boy who bears his armor and to "his brother" who accepted his armor some time back; David is also named as Saul's armorbearer (16:21), not the last to fill that role (31:4). These phrasings also are double, in that they rerun language already rehearsed between Jonathan and David (20:20–23), now in fresh circumstances. Though most commentators are understandably impatient with this fake flurry of arrows shot in accordance with an earlier plan in a scene which no longer wants such elaborate subterfuge, the narrator's choice to spend time on it suggests it needs scrutiny.[11] So Jonathan bids the boy (round 11, 35–36) to run: "to run..." is the permission David requested in verse 6. And the boy ran, comments the narrator, in lieu of the character's verbal response.

When in round 12, 20:37, the boy has come to the place of the arrows which Jonathan had instructed, Jonathan calls, "Is not the arrow behind you [i.e., farther on]?" The wording suggests the boy has turned to face his master, awaiting further cue. The other waiting figure has been instructed in 20:22 to read such a cue as: "YHWH sends you away." In that scenario envisioned days before, Saul is not the one demanding that Jonathan send David to him, but God is sending him away. Saul is at cross-purposes with God, pointlessly, it seems, perennially. The response to this utterance is not clear at first, but we can see almost at once that it is delay, or hesitation.

11. E.g. Campbell (209–17) insists that the ritual is not properly observed; Fokkelman, at the other extreme, spends pages (318ff.) excavating its possible layers of signification. It is my hope to take a middle path. It is important but not endlessly mysterious.

"Hurry, be quick, do not delay," is consequently the next command (20:38–39, round 13) observed well by the one boy, prompting the other as well. And the narrator assists us, points our vision: the one knew, the other did not.

"Jonathan gave his weapons to the boy and said, 'Go, carry them to the city'" (20:40, round 14). A reprise of the transfer of armor in 18:4, matched there by a narratorial comment that David was successful wherever Saul sent him. Saul's fingerprints are pressed upon this scene. Saul collaborating with God, whether the king knows it or not?

The last utterance (round 15, 20:41–42) is again Jonathan's alone, blending the former oaths of covenant partners with the presence of YHWH's protection and guarantee, reiterating his own words of 20:12–16, which Jonathan exacted from David too. David is wordless here, his prostrations and tears clearly responsive but difficult to read with precision. After the narrator provides, finally, assurances of mutuality between David and Jonathan, the next swing verse (MT 21:1) indicates that David rose and left and Jonathan went into the city, after the boy.

Since it seems obvious that this portion of the narrative is not really "needed," which is to say it renders little new information, it must be scrutinized rather for its mode and object of representation. It might seem that the point of the scene is for David to learn of his fate; that is true, but in fact little is made of David's learning except to register his strong emotion. At the level of David's reaction, the scene is all but wasted. David has in fact temporarily receded, both in terms of plot, as Jonathan precipitates events, and in narration, as Jonathan inhabits David's discourse. David is primarily now an object: sent, as he asked by Saul, by Jonathan, by YHWH, and of course by his own devising. The verbal code which cues him is made otiose as we look on. Once the arrows have been arranged, the two planners interact directly, as indeed they can have done in any case. The code, then, is for us, directs our attention back to chapter 14, where Jonathan and the armor bearer plan and succeed, evidently with God's approval, at the expense of Saul's position and at the apparent risk of Jonathan's life. And the arrow scene directs us ahead to chapter 31, where both king and prince are thwarted in their rule, a royal armor bearer in attendance but not acting, and where the deity again seems to abet the human machinations. David appears, by the end of chapter 20, to have made unmistakable the wedge between father and son and between his royal patron and himself. And yet, counterintuitively, the split is not final, in either case. Jonathan is not parted from Saul (as we shall see in 31 and as David himself will affirm in 2 Samuel 1:23), and David and the old king will remain locked together for some time ahead.

Converging the "Jonathan" Scenes

It remains simply to re-view the other "Jonathan scenes" in 1 Samuel. In chapter 14, Jonathan and his armorbearer act at cross-purposes with King Saul; by the scene's end, the heir has been sentenced to death on oath but reprieved (14:45). The armorbearer has disappeared. By the long story's end, both king and prince are dead, together, eulogized efficiently; the armorbearer has an ambiguous, undecidable and controversial role.

In the other two scenes, less complex, Jonathan seeks first to deny his father's sense of David as threat (19:1–7), only to own its truth in the concentrically matching moment (23:17). Jonathan has, thanks to an education experience we oversee, ceased to resist or reform his father in the matter of David. The representation is powerful and poignant, with resonance both political and personal. Bakhtin's astute sense of the tiny utterance genre has enabled us to read with careful discrimination the intersecting responsibility for what has happened.

Location, Location, Location:
Tamar in the Joseph Cycle

Judy Fentress-Williams

The Joseph cycle stands in contrast to the material that precedes it in Genesis because it is carefully crafted and intentionally literary. This beautifully composed narrative, which is classified as a novella, portrays Joseph in chapter 37 as the dreamer of dreams and the delight of his father Jacob. Joseph's dreams and the obvious favoritism of his father create tension among his brothers to the point where they conspire to kill him. Two of the brothers, Reuben and Judah, intervene. Instead of murdering the beloved son of Jacob, the sons of Leah sell Joseph into slavery for twenty pieces of silver. They take the coat of Joseph, the one given to him by his father as a symbol of his special status in the family, dip it in blood and deliver it to Jacob, saying, "see/*recognize* now whether it is your son's robe or not." From the bloodied robe, Jacob concludes the inevitable. "It is my son's robe! A wild animal has devoured him. Joseph is without doubt torn to pieces" (37:33). The chapter concludes with Jacob in mourning while Joseph is sold to Potiphar and an uncertain future. What will become of Joseph? Will he survive? Will his father ever discover the truth? It is with anticipation that the reader turns to the following chapter only to discover that the narrator has shifted gears and is now telling what appears to be a completely different story—one having to do with Joseph's brother Judah.

Scholarship has been fairly consistent in its characterization of Genesis 38 as a separate unit that interrupts the surrounding narrative:

> Every attentive reader can see that the story of Judah and Tamar has no connection at all with the strictly organized Joseph story at whose beginning it is now inserted. (von Rad: 351)

> This narrative is a completely individual unit. It has no connection with the drama of Joseph. (Speiser: 299).

> This peculiar chapter stands alone, without connection to its context. It is isolated in every way and is most enigmatic. (Brueggemann: 307)

Genesis 38 is treated as an interpolation because it interrupts the "continuous" narrative of the Joseph story. If the message of the text is to be conveyed via a single voice or perspective, then chapter 38 is a diversion. Or if resolution of the situation at the end of chapter 37 is the goal of the reader, then chapter 38 is a deterrent.

The interruption of one story by another, abrupt endings without explanations, and disregard for narrative continuity are the unfortunate characteristics of the Bible. The text in its final form is a composite. It originally existed in oral form and was edited over time. Contemporary readers tend to sift through the various strands in the hope that by isolating the individual voices of the narrative we can find respite from the cacophony of voices that contribute to the text. Unfortunately, this expectation is rarely met in the Bible.

Some literary readings offer an alternative by demonstrating ways in which chapter 38 is related to the surrounding narrative. In *The Art of Biblical Narrative*, Robert Alter uses Gen 38 to demonstrate not only that Gen 38 employs literary artistry to convey meaning but that the independent unit inserted into the Joseph narrative "interacts" with the surrounding material. The interpolation and the surrounding material are connected by "motif and theme," conveyed by a "whole series of explicit parallels and contrasts" (Alter: 4).

My use of a dialogic approach, based on the work of M. M. Bakhtin, goes further in asserting first that Gen 38 is not simply related, or secondary to the surrounding narrative, but forms a dialogue with chapters 37 and 39–50. Second, our understanding of Gen 38 is impossible without a discussion about the relationship, that is, dialogue between this chapter and the surrounding narrative. Moreover, this approach will argue that the meaning of the surrounding material would be limited with the omission of chapter 38 in much the same way one's understanding of a conversation is limited if only one conversation partner can be heard. Third, I will use the concept of chronotope, or "time-space," that offers insights into how meaning is built into the very structure of the narrative.

For the purposes of this study, I will offer a working definition of language as "dialogic" and chronotope based on Bakhtin's theory of language. Central to Bakhtin's thinking is the concept that language is dynamic and dialogic in nature. Every word carries a multitude of possible meanings, and perception or understanding is affected by the presence of another

> regardless of the position and the proximity to me of this other human being whom I am contemplating I shall always see and know something that he, from his place outside and over against me, cannot see himself: parts of his

body that are inaccessible to his own gaze (his head, his face and its expression) the world behind his back ... are accessible to me but not to him. As we gaze at each other, two different worlds are reflected in the pupils of our eyes ... to annihilate the difference completely, it would be necessary to merge into one, to become one and the same person. (Bakhtin:1990:22–23)

Bakhtin's theory assumes that the individual in isolation has limited perception. The other sees, completes the individual in a way she could not do herself. Similarly, a word in isolation is limited in its ability to realize its fullness of meaning. Meaning in language is achieved as a result of words, phrases and other units of language in dialogue with each other. Each written and spoken word exists for the purpose of working towards meaning *in dialogue* with other words. Spoken and written language is *inherently* dialogic. The dialogic nature of language creates ongoing possibilities for new meaning. This is known as unfinalizability.

For this reason, the hearer/reader can never completely understand an utterance in isolation. Meaning can be achieved only as the result of words, phrases, and other units of language being in dialogue with each other. For the purposes of our analysis of Gen 38, this means our understanding of the passage can only result from the dialogue between this chapter and the surrounding narrative.

The dialogue between Judah and Tamar in chapter 38 demonstrates another aspect of Bakhtin's theory of language, namely, that language contains two forces; the official voice and the "other." One force seeks unity. The other is disruptive and challenges the assumptions of the official voice. In Gen 38, Judah hears and understands the official voice, and Tamar exploits the "other." Judah and Tamar's encounter and dialogue takes place within a specific contextual framework or field of parameters that highlights the two forces in language and all its possibilities. This specific moment in a specific space is what Bakhtin refers to as chronotope.

Bakhtin's notion of chronotope is also of tremendous use because it seeks to redefine the "interruption" instead of attempting to explain it. The term *chronotope* literally means, "time-space." It is the:

> organizing center for the fundamental narrative events of the novel. The chronotope is the place where the knots of the narrative are tied and untied. It can be said without qualification that to them belongs the meaning that shapes the narrative. (Bakhtin: 1981:250)

Bakhtin contends that every genre of literature has a different understanding of space and time. With each genre comes a field that determines the parameters of events and possibilities for action. We expect certain things from an adventure or romance and different events in history. The field that determines these parameters is the chronotope. It is a field of possibilities.

Bakhtin identifies certain motifs, such as meeting/parting, loss/acquisition, search/discovery, recognition/nonrecognition as chronotopic in nature. Of these motifs, the motif of *meeting* is dominant, and it is closely related to the motif of *recognition/nonrecognition* (Bakhtin: 1981: 97). The presence of these motifs in Gen 38 invite us to think about the role of chronotope in understanding this narrative.

These definitions of dialogic language and chronotope have tremendous implications for Gen 38. First, I will focus on the dialogue within the chapter itself. Who speaks to whom? What are the disruptive and unifying forces at work in the dialogue? Who understands and who is deceived by the dialogue? What meaning can be found in the exchange between Tamar and Judah? Second, I will examine the dialogue that is created between Gen 38 and the larger Joseph narrative into which it appears to be inserted. Third, I will explore the extent to which the narrative is temporally structured and how an understanding of chronotope assists our navigation of this passage. Specifically, I will focus on the motifs of *meeting* and *recognition/nonrecognition* in the narrative.

After reading the first chapter of the Joseph cycle, the reader comes to chapter 38 anxious to find out what will happen next and encounters these words: ויהי בעת ההוא "*At that time,* Judah left his brothers and went down to stay with a man of Adullam named Hirah. There Judah met the daughter of a Canaanite man named Shua." True to its inimitable style, the Bible shifts to what appears to be a different story. The narrative moves swiftly in the first eleven verses of the chapter. In verses 1–5, Judah marries and has three sons who are named Er, Onan, and Shelah.

The sentence structure is simple, and, as we would expect, the verbs direct the action. In the first verse Judah "leaves" his brothers and "spreads out" with Hirah. In verse 2 he "saw," "took," and "went into" Bat Shua. From that point on, the verbal action includes her. She conceives and bears a son. In verse 3 Judah "names." In verse 4 Bat Shua conceives, bears, and names. In verse 5 she conceives, bears, and names the second and third sons.

In verses 6–11 Tamar is introduced to the narrative as the wife procured for the oldest son Er. Based on what precedes, the reader anticipates more of the same. Er, like his father, should "take" and "go into her." Tamar should then conceive and bear sons. The *waw* that begins verse 7 is the break with what has preceded. "But Er, Judah's firstborn, was wicked in the sight of God, and YHWH put him to death." Verses 6–11 move in rapid succession like verses 1–5, but the narrative is off course. The line of succession, the taking of a wife and producing of children, is detoured with the death of Er. In response to this detour, Judah speaks in the narrative for the first time. He tells his son to perform the duty of a *levir* for his brother's widow. Judah speaks to Onan, but we do not have a record of Onan responding in words. Instead, the narrator speaks to the reader and informs us that Onan did not want to cooperate and devised a plan whereby he appeared to perform the duty of a *levir* but "spilled his seed on the ground." Onan's action was displeasing in the eyes of YHWH, and he too was killed. In verse 11 Judah speaks again, this time to Tamar. In verse 8 he commanded Onan to "go." Here in verse 11 he commands Tamar to "return" to the house of her father. Tamar enters the narrative in verse 6 as the wife of Er. By verse 11 she has been married and widowed twice with no heir to show for it.

Up to this point the reader has few indicators regarding the passage of time. The narrative moves with such speed so as to suggest things happen in rapid succession. The first 11 verses of the text seem to be rushing towards some unknown destination when, in verse 12, we encounter these words, וירבו הימים "after some time," literally, "many days." It is after this period of time that the two women mentioned in the narrative will affect the course of action, one intentionally and the other unintentionally. First Bat Shua, wife of Judah, dies. In response to her death Judah goes through the period of mourning. This parallel action of mourning alerts the reader that Tamar has been in mourning "many days." What has happened to Shelah? Is he of age? Will Judah keep his word? Will the promise be fulfilled?

In verse 13 it was "made known" (נגד) to Tamar that her father-in-law was going to Timnah for the sheep shearing. Tamar removes her widow's clothing, which mirrors what Judah does at the end of his mourning period. Her action alerts the reader to the fact that Tamar's period of mourning has gone on for quite some time. She then covers herself with a veil and, like Judah, takes a trip. Her journey takes her to the entrance to Enaim, בפתח עינים, literally, the "opening of the eyes," on the road to Timnah. Verse 14 is beautifully crafted in that it first describes Tamar's actions, which only imply her intentions, and then provides the motive. She did these things because, she "*saw* [ראה] that Shelah was grown up, yet she had not been given to him as wife."

Certainly the events that will take place are set in motion by Tamar, whose eyes have been opened. And her actions will result in an eye-opening experience for Judah. Tamar's two actions, the removing of one type of clothing and the putting on of another type, not only mark a transition in Tamar's status from one who mourns to one who is ready to act but is symbolic of the activity in this story. Judah and Tamar's interactions take place around prescribed roles and identities and the uncertainty and deception around those roles. Some roles are associated with clothing. Judah is responsible for Tamar once she becomes a part of his household, but out of fear for his youngest son's life, he sends her back to her own father's house. In so doing, he abandons his role as her provider, and he does so deceptively, inasmuch as he promised Tamar she would someday marry Shelah. Similarly, by changing her attire, Tamar abandons her role as widow and daughter-in-law for another role. She is intentional in her selection of clothes. The text states, "she covered herself with a veil to cover herself" (ותתעלף ותכס בצעיף). Covering oneself is often associated with mourning. Here Tamar's covering works toward a different purpose, to end the period of mourning and to continue the line.

As is the case in the surrounding Joseph narrative, garments convey status, position, favor, or role. They also have the power to conceal or reveal identity. In the story of Joseph, the robe his father gives him is a visible sign of favor, and that same robe is used to deceive Jacob about his beloved son's death. Upon hearing of Joseph's demise, Jacob tears his clothes and replaces them with sackcloth, the garb of mourning. In Egypt, Potiphar's wife uses Joseph's robe to connect him to an offense he did not commit. When Joseph is restored in Pharaoh's house he receives a new wardrobe of fine linen, and Joseph's appearance keeps his identity hidden from his brothers when they encounter him years later. Similarly, Tamar's new garments apparently conceal her identity from Judah, who mistakes her for a prostitute, זנה. Upon seeing her he initiates a business transaction. We assume from the sparse details of the narrative that Judah deduces Tamar is a prostitute because of her location (why else would a woman be sitting alone outside the entrance to a city) and her attire (the veil). The only other mention of this term for "veil" (צעיף) comes in the story of Isaac and Rebekah. Rebekah dons a "veil" (צעיף) before she meets Isaac. The point here is that the veil is heretofore associated not with prostitution but with marriage. Thus in one verse Tamar's action of changing her attire is simultaneously associated with mourning, covering for mourning, marriage, and *possibly* prostitution. The uncertainty around the purpose of the veil directs the reader to all the possible roles associated with this woman. Tamar uses perceptions and misperceptions about who she is to achieve her goal. That she is associated with a number of roles is further substantiated by the text's reference to her in verse 16. When Judah saw her, he did not "know" (ידע) that she was his "daughter-in-law." Here the term for "daughter-in-law" (כלה) also means bride. Tamar is a daughter-in-law about to become a bride, and although Judah does not "recognize" (ידע) her, he is about to *know* her in a most intimate way.

The words function like garments in the Tamar narrative. They convey meaning and have the ability to reveal and conceal. And the reader, like Judah, will only understand the fuller meanings of the words in a dialogical process.

Now we move to the encounter and dialogue. Until verse 16 Judah speaks, and there is no verbal response in the narrative. In other words, Judah's communications are commands (38:8, 11, 13) or internal thoughts (38:11). In verse 16 Judah speaks, but this time he is answered by the veiled woman. Her voice in the text changes the course of action.

Judah: Come, let me come into you.
Tamar: What will you give me that you may come into me?
Judah: I will send you a kid from the flock.
Tamar: Only if you give me a pledge until you send it.
Judah: What pledge shall I give you?
Tamar: Your signet and your cord and the staff that is in your hand.

The dialogue consists of three verses. Judah initiates the conversation and Tamar responds with a question (38:17). Judah responds and Tamar issues a rejoinder (38:18). Judah asks a question in response to the new demand and Tamar answers (38:19). The pattern of the exchange is as follows:

Judah makes a proposition	Tamar asks a question
Judah answers the question	Tamar makes a different proposition
Judah asks a question	Tamar answers a question

Judah initiates the dialogue, but it is the veiled woman who has the last word in this exchange. Moreover, as a result of this verbal exchange the business of procreation that was detoured in verses 6–11 resumes. The phrase ויבא אליה ותהר לו, which we saw in verse 2, is repeated in verse 18, "he went in to her, and she conceived by him."

Having completed her mission, Tamar changes clothes once again, removing the veil and returning to the widow's garb, but nothing is the same. The changes that have taken place will not be hidden by her clothes for long. The repetition of the phrase, "he went in to her, and she conceived by him" (ויבא אליה ותהר לו) is like Tamar putting the widow's attire on again. The words and the clothing look the same, but everything has changed. Language in repetition, like the clothes to which Tamar returns, hold much more than the earlier meanings, and it is the repetition itself that serves to highlight the polyphony. The dialogue that takes place between Tamar and Judah is central to the narrative and now nothing, not the same clothes and certainly not the same words, has the same meaning.

The following verses detail Judah's attempt to send payment to the "prostitute." He sends his friend Hirah the Adullamite, but Hirah was unable to locate the shrine prostitute. The term here for cult or shrine prostitute is

קדשה. This term is in contrast to זנה, a common prostitute that was used earlier to describe Tamar. The cult prostitute was condemned as a corrupt Canaanite practice. However, it is condemned with such frequency that we can infer that it was pervasive. The harlot, or run-of-the-mill-prostitute, if you will, was tolerated as long as she was not married (Jeansonne: 104).[1] When Hirah reports that the men of the city said, "no harlot has been here," the reader sees the irony that Judah still does not get. There never was a harlot, only a widow securing her right to progeny (104). Judah decides that the prostitute should keep his personal items lest they become a laughingstock. That Judah wants to make sure the prostitute gets what is owed her stands in stark contrast to his lack of concern over Tamar, who has not received her due. Ironically, in "playing the harlot" Tamar secures for herself what she was unable to obtain as a daughter-in-law.

In verses 24–26, a final albeit indirect exchange occurs between Judah and Tamar. Here we see the phrase "it was made known" or "told" (נגד) to Judah, which mirrors the same phrase from verse 13, where Tamar was told about the activities of Judah. In both cases the agent of the information is unknown. In both verses the information is the basis for action. In verse 24 Judah hears of Tamar's pregnancy and orders her death. Unlike Judah's commands issued in the earlier part of the chapter, the command to have Tamar stoned is met with a response. Tamar sends Judah's personal effects with the message, "it was the owner of these who made me pregnant…. take note/ *recognize*, please, whose these are, the signet and the cord and the staff." Judah's response to seeing his personal effects forms a corrective dialogue with Jacob's response to Joseph's bloodied coat. Jacob sees the bloodied coat and forms the wrong conclusion. Judah sees his signet, cord, and staff and *recognizes* that Tamar is "more in the right than I." Judah is able to move from nonrecognition to recognition after his encounter with his personal items sent by Tamar. In verses 27–30 the text discloses that one long-awaited pregnancy produces two sons. Perez breaks forth into the world in much the same way that the Tamar narrative breaks into Joseph's story. The crimson thread tied on the wrist of the second-born son symbolizes the blood line that continues through Tamar and Judah.

Tamar's pregnancy does more than resolve the tension in the narrative. The revelation of her pregnancy forces the narrative into real time. Verse 24 begins with a specific temporal reference: "three months later…." This reference marks the time when Tamar's pregnancy would have become evident.

---

1. This opinion is not shared by a number of biblical scholars. See Gail Corrington Streete's discussion (1997) of זנה and קדשה.

In this sense it stands in contrast to the other references to time up to this point in the narrative. For example, it is not clear how much time passed in the first section of the narrative (38:1–5) where Judah marries, has three sons, and Er is eventually old enough to take a wife. Nor is it clear in verses 6–10 how long Tamar was married to Er before God took his life or how long Onan pretended to act as *levir* before God took his life as well. In verse 11 Judah asks Tamar to remain at her father's house for an unspecified length of time, "until my son Shelah grows up." In verse 12 we have the reference "a long time afterward" to mark the time of the death of Judah's wife. Time moves at its own pace in this narrative, but the specific time marker in verse 24 introduces the resolution of the story.

The temporal shift introduced in verse 24 is followed by another specific time reference in verse 27, "when the time came for her to give birth…." This brings us to the climax of the narrative. The birth of the twins, Perez and Zerah, assures the continuation of the line and offers a foreshadowing of the fulfillment of the promise in the Joseph cycle. Although the story ends structurally in much the same way it begins, with birth and naming, in this final segment of the narrative, it is not Judah who names the first-born son. Here the midwife's comment about the second-born who makes himself first, "what a breach [פרץ] you have made for yourself," becomes the name of the child. The red cord the midwife ties on the would-be first-born becomes the basis for his name as well. The story in chapter 38 achieves resolution, but the path by which the promise is fulfilled is unconventional. The reader will return to the Joseph narrative, but the lesson in Gen 38 is that the path to God's promise is a circuitous one. Joseph's path to the fulfillment of God's promise to Abram will be one of delays, imprisonment, exile, and reversals.

In its final form, Gen 38 functions as an interruption only when we read the entire story chronologically. If one sees Gen 38 as a chronotope, a play within a play that contains the thematic elements of the surrounding narrative, we can make the following conclusions. First, garments are key to understanding the Tamar/Judah story and the surrounding Joseph narrative. In both stories the garments have the potential to conceal/deceive and reveal. Second, words in both narratives function like the garments. They contain unifying and disruptive forces that have the power to conceal/deceive and reveal. Third, the heroine/hero in the two narratives is the individual who is able to "perceive," נכר, (or recognize) rather than simply "see," ראה. Fourth, the ones who perceive, Tamar and Joseph, are the ones who take the necessary steps to preserve the line. They function as the links between the promise of God and the fulfillment of God's promise.

Moreover, the motif of encounter, recognition/nonrecognition functions not only in chapter 38 but between chapter 38 and the surrounding narrative. The location of the Tamar story forms a meeting/encounter with the Joseph story, and it is up to the reader to recognize the function of the narrative. The Tamar/Judah story alerts the reader to the fact that those things that appear to stand between the promises of God and the fulfillment of those promises are illusions. The chronology of the narrative is not the only way to follow the narrative. To the contrary, the story of Joseph and that of Israel, for that matter, can be characterized as a series of encounters and meetings. The motif of encounter/meeting creates opportunities for the exploitation of language in dialogue. Tamar and Judah speak the same language, but they use language differently. As is the case in this narrative, the meeting/encounter brings with it the possibility for recognition. The exchange between Judah and Tamar demonstrates that the existing power structure can be challenged by the one who can *recognize* or *perceive* new possibilities within the existing language.

DIALOGIC FORM CRITICISM: AN INTERTEXTUAL READING OF LAMENTATIONS AND PSALMS OF LAMENT*

Carleen Mandolfo

Martin Buss has called for a more relational approach to our form-critical endeavors. In his attendance to the connection between form and life, Hermann Gunkel's work presaged this call, but in the end his categories were too narrow:

> In observing connections between aspects of literary form, biblical scholarship can go further than Gunkel did, for he reflected on their nature only intermittently. One can ask on a more regular basis, "How does this language go with certain thoughts and feelings, and how do these go with a given kind of situation?" (1999:415).

Bakhtin's insistence on the dialogic nature of language and life, from units of language as fundamental as the word to the most complex of utterances, can contribute to the goal Buss outlines. Both Gunkel and Bakhtin were interested in speech/texts in their contexts, but Gunkel stressed the fixity of genres, while Bakhtin stressed their fluidity. For Gunkel, genres, when altered, become impure (Buss 1999:259);[1] for Bakhtin, that is what genres do—change—depending on the situation of the "user," that is, either the speaker/author or addressee/reader. According to Bakhtin, "Speech genres in general submit fairly easily to reaccentuation; the sad can be made jocular and gay, but as a

---

* This essay is based on chapter 3 of my *Daughter Zion Talks Back to the Prophets: A Dialogic Theology of the Book of Lamentations* (SemeiaSt 58; Atlanta: Society of Biblical Literature, 2007).

1. According to Buss, Gunkel held to an Aristotelian essentialism in believing that genres have a distinct "pure" form. Many others during Gunkel's day held to a more flexible view of genres (Buss 1999:255–56).

result something new is achieved" (1986:87).[2] As such, the intermixing and evolution of genres is a form of artistic expression, not corruption.

Communication is enabled because of the way in which we manipulate the features of our generic inheritances (Van Leeuwen: 74–75). In order to move "beyond" form criticism, we need to read form dynamically as content given shape by a living, situated human being and to recognize that the text has relationships and is responsive to related texts and forms. Newsom makes this observation a cornerstone of her understanding of genre and approach to reading biblical forms:

> [T]exts do not "belong" to genres so much as participate in them, invoke them, gesture to them, play in and out of them, and in so doing continually change them. Texts may participate in more than one genre, just as they may be marked in an exaggerated or in a deliberately subtle fashion. The point is not simply to identify a genre in which a text participates, but to analyze that participation in terms of the rhetorical strategies of the text. (2003:12)

In their comprehensive overview of the current state of form criticism, Sweeney and Ben Zvi also recognize that the method's future lies with this insight:

> Form-critical studies will no longer concern themselves only or mainly with the typical features of language and text. Rhetorical criticism and communication theory have amply demonstrated that the communicative and persuasive functions of texts depend on the unique as well as the typical. Moreover, in considering the rhetorical or communicative aspects of texts, form-critical scholars will no longer presume that genres are static or ideal entities that never change. Rather, they will recognize the inherent fluidity of genres, the fact that they are historically, culturally, and discursively dependent, *and they will study the means by which genres are transformed to meet the needs of the particular communicative situation of the text.* (2003:9–10, emphasis added)[3]

Accordingly, a proper definition of genre must stress flexibility as much as stability: "[T]he fact that a genre can retain its identity in the face of sometimes radical changes in its linguistic and cultural environment illustrates the flexibility of the genre's rule and its ability to absorb 'culture shock' " (Fishelov: 8, 17). In this essay I will read Lam 1–2 as a product of the "culture shock" of

---

2. But Bakhtin did acknowledge that the high and official genres are "compulsory and extremely stable" (1986:79).

3. Tull 1997:327 addresses exactly this point.

587 B.C.E.[4] and in so doing will explore the ways in which it remains identifiable as a member of the lament genre, as well as the way it is transformed "to meet the needs of the particular communicative situation of the text." In my reading, the ultimate rhetorical purpose, however, for reworking the traditional generic lament features is to craft a response to the prophetic rhetoric that exploited the marriage metaphor as a staging ground for its accusations against Israel.

An anecdotal analogy may prove a useful starting point: I spent the month of July 2004 in Manhattan involved in a research colloquium,[5] where I had the opportunity to attend a Broadway musical that illustrates the way genres morph in order to remain compelling in new contexts. *Wicked* is a retelling of a modern musical cinematic fairytale, *The Wizard of Oz*.[6] It was perfectly recognizable structurally and semiotically as drawing on the conventions of that genre—music, good versus evil, talking animals, didactic motifs, overcoming fearsome situations and opponents, and so forth—but it reshuffled its signifiers to suit its postmodern/postcolonial intentions. The story is retold from the perspective of the wicked witch, who is merely trying to defend the subjugated (subaltern), indigenous creatures in her kingdom from the oppressive policies of the Wizard, which include the removal of their ability to speak, literally. The witch, who in this version is given a name, "Elphaba," a twist that is crucial to underlining her subjectivity, is given the opportunity to tell her side of the story and thus is able to construct a persona that defies the construction previously applied to her by the Wizard and the story/genre itself. The unmasking of the perceived redeemer as an oppressor is a theme that is readily comprehensible, even embraced, among large segments of contemporary American society. In fact, the play has been wildly popular, selling out for months and months and garnering a remarkable ten Tony Award nominations. This clearly has much to do with the fact that a postmodern reworking of the mythic conventions of fairytales (good versus evil, the hero's journey, etc.) resonates with some Americans at this time in a way that the original no longer does. A remake that strove to remain rigidly loyal to the original would seem quaint rather than compelling.

---

4. For an appreciation of the devastation suffered by the Judeans at the hands of the Babylonians, see chapter 2 in Smith-Christopher 2002.

5. I am very grateful to *CrossCurrents* for their support of this project while I was their guest as a Coolidge Fellow.

6. I am comparing *Wicked*, the theatrical version (as opposed to the book by G. Maguire) to the 1939 screen version of the movie *The Wizard of Oz* rather than to the original book (*The Wonderful Wizard of Oz*) by L. F. Baum because of the film's iconic status and the fact that the creators of *Wicked*, the musical, were working from a similar assumption.

As crucial to the definition of genre as the notion of flexibility is, however, the more common and integral observation is that genres also exert a restrictive, if pliable, influence on our expression. Ironically, this constraint is necessary for individual creativity. *Wicked* would not have been nearly so effective from a creative standpoint had it disregarded completely the features of the original form. In fact, much of the play's power derives from its recognizability: Elphaba is still green, still dressed in black, and still unleashes that cackle when vanquishing her enemies. She is completely identifiable on an iconic level, but no one who sees *Wicked* can ever "read" her character the same way again. Likewise, a committed reading of Lam 1–2 compels a reappraisal of Daughter Zion as she is construed in a number of prophetic texts. As I will suggest, the poet of Lamentations draws part of his rhetorical impact from the maintenance of the female metaphor for Israel. In this way, the poet provides his audience with a recognizable voice for their pain. Repeating the shameful figuration of Israel as female might seem an odd choice if the goal is comfort, but in light of the treatment this figure receives at the hand of YHWH in the prophetic texts, granting this voice subjectivity makes a powerful theological statement.

The Set-Up

Israel had at least one indigenous genre (or two related genres), besides the dirge, that could be deployed in situations of individual and corporate anxiety: individual (and communal) psalms of lament, or complaint. Surely many of them, like Lamentations, were composed or preserved, at least, in response to 587 B.C.E. A look at the first two chapters of Lamentations, however, suggests that some members of the community needed an outlet for their grief that, while still drawing on established generic traditions, was tailored to this particular situation. This paper will focus on some of the particulars of how the poet went about his task, but only insofar as this helps to answer a more far-reaching question: Why did the poet make the choices he did; in other words, what ideological goals did he hope to accomplish? Trying to unravel ideological motivations necessarily involves attending to generic usage:

> The choice of genre over and against other conventional literary discourses is already an ideological act. Motivations might be recovered by asking questions such as: *How does the text conform to the conventions of the genre, and how does it depart from them? It is in these departures that the text reworks the ideology that intrudes between it and history.* (Yee: 26, emphasis added)

I am focusing on the two chapters of Lamentations in which the people are figured as a woman (*bat Zion*) because they hold together as a unit through the use of the feminine metaphor. Furthermore, the metaphor gives me a point of entry for discussing in the most tangible ways possible my proposition that these two chapters function as a "response" to both the devastation of 587 and the way in which the devastation was prefigured in the marriage metaphor rhetoric of the prophetic texts. Generic responsivity is integral to Bakhtin's dialogic linguistics:

> Every utterance must be regarded primarily as a response to preceding utterances of the given sphere (we understand the word "response" here in the broadest sense). Each utterance refutes, affirms, supplements, and relies on the others, presupposes them to be known, and somehow takes them into account.... It is impossible to determine its position without correlating it with other positions. (1986:91) [7]

In short, I understand the rhetorical (if not sociopsychological) impetus of Lam 1–2 as providing Daughter Zion a voice to speak back to the accusations leveled against her in the prophets, and I see the reworking of the lament psalm as the means of reaching that goal.

I will chart the "development" from lament to Lamentations primarily by attending to formal features, specifically the way voices are aligned in the various texts. As I have demonstrated elsewhere (Mandolfo 2002b), many individual laments are, in spite of a history of monologic interpretation, actually double-voiced. I will flesh this out more thoroughly shortly, but suffice it for now to say that the supplicant's voice is combined in these psalms with what I have called a "didactic voice" (hereafter DV), a third-person voice that speaks of and for, rather than to, God, and is thus a didactic rather than prayerful discourse. The interplay of the DV and the supplicant results in an ideologically tensive discourse that remains open-ended and unresolved throughout the Psalter. Lamentations 1–2, even more explicitly than the psalms, features two voices—the supplicant, Daughter Zion; and an objective or third-person voice—but in this case the third-person voice is co-opted into the ideological world of the supplicant's discourse, with the result that the tension that prevails in the lament psalms seems somewhat relieved in Lamentations. This rhetorical relief, however, comes at the cost of stable or comforting theology. Whereas the DV in the psalms of lament could be construed as speaking in support of the prophetic utterances regarding divine retributive justice, that same voice in Lam 1–2 has structurally reversed its

---

7. Interestingly, Buss notes that the Jewish thinker Israel Abrahams, in his 1920 study *Poetry and Religion*, understood the psalms as a "response" to God's speaking through the prophets (Buss 1999:375).

former perspective and now stands with the supplicant, more or less against the deity and the prophets through whom the deity speaks. Lamentations 1–2 is the only dialogic text in the Bible of which I am aware where this alignment takes place. Even in Job, an intensely dialogic and confrontational text, the countervoices, manifested in the persons of the friends, uphold a "prophetic" point of view, as in, "Does God pervert justice?" (Job 8:3).

Although I have carefully laid out my dialogic reading of psalms elsewhere, I will outline it here in terms of my thesis regarding Lamentations. In many psalms of lament, particularly those usually referred to as "individual," the supplicant's second-person discourse directed toward God is interrupted by a didactic voice that speaks of God in third-person descriptive terms or speaks to the supplicant in the form of a command. This latter voice could be understood as revelatory insofar as it speaks as a mouthpiece for, or in defense of, the deity. Biblical speech includes both receptive/revelatory (prophetic and priestly) and active speech (prayers and wisdom), but these two come together in psalms of lament (Buss 1999:26, 29). This configuration is fairly clear in Ps 7 (the underlined sections belong to the DV):

1:      A Shiggayon of David which he sang to YHWH concerning the
        deeds of Cush, the Benjaminite.

2:      YHWH, my God, in you I trust.
        Save me from all who pursue me, and rescue me,
3:      lest he rend my soul like a lion, tearing [it] apart,
        and there is none to rescue [me].

4:      YHWH, my God, if I have done this,
        if there is iniquity in my palms;
5:      If I have repaid evil to one at peace with me
        (instead, though, I have delivered, in vain, the one vexing me.),
6:      let the enemy persecute my soul, and entrap,
        and trample my life to the earth; and lay my honor in the dust.

7:      Arise, YHWH, in your anger;
        lift yourself up against the fury of those vexing me.
        Rouse yourself on my behalf.
        Ordain fairness!
8:      Let the congregation of the tribes encompass you,
        and for their sake return to the high place (seat of judgment?).

9:      YHWH arbitrates between the peoples;

Judge me, YHWH, according to my innocence,
and according to my integrity within me.
10:    Let the wickedness of the evil ones cease,
and establish the just.

The one who tests the thoughts and emotions is a just God.

11:    My defense depends on a God
who saves the upright of heart.

12:    God is a just judge, but a God who is indignant every day.
13:    If one does not turn back then He whets his sword,
He has bent his bow and readied it.
14:    And He has readied for himself instruments of death—
He has made arrows into burning ones.

15:    Observe! He pledges iniquity, and conceives trouble,
and gives birth to falsehood.
16:    He has dug a ditch and hollowed it out,
and fallen into the pit he made.

17:    His trouble will return on his own head
and upon his scalp his violence will descend.

18:    I will praise YHWH according to his justice,
and I will sing the name of YHWH Elyon.

Without going into exegetical detail, note how the DV counters the supplicant's shaky faith in God's justice (or at least deity's current application of it) and insists that God delivers justice according to deserts. The two voices seem to respond to one another until the end, where the supplicant seems satisfied by the insistence on God's fairness. In such a case it is possible to imagine the DV's discourse as an oracle that when delivered eased the supplicant's anguish.[8] Be that as it may, the point that interests me most is the rhetorical interplay of these voices and the way they offer a dialogic theological point of view: one that implies the manifest unfairness of much of existence ("Ordain fairness!"); and the other that posits the "normative" theology of the Bible that proclaims "God is a just judge!" What makes these dialogical, in the Bakhtinian sense, is not merely the form of dialogue that I suggest for them

---

8. On oracles, see Mowinckel: 53 and Gunkel and Begrich: 370–75.

(dialogue can be monological), but the perception that two worldviews are interacting. Both are altered by the interaction and forced to "tilt" their position, so to speak. The DV's worldview is decentered, its centripetal tendencies resisted, while the supplicant's complaint is clearly constrained by the generic demand, imposed by the cult, no doubt, to avoid blasphemous speech. This tension characterizes nearly all laments, suggesting it is a requisite feature of the genre, a feature Lam 1–2 will nevertheless subvert.

When close attention is paid to the dialogic form of laments, the decentering force each voice exerts on the other becomes manifest, but the overall control the DV, as the "revelatory" voice, exerts is still hard to gainsay. The genre is, after all, a religious or cultic creation and is primarily in the service of upholding God's authority. In fact, it is the forms of ritual (and lament psalms are surely the verbal portion of what was a more encompassing lament ritual) that create and maintain a type of religious and sociopolitical authority known as "traditional authority" (Bloch: 71). The lament genre has a specific ideological agenda, and all voices contained within it are compelled, more or less effectively, to be at its service. Hence, scholars rarely emphasize those aspects of lament that suggest YHWH is unreliable or unfair (but see Mandolfo 2002b). This has much to do with the form itself: the way in which the protests are generally presented in the first and second person makes the supplicant's speech more personal, subjective, less authoritative. Conversely, the DV's viewpoint is expressed almost exclusively in the third person, lending it an air of objectivity and prestige. As Morson and Emerson report about highly authoritative utterances (of which they cite scripture as an example), "There [is] a tendency to 'depersonalize' and 'disembody' the authoritative figure's speech, so that it is not perceived as merely one person's opinion" (Morson and Emerson 1990:164). Meanwhile, in Lam 1–2 the voice of the supplicant does not have to compete with a countervoice. The DV's authoritative third-person structure lends clout to *bat Zion*'s discourse. Regardless, commentators have still persisted in privileging a theologically normative voice over the voice of protest: Zion got what she deserved.[9] The theological orthodoxy of the DV is a generic feature of laments that the poet of Lam 1–2 amends to disquieting effect.

Thus far, I have been assuming that Lam 1–2 is a *type* of lament, but the designation of a genre is an ongoing dispute in Lamentations scholarship. Most agree that Lamentations constitutes a mixed genre—*qinah* (or dirge) and lament (Berlin: 23; Dobbs-Allsopp 2002:54)—although exceptions such

---

9. This interpretation is getting less play in recent commentaries by Berlin and Dobbs-Allsopp 2002, among others.

as Lam 3 and 5 follow the typical form of psalmic laments almost exactly. The fact that *qinot* contain no appeal for deliverance, unlike laments, strengthens their tie to Lam 1–2, which also omits any explicit appeals.[10] No *qinot* have survived in the Bible; we are left with only literary creations crafted for narrative (e.g., 2 Sam 1:17) and prophetic (e.g., Jer 9:9) purposes. Although Lamentations clearly also has affinities with Mesopotamian city laments, it is impossible to determine the precise connection between the two.[11] Despite the formal similarities (such as the feminization of the city, which obviously is of no small consequence to this study), there are some significant differences. The Mesopotamian city laments seem to have as their primary function the rebuilding of the city and the return of the gods to the city. This comic trajectory seems more comparable to Second Isaiah than to Lamentations, which takes a tragic tack (Dobbs-Allsopp 2002:11). And theologically, they could not be more dissimilar. The city laments portray gods that have acted capriciously in their destruction of the city,[12] while in Lamentations, of course, it is implied that YHWH is inflicting a reasonable punishment (although I will problematize this notion later in the paper).

Whatever the influence of the city laments, Adele Berlin makes the claim that the combination of *qinah* and lament in Lamentations (and some psalms) results in a new genre, which she calls the "Jerusalem lament" (24–25).[13] Berlin is sensitive to the complexity that attends the changes that genres undergo and says that the Jerusalem lament is more than the mere combination of *qinah* and lament (25). She also recognizes the generative role social context is bound to play: "This new genre or subgenre arose from a new historical situation [destruction of Jerusalem] and a new theological need" (25). Lamentations as a whole may have some similarities to the psalms she has labeled Jerusalem laments, but these similarities are mainly thematic, arising from a shared historical situation. Moreover, taken independently, Lam 1–2 certainly does not have enough in common with Berlin's new genre to share a designation. While not feeling obliged to support her opinion that a new genre that became standardized in other texts emerged out of 587, I do agree with her basic thesis that 587 was enough of a rupture to the sociopsychological fabric of ancient Israel that it provoked the emergence of a fresh, if not

---

10. Hillers (xxvii) calls Lam 1, 2, 4 dirges, for the most part, but sees them as very mixed genres.

11. Dobbs-Allsopp (2002:9–11) considers the city lament the most "important" generic influence on Lamentations. For a skeptical assessment of Mesopotamian influence, see Berlin: 27.

12. The Curse of Agade is an exception.

13. Other examples of a Jerusalem lament are Pss 44; 69; 74; 79; 102; and 137.

sustained, version of lamentation and that the generic ingredients that went into this new form of expression are multiple, so that the influence they exert is too complex to chart with precision.

Since we do not have a solid example of a *qinah* in ancient Israel, this study will not attempt to explain how Lam 1–2 evolved from that direction, and Dobbs-Allsopp (1993) has already done a thorough evaluation of the relationship between Lamentations and the city laments. By suggesting that Lam 1–2 represents a development of the lament tradition, I am not trying to make a positivistic claim about genre, that Lam 1–2 is somehow more closely related to lament psalms than to dirges or city laments. I do feel justified in making the claim, however, that there are clearer "family resemblances" between the two.[14] If nothing else, Lamentations is a form of lament, sharing such elements as subject, values, mood, attitude, occasion (i.e., threat), and to some degree style and task.[15] And, in terms of the biblical corpus as a whole, they are among the few texts that speak in large part *to* YHWH rather than *about* YHWH. The poet of Lamentations surely borrowed freely from the generic traditions that surrounded him without engaging in much theoretical reflection, but because we have inherited a well-established lament tradition in the Bible, from a readerly perspective, at least, it is natural for us to read Lamentations as a lament (and lexical connections between Lamentations and Psalms have long been noted; Hillers: xxii).

The Reading

My focus on the links between Lam 1–2 and psalmic laments will involve both content and formal/stylistic features. As mentioned, Lam 1–2, far more explicitly than psalms of lament, is a double-voiced utterance. The speech of "characters" is clearly delineated, and voices/discourses alternate in ways quite like some of the psalms. I will concentrate on only two double-voiced laments—Ps 22 and Lam 3—although I will touch on others to make certain points.[16] Psalm 22 provides a fairly clear contrast to the rhetoric of Daughter Zion in Lamentations, and Lam 3 is a classic lament that because of contiguity serves as a good counterpoint to the poems that precede it.

---

14. See Fowler for a discussion of texts within a genre as representing types that share traits, rather than as fixed entities. It is useful to keep in mind the qualification of Berlin (24), that we cannot know whether Lamentations is more *qinah* than lament or vice versa, nor do we have to choose to produce a "good" reading.

15. These are some of the generic categories established in Fowler: 61.

16. This paper is part of a larger book project (Mandolfo 2007); a more systematic treatment of these issues will have to await a less-restricted venue.

Lamentations 1 begins with a cry (איכה) more appropriate to a dirge than a lament, but many of the later verses in which Zion speaks could be placed into the mouths of the psalmic supplicants. Lamentations 1 continues with third-person speech for several verses. We do not hear Zion speak until verse 9. In contrast, but in accord with most lament psalms, Ps 22 begins with the speech of the supplicant and a traditional statement of lamentation: "My God, my God, why have you abandoned me? Why are you so far from saving me, from the words of my complaint?" "Why" is frequently used in laments as a form of complaint against divine inattentiveness: "God, why have you cast us off forever? Why does your anger smoke against the sheep of your pasture?" (74:1); "Why do you hide your face, and forget our affliction and our oppression?" (44:25). Even in the absence of the interrogative, several psalmic supplicants suggest God's culpability in their suffering. Psalm 38, for example, opens up with a plea that emphasizes many of the same concerns that haunt Daughter Zion's rhetoric: God's wrath and his *direct* involvement in the suffering of the supplicant.

> Yhwh, rebuke me not in your anger
> nor chasten me in your wrath!
> For your arrows have sunk into me,
> and your hand has come down on me. (38:2–3)

Similar statements are peppered throughout the more impassioned laments: "You have laid me in the lowest pit, in darkness, in the deeps. Your wrath lies hard upon me, and you overwhelm me with all your waves" (88:7–8). A request that naturally arises in the context of such complaint is, however, absent in *bat Zion*'s discourse. Although Daughter Zion frequently demands that her situation be noticed, both by Yhwh and passersby, interestingly, she never explicitly requests succor from God.[17] Psalm 22:20–22 is typical of what we are usually treated to:

> But you, O Yhwh, be not far off;
> my strength, hasten to my aid.
> Save my life from the sword,
> my precious life from the clutches of a dog.
> Deliver me from a lion's mouth,
> from the horns of wild oxen rescue me.

---

17. This may suggest a significant argument against categorizing Lamentations along with Berlin's other Jerusalem laments.

Not only does Daughter Zion neglect to ask Yʜwʜ for assistance, but she also, tellingly, fails to address Yʜwʜ by any of the appellations in Ps 22 that refer to his saving abilities, such as "my god" and "my strength." In fact, none of the typical metaphors connected to Yʜwʜ in lament psalms (rock, fortress, just judge, king, benefactor) are used in Lam 1–2.[18] The one occasion on which she requests that God intervene on her behalf—but only to exact vengeance on her enemies—betrays little hope that God will directly improve her situation (1:21–22). Even when the DV/narrator in Lam 2 beseeches her to cry out to God as her only hope (2:18–19), she responds by indeed crying out to God, but only to pour out her rage, not to ask for his mercy (2:20–22).

Like many double-voiced psalms (see Ps 7 analysis), after the initial complaint there is a counterdiscourse that begins at Ps 22:4. The voice does not shift grammatically, but it serves the same rhetorical function as the DV in Ps 7, such as to balance out the theologically destabilizing complaint that preceded it: God is "holy" and to be "trusted." Lamentations 1–2 includes no such proclamation of confidence. Psalm 22 then rapidly shifts back to complaint— "But I am a worm, and no man; a reproach of men" (22:7)—and echoes *bat Zion's* self-description in Lamentations: "Look Yʜwʜ, and see how worthless I have become!" (Lam 1:11). Psalm 22:12 laments that "there is none to help," similar to *bat Zion's* cry that she has "no one to comfort" her (1:21). In both, this proclamation is coupled with the observation that enemies are the cause of the problems. Both also suggest that God is behind the enemies' success, although in Ps 22 this suggestion is subtle (mentioned only once in 22:16), while in Lamentations it is declared overtly over and over again by Zion herself (1:12, 13, 14, 15; 2:20–22), not to mention the numerous times the assessment is affirmed by the narrator/poet in both chapters (but especially in ch. 2). From verse 23 until the end of Ps 22 the discourse of the DV takes over (except for a brief reversion to second-person speech in 22:26a). The voicing switches to speech about, rather than to, the deity and, it follows the standard line we find in the didactic discourse of so many laments. Of special interest for a comparison with Lam 1–2 is Ps 22:25: "For he has not despised nor abhorred the affliction of the afflicted, nor has he hid his face from him, but when he cried to him, he heard." Most laments end with similar thanksgiving, but praise of any sort is foreign—and moreover, antithetical—to the third-person discourse featured in Lam 1–2. In the midst of Zion's grievance in chapter 1 is inserted, instead, third-person speech that reports a purely negative assessment of Zion's situation vis-à-vis God.

---

18. As Dobbs-Allsopp (1993:30) points out, the only metaphor used to describe God in Lamentations is some version of "warrior."

Zion stretches out her hands,
but there is no one to comfort her;
YHWH has commanded against Jacob
that his neighbors should become his foes;
Jerusalem has become a filthy thing among them. (Lam 1:17)

While in chapter 1 the DV's assessment of Zion's situation still acknowledges some responsibility on her part for what has befallen her (1:5, 8), the DV in Lam 2 moves much further from the normative theological position of the psalmic DVs. Amassed, the verbs used, along with their qualifiers, are uniquely fierce.

How YHWH in his anger
has humiliated daughter Zion!
He has thrown down from heaven to earth
the splendor of Israel;
he has not remembered his footstool
in the day of his anger.

YHWH has destroyed without mercy
all the dwellings of Jacob;
in his wrath he has broken down
the strongholds of daughter Judah;
he has brought down to the ground
in dishonor the kingdom and its rulers. (Lam 2:1–2)

In accord with this harsh appraisal of YHWH's activities and presaging Zion's own rhetoric in 2:22, the DV in Lam 2:4–5 refers to YHWH as an "enemy." The poet (or later editor) tempers that assessment somewhat by inserting the preposition כ, thus making YHWH "like" an enemy, a qualification Zion herself does not bother with when she refers to YHWH as "my enemy" at the end of chapter 2.[19]

Psalm 22, in contrast, ends with the DV assuring the supplicant that "The poor shall eat and be satisfied!" (22:29); and future generations shall praise YHWH:

Their progeny will serve him;
it will be told of YHWH to the coming generation.

_____

19. Dobbs-Allsopp (2002:83) suggests that the preposition is a later addition. Xuan (98) says that it means "exactly like."

They will come
and will declare his justice to a people not yet born,
that he has done this. (22:30–31)

Abandoning for a moment the usual third-person address, the DV of Lam 2 (although it is plausible the address belongs to Zion herself) comments on the issues of food and children as well, but from an opposing perspective:

My eyes are spent with weeping;
my stomach churns;
my bile is poured out on the ground
because of the destruction of my people,
because infants and babes faint
in the streets of the city.

They cry to their mothers,
"Where is bread and wine?"
as they faint like the wounded
in the streets of the city,
as their life is poured out
on their mothers' bosom. (2:11–12)

Not only is Yhwh not providing food, but he is withholding it, ensuring that no "progeny will serve him." This hasty comparison of Ps 22 and Lam 1–2 is not meant to suggest that the poet of Lamentations had Ps 22 in mind when he was reworking the genre, only to suggest that the situation of 587 compelled some reassessment of how to communicate with God within the tradition of Israelite lament, utilizing well-rehearsed themes and structure. This exercise could be repeated with many lament psalms, but it will suffice to conclude by looking at what amounts to a lament psalm transposed to or crafted for the Book of Lamentations (Dobbs-Allsopp 2002:105).

In conformity with most laments, the supplicant in Lam 3 is primarily focused on his own suffering and grief, rather than, for example, Lam 1–2's focus on the children. Chapter 3 features a male supplicant, whose discourse opens the poem. The poem is basically divided into three fairly balanced sections: 3:1–21 consists of speech to the deity from the supplicant; 3:22–42 are spoken by the DV (except for 3:40–42, which includes mixed voicing); and 3:43–66 switches back to the supplicant speaking to the deity, the first part of which reprises the complaint of the first section, the second part of which professes faith in Yhwh. Such tight organization suggests a nearly stylized lament, perhaps explainable by the lateness of the poem as well as the liturgical and emotional needs demanded by the calamity to which it is responding. Much of the supplicant's discourse about God in chapter 3 matches in intensity and pathos that of Daughter Zion's in the two previous chapters.

> He is to me like a bear lying in wait,
> like a lion in hiding;
> he led me off my way and tore me to pieces;
> he has made me desolate;
> he bent his bow and set me
> as a mark for his arrow. (Lam 3:10–12)

It is in the objective discourse of the DV/narrator where the differences become apparent. In verse 22, following hot on the heels of quite impassioned complaint rhetoric, the tone completely shifts and the DV proclaims: "The steadfast love of Yʜwʜ never ceases; his mercies never come to an end!" The DV proceeds in a similar vein through verse 39. The placement of this normative voice in the center of the poem, as well as the poem's placement in the center of the book, suggests a conscious attempt to ideologically centralize the DV's theological position. As such it acts as a counterbalance not only to the first twenty-one verses of its own chapter but also to the first two chapters of the book. The inclusion of a traditional DV in Lamentations serves to mitigate Daughter Zion's insubordination. It is essentially the intrusion of divine discourse into what is otherwise theologically troubling human speech.

> Yʜwʜ is good to those
> who wait for him,
> to the *nefesh* who seeks him.
> It is good that one should wait quietly
> for the salvation of Yʜwʜ. (Lam 3:25–26)

A focus on the juxtaposition of complaint and praise in a traditional lament highlights the way in which the poet of Lam 1–2 strove to say something new about his particular situation. In Lam 1–2, the objective voice, the voice of authority does not bother with defending God's righteousness but rather puts all its weight behind Daughter Zion's complaint.[20]

---

20. I am not much interested in issues of authorship or redaction, but the structural and theological discrepancies between Lam 1, 2, and 3 makes reasonable the suggestion of many commentators that chapter 3 comes from a different hand than the Daughter Zion supplications.

YHWH determined to lay in ruins
the wall of the daughter of Zion;
he marked it off by the line;
he restrained not his hand from destroying. (Lam 2:8)

Newsom uses Lam 3 as a way to discuss Job's reconfiguring of the lament tradition, but her observations are equally illuminating for the way *bat Zion* reworks the lament.

> In Lamentations [3] the extensively described violence (Lam 3:1–20) serves as prelude to a word of hope (3:21), grounded in a conviction of the mercies of God (3:22–24).... Consequently, one should engage in self-examination and confession (3:40–42), drawing attention to one's suffering as motive for divine compassion (3:43–48). Job's act of resistance to this religiously sanctioned violence is to violate the form of the lament.... What the rhetoric of lament configured as legitimate punishment, Job...reconfigures as murder. The ravaged body serves not as the basis for compassionate appeal, as in Lam 3:43–48, but as the basis for accusation. (Newsom 2003:137)

The call for self-reflection in Lam 3:40–42 finds no echo in the chapters that precede it. Even when the DV alludes to Daughter Zion's transgressions, it comes across as no more than an aside, certainly not as denoting she deserves YHWH's choice of punitive response. Like Job, Zion's presentation of her ravaged body signifies a departure from the normative theology of lament. In contrast to Job, however, who has no defender, much of the effectiveness of Lam 1–2's reworking of the lament tradition comes from the redeployment of the DV, as much as from Zion's own presentation of her suffering.

It seems plausible to suggest that it is in part the influence of the city lament tradition in Mesopotamia that contributed to the poet's license in altering the rhetorical position of the DV. In both Lam 1–2 and the city laments, the "narrator's" function is to report on the deity's dealings with the city.

> Enlil afflicted the city with something that destroys cities,
> that destroys temples;
> He afflicted the city with something that cannot be withstood with
>   weapons;
> He afflicted the city with dissatisfaction and treachery. (Michalowski:
>   lines 296–299)

Still, the DV of Lamentations expresses itself in much less stylized and more personal, pathos-filled utterances, a quality that surely comes from an indigenous Israelite literary tradition, perhaps a combination of lament and *qinah*, and moreover inspired by a more democratic covenant tradition.

To summarize the generic situation, both the lament psalms and Lam 1–2 are double-voiced poetry. They share features in the area of content and structure. Attending to the formal and thematic features, however, leads us to observe a major structural difference that has theological repercussions. While the supplicants' discourses are not substantially different (Zion's may seem rather more harsh than most psalmic supplicants, but note Ps 88 for an example of how close they can be), the discourse that is generally characterized by third-person speech has essentially flipped 180 degrees. The function of the DV in the psalms seems to be to defend Yhwh's goodness or justice, or, in a more pastoral sense, it might be understood as offering reassurance to the supplicant. In Lamentations, however, one cannot discern a parallel function. The narrative voice understands the supplicant's situation from her perspective, has seemingly internalized her pain (and so in a sense could also be seen as performing a pastoral function). What does it mean, theologically, when the voice traditionally representing the divine position, the voice of authority, speaks against its own interests and from the perspective of suffering humans? Scott might provide a clue to the rhetorical impact of such speech when he speaks of the disproportionate impact elites wield when they stand up against the very system that has supported their interests: "those renegade members of the dominant elite who ignore the standard script ... present a danger [to the status quo] far greater than their miniscule numbers might imply" (Scott: 67).

BAT ZION AND THE PROPHETIC MARRIAGE METAPHOR

Lamentations 1–2 transforms the language of the lament psalms and wrests the DV over to her point of view. Zion does what the psalmic supplicants could or would not: she silences the divine/didactic voice. God is utterly silent in these two chapters, as are his typical defenders. Insofar as the traditional DV can only articulate the normative position—as often articulated in the prophetic accusations—it has no place in this poetry; the "party line" of the DV/prophetic voice would impose a nearly unbearable dissonance in this context. This modification to the lament provides Zion with a fitting response to the accusations leveled against her in the prophets through their deployment of the marriage metaphor. It further serves to emphasize how far apart husband and wife have become (before a move toward reconciliation is attempted in Second Isaiah[21]). In a patriarchal context of honor and shame,

---

21. Plenty of work has been done discussing the way God's voice is transformed in

the marriage metaphor is a potent and effective rendering of God and Zion's troubled relationship in the prophets. It constructs a discursive world in which the people's actions are construed as morally reprehensible and without defense. Absent the imaginative world created by the metaphor, the "disloy-alty" of Israel becomes more morally ambiguous. Outside of rigid Yahwism, adultery simply does not equal polytheistic practices. It is surprising, then, that Lamentations preserves the metaphor, but Dobbs-Allsopp contends that Lamentations draws on this metaphor for its own rhetorical purposes.

> [I]t may be assumed, insofar as the poem is culturally situated in a context where adultery is defined asymmetrically in terms of the rights of the hus-band as head of the household, that the poet means to tap into the motif's cultural symbolism, including the idea that the assault results from and is (partially) justified by Jerusalem's sin. Yet there are subtle but significant dif-ferences in how the motif is realized in this poem as compared with the prophetic literature that ultimately cast the imagery in a different light, cre-ating tensions that shift the focus away from the issues of sin and guilt and toward the experience of pain and suffering. (2002:63–64)

Daughter Zion wrests the motif out of divine control and uses it to recon-struct the moral discourse swirling around her. For space considerations, a brief survey of how this motif is recapitulated from Jer 2 and Ezek 16—both texts that employ the marriage metaphor to horrific effect—should suffice to make the point (see Mandolfo 2007 for a more detailed analysis of these texts). Both prophetic texts portray Jerusalem as an adulterous woman, with Yhwh as the betrayed husband. In Jer 2 Yhwh remembers with nostalgia his once innocent and loyal bride (2:2). But she eventually "rebels" and is quoted as proclaiming "I will not serve!" (2:20), and consequently she starts "playing the whore" with every Tom, Dick, and Baal (2:20–28). In Ezek 16:15–20 she is called a זנה and is accused of the additional charge of slaughtering her and Yhwh's children. According to Yhwh, her response to these accusations is to insist on her innocence (Jer 2:35a), a claim that seems to outrage the deity, for immediately following this quote he responds, "Now [הנני], I will bring you to judgment *for saying*, 'I have not sinned'!" God's "judgment" includes gang rape and dismemberment (Ezek 16:39–40). Never in these texts is Zion shown to speak in her own voice; it is always filtered through indirect dis-course. Baumann comments on the deity's rhetorical disregard for Zion's subjectivity: "Another problematic aspect of the depiction of Israel is that the

---

Second Isaiah, the way he appears to respond to her grievances in Lamentations. See Tull 1997.

female figure almost never has a word to speak and when she does, it is only
in supposed quotations that establish her compulsive pursuit of the Baals and
make it clear that she lacks any sense of guilt (2003:23, 25). The text speaks
about her from an exclusively male perspective; her own voice, her own will,
even as regards her 'marriage' to YHWH, is not recorded" (Baumann: 125).
While ostensibly an accurate reflection of her response to his accusation, in
God's mouth her proclamation of innocence is put to work for the deity's ideological purposes.

> The truth about a man [*sic*] in the mouths of others, not directed to him
> dialogically and therefore a *second-hand* truth, becomes a *lie* degrading and
> deadening him, if it touches upon his "holy of holies," that is, "the man in
> the man." (Bakhtin 1984a:69–70)

In Lam 1–2 *bat Zion* responds not by countering the charges but by portraying in no uncertain terms that YHWH's punishment has transgressed the
bounds of fairness and that his story about her is not the whole story. As is
not uncommon in lament psalms, she does admit to having sinned (Lam
1:18), but it is an admission that comes across in its new context as more
ironic than heartfelt, perhaps uttered to emphasize the disproportionality
between sin and punishment.[22] Terms used in the prophets referring to her
sin—"whoring," "committing adultery," and the like—are entirely absent in
Lam 1–2 (Baumann: 171). Given YHWH's response in Jeremiah to her claim of
innocence, it is no wonder that Zion does not take that tack in Lamentations.
Since his words about her carry a disproportionate amount of discursive
power, her confession might be read as coerced, perhaps with a hint of
mockery. A more derisive, or "inflected," reading of Lam 1:18 aligns with
Bakhtin's understanding of double-voiced discourse, when an "other's" words
are recontextualized in one's speech;[23] in this case it is the subordinate party
who recontextualizes the language of the dominant (Bakhtin 1984a:189). As

---

22. Irony, in this case, evokes Bakhtin's notion of "excess vision," whereby Zion is able
to see God and God's actions from a perspective that is inaccessible to him. Theologically,
this has obvious difficulties, but it seems rhetorically plausible.

23. Newsom (2003:28) notes the way double-voiced discourse works: "In ordinary
speech the words one speaks are always partly one's own and partly those of someone
else. This phenomenon can buttress one's own speech by invoking the words and phrases
associated with someone or some discourse the speaker treats as authoritative. Or it can
undercut another position, as in parodic speech. In both cases the speaker's own accents
as well as those of the other posited speaker are present and actively engaged in dialogic
relationship. While the discourse that constructs Zion as a sinner definitely belongs to
the authoritarian discourse of the deity, and thus might demand an admission of sin from

has been demonstrated of women situated in patriarchal discursive contexts, Zion cannot help but try to express herself through the language of the dominant discourse.[24] "[T]he dialogic perspective is preserved in the face of power only by being forced underground. What it cannot say outright it hints at through possible double or triple meanings" (Newsom 2003:30).[25] Given the intensity of her complaint throughout these chapters, an ironic or ambiguous reading of her confession makes more sense than the straightforward reading that claims she is taking responsibility for the suffering she is experiencing. Rather, whether she has sinned or not seems nearly beside the point from where she is standing. Yнwн's indiscriminate brutality takes center stage and thus mitigates the gravity of the charges against her.

Yнwн announces judgment against His errant wife (whom he calls "whore" [זנה]): "I will gather all your lovers.... I will gather them against you from all around and will expose your genitals for them.... I will deliver you into their hands, ... and they will gang rape you and stone you and cut you to pieces with their swords" (Ezek 16:37–40). She counters his charges of adultery and infanticide by pointing out the perversity of punishing her for such crimes by having her raped and her children slaughtered. In Lam 2:19 we read of the destruction of Zion's children, "who faint for hunger at the head of every street." Zion directly contradicts God's construction of her and turns the prophetic rhetoric back against her accuser when she states: "Those whom *I cherished and reared* my enemy has consumed" (from the root כלה, to finish, exhaust, consume [2:22]). The prophets and God enact a false construction of Zion's body. It is a body of lust and treachery, not a body that births and nurtures children. But with this final proclamation, she wrests back some of her subjectivity by transforming the deity's sexualized and violent portrait of her into one that powerfully evokes maternity, as well as simple humanity. And the DV, formerly an instrument of divine privilege, lends its weight to her case. Reading Lam 1–2 in relation to lament psalms, as well as particular prophetic texts offers us a polyphonic view of truth, as Bakhtin understood it,

---

Zion, it still seems reasonable to read her admission in a dialogic, almost parodic, manner; Zion is holding two positions in tension.

24. For a linguistic study that addresses this phenomenon, see Lakoff 2004.

25. Newsom further notes that the friends have an easy relationship with the language/tradition from which they are drawing, while Job "picks his way through a shattered language that he can wield only in fragments" (2003:131). Similarly, the prophets are understandably at home with the words they speak, since those words emanate from the source of their language/tradition itself. In contrast, Daughter Zion struggles for coherence. Her words are fragmented and often contradictory. The *qinah* meter contributes to the sense of asymmetry.

and Newsom specifies theologically: "[T]he truth about piety, human suffering, the nature of God, and the moral order of the cosmos can be adequately addressed only by a plurality of unmerged consciousnesses engaging one another in open-ended dialogue" (2003:24).

The utter silence of God in these chapters suggests that the largely myopic but consistent conviction that characterizes the discourse of the prophets and DV in the psalms dissolves into an inability to articulate a clear moral and, by implication, theological judgment in Lam 1–2.

> What can I say for you,
> to what compare you, Daughter Zion?
> To what can I liken you,
> that I may comfort you, virgin Daughter Zion?
> For vast as the sea is your ruin;
> who can heal you? (2:13)

The DV of the psalms, on the contrary, is never at a loss to respond to the suffering of the supplicants. For them, God's governance of the universe is in complete alignment with human notions of justice. I have elsewhere characterized Psalm 37 as one long Didactic Voice. It seems composed to assuage every lament ever voiced.

> Fret not yourself because of the wicked,
> be not envious of wrongdoers,
> for they will soon fade like the grass,
> and whither like the green herb.
>
> YHWH knows the days of the blameless,
> and their heritage will abide forever;
> they are not put to shame in evil times,
> in the days of famine they have abundance. (Ps 37:1–2, 18–19)

Such a response is not to be found in Lam 1–2. If we imagine the juxtaposition of this psalm with Daughter Zion's speech—

> Look, YHWH, and consider!
> To whom have you done this?
> Should women eat the fruit of their womb,
> the children they have borne? (Lam 2:20)
>
> Trust in YHWH and do good;
> dwell in the land and enjoy security. (Ps 37:3)

—it is patently clear how inappropriate the typical DV would seem in the context of Lamentations. Confronted with Zion's perspective on God's justice, Psalm 37's DV would come across as haughty disregard for her suffering and would set up a situation of irreconcilable dissonance for those living her words.

In the same way the creator of *Wicked* preserves the signifiers of Elphaba by which she had traditionally been epitomized as evil, the poet of Lam 1–2 preserves the metaphor of Israel as a woman, a metaphor that in the discourse of the prophets is meant to humiliate and dehumanize the people, and imbues it with pathos and subjectivity. Elphaba is still green, Israel is still the adulterous wife, but no one who finally hears their story from their own mouths can make the same easy moral assessments that were possible when their stories were shaped only within the discourse of the Wizard and God, respectively.

The gap between God and Daughter Zion in this text may seem nearly unbridgeable, but of course, this is only one moment in an ongoing relationship. The very fact that Zion cries out her anger attests to a future for the two.

> [C]omplaint ... reaffirms the radically relational nature of the divine-human relationship that undergirds biblical faith....In one respect, complaint is the lifeblood of the biblical notion of covenant: it ensures that the relationship is alive, dynamic, and open. Here faith is real, contested, actively negotiated. (Dobbs-Allsopp 2002:38)

The terror and incomprehensibility of her situation compels Zion to try to find language within her generic traditions to account for what has happened by countering and navigating the prophetic language that ostensibly already provides a rationale for her experience. The traditional account is no longer tenable in the culmination of what it prophesied. She constructs an alternative story, more authentic to her experience, by drawing on the language of lamentation, combined with elements of city lament (which, e.g., employs a sympathetic "narrator" and supports the use of a female supplicant) and dirge (which contributes meter, vocabulary, and tone). Because the DV is the one place in the lament psalms that most logically lines up with the divine position of the prophets, it is that piece that must be reworked to reflect her point of view so that her lament can resonate better in its particular context.

Polyglossia and Parody: Language in Daniel 1–6

David M. Valeta

Introduction

The presence of two major languages in Daniel that do not correspond to accepted genre boundaries is one of the most difficult questions in Daniel research. The court tales of Dan 1–6 and the apocalyptic visions of Dan 7–12 are divided into the Aramaic section of 2:4b–7:28, sandwiched by the Hebrew sections of Dan 1–2:4a and Dan 8–12. This perplexing and persistent problem as yet admits no adequate solution. The existence of Aramaic and Hebrew in Daniel continues to puzzle scholars. Proposals that explain the development of the text diachronically by means of various source theories have led to an impasse. Others attempt to explain the change through reference to the translation history of the book.[1] This has led to more gridlock. This study suggests that the work of Mikhail Bakhtin, particularly his concept of heteroglossia/polyglossia, may provide some new avenues of exploration toward understanding this perennial conundrum.

Language as a Context-Driven Phenomenon

Recent narrative and sociological studies have suggested intriguing new avenues to explain the presence of the two languages in Daniel. Daniel C. Snell posits that the reason for Aramaic in Daniel and Ezra is to lend authenticity to reports about foreigners and statements to them (32). Arnaud Sérandour argues that Hebrew represents a local and sacred idiom, while Aramaic signifies the official international and political language of profane use (345). Thus both these theories suggest from a narrative viewpoint that when the servants of the king begin to speak in Dan 2:4b, they naturally speak in Aramaic,

---

1. For good summaries of these issues in Daniel, see Collins 1993:24–38; Redditt: 20–34.

representing the official language of the royal court. The text simply reflects this expected state of affairs and lends authenticity to the account. These suggestions are interesting because their starting point is that the change of languages from Hebrew to Aramaic is intentional and part of the rhetorical strategy of the book rather than an accident of the translation or redaction process. Hedwige Rouillard-Bonraisin adds another layer of rhetorical intentionality with the suggestion that the language division in Daniel is a function of openness and hiddenness. Her argument is that over time Aramaic became the more commonly spoken language, while Hebrew became more progressively a language of the elite. The Aramaic stories, recounting the distant past, are retained in that language because they are popular, accessible, and non-threatening. The apocalyptic visions are written in Hebrew because they deal with currently sensitive political realities and thus are recorded in a relatively more obscure, less-accessible idiom (162).

The proposals of Sérandour and Rouillard-Bonraisin add a sociological component that is particularly important because they recognize that when two or more national languages exist in a culture and in works of literature, they each embed an ideology, a key Bakhtinian concept (Bakhtin 1981:296). Heteroglot difference can produce a variety of effects, related to time, space, class (Vice: 21). Bakhtin notes that heteroglossia "represents the co-existence of socio-ideological contradictions between the past and the present, between differing epochs of the past, between different socio-ideological groups in the present, between tendencies, schools, circles, and so forth, all given a bodily form" (1981a:291). In the multicultural, polyglottic world of the Hellenistic Judea, language was an important indicator of self-identity (Jaffee: 37). Certainly the preservation of indigenous languages was a means of cultural and nationalistic conservation (Mendels: 17). Moreover, evidence exists that throughout history, in times of crisis, Hebrew literature consistently revived as an expression of resistance and survival (Aberbach). It may be an overstatement on Rouillard-Bonraisin's part to consider Hebrew a language for keeping secrets and thus inaccessible to outsiders. The multicultural nature of Hellenistic society precludes the plausibility of such a scenario. Nevertheless, her instincts are correct that this document purposefully utilizes several languages. Languages are carriers of ideology that assists the book in relaying its message.

Another recent study suggests that the change to Aramaic occurs because of literary artistic considerations related to ideology. Bill T. Arnold contends that the author uses Hebrew and Aramaic intentionally in order to express differing ideological perspectives (1996:11–13). The two languages are utilized as rhetorical devices to express the narrator's shifting point of view, and it plays a large compositional role in Daniel. He explains that in Dan 1 the author's point of view is evident on two levels. First, the author is internal to the narrative, as revealed by the consistent use of the Hebrew names for Daniel's friends throughout Dan 1. Second, the author's assessment of Daniel's determination to resist the royal diet in 1:8 and the report of God's blessings toward the Hebrew heroes in 1:17 indicate that the chapter's ideological point of view is clearly oriented toward Daniel and his friends. Thus, the author's internal position, both phraseologically and ideologically, is consonant with the use of Hebrew in the opening chapter of this bilingual document. The point of view clearly shifts, however, in Dan 2. First, while Dan 1 opens with a Judean date formula, Dan 2 begins with a Neo-Babylonian one. Second, the narrator is moving toward an external viewpoint manifested in part by the use of actual rather than reported speech. Daniel 2:4b begins with the words of the courtiers of Nebuchadnezzar, who speak flattering words about the king even as they try to hide their inability to meet his requests. When the king's servants begin to speak, it appears that they naturally speak in Aramaic, the official language of the court, and the text is simply reflecting this expected state of affairs. The switch to Aramaic in 2:4b confirms the shift of the narrator's point of view to the external. The use of two languages lends authenticity to the account and contributes to the literary artistry in the composition of these court tales. The use of both Hebrew and Aramaic, as well as the smattering of Greek, in the book of Daniel is intentional, and it serves both artistic and ideological purposes. This new movement in Daniel studies concerning its multilingualism is going in the right direction. The following analysis builds on this prior work.

BAKHTIN AND POLYGLOSSIA

According to Bakhtin, there are two extremely important factors in the prehistory of novelistic discourse, laughter and hetero- or polyglossia (1981:50). Bakhtin argues that every prenovelistic literary creation has the attribute of heteroglossia or the presence of multiple conflicting voices in a text. This is typically indicated by the presence of different ideological voices in the text and is occasionally made obvious by the presence of two different sociological or even national languages (1981:275). This is also true of the prenovelistic menippea, a genre categorization that I have argued applies to the stories of Dan 1–6.[2] According to Bakhtin, the menippea is a multistyled, multitoned and/or multivoiced work that is dialogic and is based on the presence of

---

2. For a short discussion of my argument, see Valeta 2005:309–24. For my full treatment, see Valeta 2007.

multiple genres, voices, and/or multiple languages. The menippean construct compels new ways for thinking about the use of the multiple languages in Daniel. The languages are an intentional aspect of the text, an integral part of its menippean heteroglossic and dialogic nature.

Menippean creations are characterized by an organic unity of seemingly very heterogeneous features (Bakhtin 1984a:119). The use of several languages is therefore most likely a purposeful rhetorical and literary strategy in the formation of this narrative that contributes to its polyglossic ideological conflicts. Language is inherently ideological because it is an expression of contextualized social interaction and embodies a distinct view of the world. The interanimation and contestation of languages may, therefore, provide a venue for the testing of ideas (1984a:62). Language is the medium through which an alternative reality may be experienced. Bakhtin states of language in prenovelistic forms: "Language is transformed from the absolute dogma it had been within the narrow framework of a sealed-off and impermeable monoglossia into a working hypothesis for comprehending and expressing reality" (1984a:61). These languages also in all likelihood contribute to the book's satirical humor. Laughter and criticism suggest digging beneath surface indications to capture an alternative reality. As Bakhtin states: "[T]he corrective of laughter and criticism to all straightforward genres, languages, styles, voices, [forces us] to experience beneath these categories a different and contradictory reality that is otherwise not captured in them" (1981:59). The menippea uses and abuses genres, tones, styles, ideologies, monologic truth statements, sacred values, and more in its comical but dogged pursuit of the truth. When considering Dan 1–6 as a menippean construction, languages and voices should not be excluded from this list. Consequently, an exploration of the multiple voices and multiple languages of Dan 1–6 illustrates how they contribute to the overall menippean structure and satiric nature of the court tales.

THE MULTIVOICED NATURE OF DANIEL 1–6

Multiple voices exist in the Daniel narratives. For Bakhtin, the fundamental indicator of different voices is the presence of different ideologies. The characters clearly represent very diverse ideologies and therefore voices. Daniel and his friends represent the voice of faithful adherence to the Hebrew God. They seek kosher food to keep them strong, ask for mercy and intervention in events, are receptive to visions and apparitions from God, seek the interpretations of such, sing hymns to God, pray, and refuse to worship any god but their God, no matter what the cost. The kings, on the other hand, fundamentally worship only themselves. They destroy the Hebrew God's temple, capture his people, and desecrate his possessions. They demand dream interpretations, erect great statues to themselves, make laws in furtherance of their own grandiosity and desires, throw huge banquets, and are so prideful that they are turned into animals.

Different ideologies are also manifest in the fact that the heavenly voice of judgment continually casts a pall over the commands and desires of kings. The kings make plans, bark commands, roar decrees, and shout about the magnificence of Babylon. Meanwhile, divine dreams and apparitions portend death and disaster. All will finally be laid to waste. The voice of judgment stymies kings in their every attempt to assert real power. Their voices are cowered. The kings become puppets, singing hymns to the voice of judgment and bestowing favor on the carriers of that voice. The king's advisors also exhibit diverse ideological voices. Some of the king's advisors, such as Ashpenaz and Arioch, are people sympathetic to the Judeans. Others, such as the Chaldeans of Dan 3 and the satraps of Dan 6, work against them. These characters are more than bit players. They are another expression of the ideological tension in the book.

Different ideologies are similarly reflected in the reasoned voices of Daniel and his friends versus the wildly reactive voices of the kings. Daniel's voice, in particular, remains consistently calm and steady throughout the text. The voices of kings, to the contrary, are exploding with inappropriate passions, such as anxiety, fear, rage, and a hysterical worship of the Hebrew God. Except for the officials of Dan 3 and 6 who accuse the Judeans, the kings' officials and family generally try to talk sense into the king or smooth his way.

The voices of different characters thus represent differing levels of wisdom. The wise men of the king are never wise. Daniel, on the other hand, is always wise. Even the queen mother of Dan 5 knows this fact. She too is wise, unlike her husband and son. Moreover, diverse voices are present in different spaces. The royal court scenes, where official, stylized, and solicitous language is the norm, portray voices different from those in the scenes outside the court, such as the discussion between Daniel and Ashpenaz in Dan 1, where the conversation takes on a more informal and intimate tone, or, in Dan 3, where open rebellion breaks out.

The fact that the book of Daniel has both a public and hidden transcript indicates that it is a multivoiced work (Scott: 2). The public transcript carries the voice of cooperation with empire. The hidden transcript carries the voice of resistance. Daniel 1 exemplifies this well as the public transcript indicates that the Judean exiles are being shaped and formed through the learning of Babylonian language and arts while the hidden transcript indicates that the exiles secretly conspire with the advisor to the king to resist cultural assimilation by manipulation of their diet. These voices speak simultaneously throughout the narrative. The voices of rebellion are likewise diverse within Daniel. Most of the time, the voices of resistance are circumspect and remain part of the hidden transcript. Occasionally, however, they break into the open, as in Dan 3 and 6, where Daniel and his friends openly defy the kings' decrees regarding worship.

The voice of the narrator also reflects dialogism. The previous discussion of Arnold's view noted that the narrator switches from an internal to an external point of view between Dan 1 and 2. This is a mark of heteroglossia. Furthermore, the narrator is the only character in the text who uses different social languages within the same national language. He uses official and professional language in telling us most of this story, but he also uses slang in reference to Belshazzar's fear-induced scatological episode in Dan 5. This incidence of slang is quite grating when set against the usually high register of discourse. It flags that something far beneath royalty has just occurred. For all the high and mighty airs that kings exhibit, they are still quite human with all the frailties that go with it. The different social registers strip the king of any pretensions.

The use of so many different subgenres within Dan 1–6 is, according to Bakhtin, an expression of polyglossia. Each subgenre reflects the different voices of its use history. Moreover, the parodying of the form and use history of each genre brings another voice into the text's conversation. Daniel is a virtual chorus of generic voices.

This brief analysis of the many voices of Dan 1–6 lays bare the polyglossic satirical nature of the work. The character's voices and actions operate on a number of levels to introduce a series of diverse attitudes, ideological points of view, and narrative tones that produce laughter and scorn. Additionally, the narrator switches his narratological point of view. He also uses different social registers within one language to contrast two opposing attitudes toward royal status. This too is funny. The parodying of so many biblical genres adds more voices to the textual discourse. In light of these several levels of satiric dialogism in the text, the presence of three languages in Dan 1–6 logically reflects yet another level of the text's satiric heteroglossia. It is *intentional* to the work.

ARAMAIC IN THE BOOK OF DANIEL

The ancient Near East had been a polyglottic culture for over two millennia before the Hellenistic period. Akkadian and Sumerian sat side by side for centuries, and Akkadian eventually appropriated a great deal of Sumerian in its development. Akkadian became the *lingua franca* in regions where people spoke other languages (Caplice: 170). Aramaic supplanted Akkadian in that role during the Persian period (Kaufman: 174). After the conquests of Alexander the Great, Greek became the *lingua franca*, but Aramaic, Akkadian, Hebrew, and other languages lived on. The Hellenistic Near East was characterized by a vast and complex polyglossia.

Language development and usage is a fluid process, and languages in polyglottic areas can absorb the influence of other languages, as indicated above. Polyglots can use their languages in a separate fashion or combine them within a single sentence or speech. Polyglossia is reflected in single written documents early in human history. Archaeologists found Sumero-Akkadian interlinear bilingual compositions in Ashurbanipal's library at Nineveh (Cooper: 231). The Dynastic Chronicle uses both Sumerian and Babylonian traditions in a bilingual form (Finkel: 65–80). Letters from el-Amarna reflect "a kind of creole in which the vocabulary is mostly Akkadian (with some local words and phrases) but the morphology and syntax reflect the local NW Semitic dialects" (Huehnergard: 160). In the Persian period, it was common to find Aramaic script written on Neo-Babylonian legal tablets. This intersection of more than one language in written materials is described as macaronic literature (Bakhtin 1981:78–79). Eventually this phenomenon spread into literature and became especially present in the Middle Ages with the combination of Latin and developing national languages in a variety of literary forms (Wenzel). In this later form, it is common to see the interweaving of the languages throughout the text, which does not appear in the earliest forms of macaronic literature.

Written manifestations of polyglottism are found in the Hebrew Bible. Aramaic is embedded in the Hebrew text in Gen 31:47 and Jer 10:11. Ezra 4:8–6:18 and 7:12–26 is, of course, the greatest occurrence of Aramaic in the Hebrew Bible before Daniel. Gerard Mussies discusses the presence of Greek loanwords in the Hebrew Bible, most importantly in 1 Chr 29:7; Ezra 8:27; Neh 7:69–71; and Dan 3:5–7 (195–96). A mistaken perception exists within some circles of the biblical academy that macaronic literature is usually the result of a redactional process. This does not, however, have to be the case. The history of literature reveals that some works are originally composed in multiple languages or may quite intentionally have a sprinkling of foreign words. Wesselius makes such an argument for the intentionality of languages in Daniel (241–83).

Bakhtin observes that many prenovelistic literary forms came into being in the Hellenistic period, eventually becoming the dominant literature. These new genres were responses to the polyglossia of the Hellenistic world. In such an environment, the possibility of macaronic literature could increase radically. Because the Hellenistic milieu reflects a time of profound polyglossia, the intermingling of languages, cultures and ideological perspectives animated everyday life. The tension between majority and minority cultures created an environment where those under subjugation developed various strategies, including literary ones such as serio-comical compositions, to subvert the dominant structures of their time (Vines: 141). The reanimation of Hebrew literature in periods of crisis mirrors this peoples' constant reclaiming of their linguistic roots even while they were forced to learn and use the language of the dominant culture. It is therefore quite plausible to maintain that a prenovelistic literary composition of the time could be macaronic. The book of Daniel is one such instance.

The fact that Aramaic was the primary international language of literature and commerce in the Ancient Near East for hundreds of years is significant for its appearance in both of the books of Ezra and Daniel. It is the language of empire. In the book of Ezra, the Aramaic portion first begins at 4:8. Verse 7 states in Hebrew: "And in the days of Artaxerxes, Bishlam and Mithredath and Tabeel and the rest of their associates wrote to King Artaxerxes of Persia. The letter was written in Aramaic and translated." This verse signals that the letter will be in Aramaic, which it is (Ezra 4:11–16), as is the king's response (4:17–22). Other official documents are also in Aramaic within the text. These include a report from Tattenai and Shethar-bozenai sent to King Darius (5:7–17), a decree from King Darius (6:3–12), and a letter from King Artaxerxes to Ezra (7:12–26). Aramaic conveys official communiqués between the Persian kings and various officials in Yehud in the book of Ezra. Ezra apparently uses two languages to reflect two different literary voices, one the voice of Persian authority. Unfortunately, the interweaving of the Aramaic with the Hebrew is not perfectly consistent, for the surrounding narration is also in Aramaic (4:8–10, 23–24; 5:1–6; 6:1–2, 13–18) and one other official communiqué is not in Aramaic, the original order of King Cyrus to build the temple (1:2–4). Nonetheless, the lack of precision in this early example of Hebrew macaronic literature does not negate the fact that Aramaic seems to bear the voice of authority and a particular ideology within Ezra.

The book of Daniel uses Aramaic, the official language of the royal court until the Greek conquest, in some very unofficial ways to express humor and satire toward the king and his empire. The Aramaic conveys a satirical ideological perspective through two fundamental means. The shift to Aramaic in Daniel occurs at a point of reported speech where the counselors respond to the king's request. The king's request in Dan 2:3 is, however, in Hebrew. If the Aramaic were simply a concession to realism in the report of actual speech, one would expect the Aramaic to begin with the king's request. Instead, it begins with the advisors' response to the king. Daniel Smith-Christopher notes that the counselors' first words, "O King, live forever!" (מלכא לעלמין חיי), serve as an ironic statement that sets the predominant satirical tone of Dan

1–6 (1996:51). Each king who is greeted in this way is in the end humbled in some manner.[3] This irony provides an important clue that the introduction of Aramaic into the text is more than a simple literary device to inject realism into the dialogue and more than a mere signal of the shift of the narrator's point of view from internal to external. Rather, it is an indication that the Aramaic language is being used in a creative and sarcastic manner. The prevalence of Aramaic wordplays in the stories of Daniel confirm that the language switch is intentional, and a brief survey of some of these constructions provides the final piece of evidence that the language change is part of an calculated rhetorical strategy.

EXAMPLES OF WORDPLAY

The work of Anthony Petrotta provides a framework to illustrate the extensive use of wordplay throughout the court tale section of Daniel. He argues that instances of wordplay are more than examples of mere ornamentation but are also important in the overall message of the composition. The persistent use of wordplay techniques such as paronomasia, repetition, antanaclasis, and syllepsis demonstrate that the court tales are a highly complex creation designed to judge king and empire (Petrotta: 153). The following examples will highlight some of the most important occurrences of various wordplay techniques. There are many more occurrences of wordplay in addition to those explored below. These examples simply demonstrate that wordplay is a pervasive technique throughout the court tales of Daniel and this literary convention plays a significant role in the composition of these narratives.

DANIEL 1

Although it is written in Hebrew, this chapter does exhibit some wordplay techniques that are also used in the Aramaic stories. This demonstrates that literary creativeness using wordplay is found in all the court tales regardless of language. The most conspicuous technique is the use of the *Leitworter*, or leading word, which is the recurrence of a word or phrase that sets the tone for a passage (Arnold 2000:236). In chapter 1, the root king or rule (מלך) occurs in various forms over twenty times. This is a chapter seemingly about royal privilege and power, and yet the entire chapter describes various scenes of resistance and subversion. From the beginning, Nebuchadnezzar appears to be in control, but the reality is that the king's servants collude behind his

---

3. Other uses of this phrase are found at Dan 3:9; 5:10; 6:7, 22.

back and help the Hebrew heroes to subvert the wishes of the king. The repetition of the verb give (נתן) three times in this chapter, each time with God
as the subject who acts to allow things to happen in the story, indicates that
there is an ironical undercurrent at work throughout this chapter. The king
may claim to be all-powerful, but the story indicates that reality is indeed
quite different.

In Dan 1, King Nebuchadnezzar is portrayed as a conqueror of both the
political and cultic power centers of Judah as he defeats King Jehoiakim and
plunders the sacred articles of the temple. Then the finest of the deportees
are chosen for special education and training for imperial service. The public
transcript indicates that the king's desires are completely fulfilled, for indeed
the conscripts are trained and in the end presented to the king for royal
approval. As far as the king knows, his orders have been totally followed and
completely obeyed. However, the reader also learns that Daniel and his three
friends negotiate with the king's servants to change the terms of their subjugation. Many posit that the Hebrew heroes' concerns stem from piety and a
desire to remain ritually pure. While purity is certainly an issue, another likely
motivation, one that is apropos to the political nature of this chapter, is the
motivation to resist the royal edicts whenever possible. Their actions have the
political consequence of setting themselves apart from the king's agenda and
the Babylonian training table. Their resistance takes the form of the trickster
hero, which Scott defines as one that makes his way through a treacherous
environment of enemies not by strength but by wit and cunning (162). This
resistance is covert and invisible to the king and yet is powerfully subversive
and indicative of the true relationship between the king and his subjects. The
delicious denouement of this story is that the king knows nothing of this subterfuge, and deems the four Hebrews to be better servants than even his most
trusted countrymen (Dan 1:20–21). This commendation by the king adds to
the irony of this chapter because the heroes are in effect rewarded for their
subversive behavior. Thus the public transcript of this story attempts to affirm
the king's sovereignty, while the hidden transcript reveals that his conquered
subjects resist surrendering their identity in a variety of ways. This is a chapter primarily about power and control, not dietary scruples.

There are other clues in the text that indicate that power and control,
rather than purity issues, are the primary concern. Daniel 1:1–7 is filled with
commands that indicate that royal control is absolute, even to the changing
of the captive's names, which is an attempt to eradicate their identities (Chia:
26–29). In verse 7 the chief official gives the Hebrew heroes new names. The
Hebrew verb used here is וישם, with the sense of setting or determining.
Daniel's reaction to this determination of new names on the part of the king's
servant is not to challenge the new names, which would be risking a direct

public confrontation with an order of the king, but instead to choose another area of covert resistance. Daniel determines not to defile himself with the royal rations, and in verse 8 the same word, וישם, is used to describe Daniel's determination not to be defiled with the royal food and wine. The use of the same verb in these two different ways is an example of a wordplay technique called antanaclasis. Antanaclasis is the repetition of a single term with different senses, and here it is used to highlight the direct contrast between the actions of the royal servant and Daniel. The *patbag* (פת־בג) is royal food, and it is the political implications of such food that seems to trouble Daniel (Fewell: 19).

DANIEL 2

In this dream interpretation story there are a number of wordplay techniques that heightens the ambiguity and playfulness of the narrative. When the king asks the counselors to tell the contents of the dream to him, he uses a form of the verb to know (ידע) in verses 3, 5 and 9. His counselors respond many times with a form of the verb to declare (חוה), a technical term with the nuance to interpret. The shifting use of these synonyms highlights the cross-purposes of the king and his advisors. Once they begin to understand each other, the advisors cannot believe the king is asking them to interpret the dream without telling them its content. The king threatens to annihilate all of them. This type of wild swing of action and emotion is characteristic of each of the court tales and underlines the satirical nature of these stories. A second synonymic wordplay is the varied use of the words interpretation (פשר) and secret (רז). While the king and his advisors frantically search for an interpretation, it is God through Daniel who provides the hidden answer to the mystery, creating an ironic contrast between the supposed knowledge of the counselors and the true knowledge from on high. There is also in this scene an example of paronomasia, which is a wordplay determined by the sound of letters and syllables. Daniel, who is a son of the exile (גלו, 2:25) is the one to whom the mystery is revealed (גלא, 2:19, 22, 28, 30, 47) (Meadowcroft: 182–83). Finally in chapter 2, there is the use of lists of multiple synonyms in order to heighten the hyperbolic quality of this story. These include lists of sages (2:2, 10, 27), rewards (2:6), rulers (2:10), power (2:37), shattering (2:40), and homage (2:46) (Goldingay: 43). This is a technique that is used in many instances throughout the court tales of Daniel.

DANIEL 3

Dan 3 has been recognized by many to be an example of comedic storytelling (Avalos: 581; Gunn and Fewell: 174). The most prominent feature of this chapter is the numerous repetitive lists of government officials, residents of the empire, and musical instruments (Coxon: 95). These staccato lists paint a vivid word picture of a king and his subjects who act in mechanical and robotic ways. The ironic contrast of this lifestyle compared to the dignified behavior of the three Hebrew heroes creates a comical scene. The ludicrousness of the scene is emphasized by the repetition of references to the red-hot blazing furnace (3:6, 11, 15, 17, 20, 21, 23, 26) being heated extraordinarily high (3:19, 22) to receive the bound heroes (3:20, 21, 23). This hyperbole heightens the dramatic intervention by the angel of God. There are two other techniques worth noting. The first is an example of antanaclasis, which is the repeated use of a single term with different meanings. In verse 1 the word "image" (צלם) refers to the image of gold, the statue that Nebuchadnezzar sets up. The dimensions of this statue are quite ludicrous (Smith-Christopher 1996:61). Later in verse 19, image (צלם) is used in a description of how the king's face changes because of his fury toward the recalcitrant heroes. Meadowcroft suggests that this wordplay may suggest that the original statue was an actual image of the king (148). There may also be an allusion back to Dan 2, where the statue (צלם) is ultimately destroyed. There is also an example of paronomasia in verse 7, where all (כל) the people hear the sound (קל) of all (כל) kinds of music. This wordplay reinforces the bureaucratic lockstep obedience that the king requires, and this behavior is an ironic contrast to the dignified steadfast refusal of the three heroes to follow the orders of the king (3:16–8).

DANIEL 4

The rise and the fall of the great tree in this chapter sets forth the antithesis of human and divine kingship in no uncertain terms (Henze: 99). The synonyms great (רב) and mighty (תקף) (4:8, 17, 19, 27, 33) and king (מלך) and rule (שלט) (4:14, 22, 23, 29, 31) are used to establish this contrast. Nebuchadnezzar boasts of his greatness, but his words are hollow compared to the God of heaven who is in reality great. This is reinforced by the numerous references to the antonyms earth or ground (ארע) and heaven (שמיא) (Goldingay: 85). The hyperbolic boastfulness of the king is ironically contrasted with the true power of God. Two examples of paronomasia in verses 17 and 19 make clear the connection between the tree and the king, and that the fall of tree necessarily parallels the fall of the king. (The tree's height "reached to heaven" [4:17, ימטא לשמיא], and the king's greatness reaches to the heavens [4:19, ומטת לשמיא]. The tree's appearance is "to all the earth" [4:17, לכל ארעא], while the king's rule is "to the end of the earth" [4:19, לסוף ארעא) (Meadowcroft: 47). Another way this contrast is heightened is through the poetic wordplay techniques found in Dan 4:7–14, which emphasizes the greatness of the tree, setting it up for a great fall. Further wordplay examples are far too numerous to detail in this short article, but interested readers can access the extended list of wordplay techniques in this poem in an article published by Alexander Di Lella (247).

DANIEL 5

Chapter 5 contains numerous wordplays, including the well-known writing on the wall. In verses 2 and 3 there is an example of the literary device known as phrasal repetition, where entire statements are repeated with small but important changes (Arnold 1993:481).

The reader learns that Belshazzar causes the temple vessels to be brought forth in verse 2, but verse 3 adds that these vessels are from the house of God. The narrator subtly introduces his point of view with the addition of these words. Then there is a further wordplay based on the verb to bring forth (נפק). The verb to bring forth (נפק), is used in the haphel in these verses 2 and 3 and refers to the moving of the vessels, while in verse 5 it is used in an atypical way in the peal to describe the appearance or "bringing forth" of the writing on the wall. This paronymous wordplay underlines the ironic contrast between the human insolence of the king and the divine response towards this rebellious behavior. A second graphic instance of paronomasia is the loosening (משתרין) of the knots (קטרי) of the king's bowels in verse 6, while the same words are used in verses 12 and 16 to describe the ability of Daniel to "loosen the knots" of interpretation of the riddle (Paul: 125; Wolters 1991b:119). In verse 12 it is the queen mother who informs the king of Daniel's abilities. This advice coming from a female character adds to the sarcasm of the scene (van Deventer: 247). There is no doubt here that the king is being severely ridiculed (Brenner: 51). Then in the interpretation of the writing on the wall in verses 26–28, there is the extended paronomastic structure where three weights (מנא, תקל ,פרסין) are used as three acts of evaluation (מנה, תקילתה, and פריסת) in order make three judgments against the king (Wolters 1991b). A final wordplay that combines paronomasia, which is determined by the sound of letters and syllables, and the pun, which is determined by the meaning of words, is the fact that the weighing (תקל) of the king's actions results in the slaying (קטיל) of the king!

DANIEL 6

Meadowcroft describes Dan 6 as having a cheerful haggadic tone (94). This chapter is often compared to chapter 3, which has a plethora of repeated lists.

While there are fewer lists in Dan 6, there are many words that are used again and again, which lends a stilted parodic quality to the narrative (Goldingay: 124). Arnold proposes that the words "seek" (בעה) and "find" (שכח) are used as *Leitworter*, or leading words (1993:482). Daniel's enemies seek (בעה, 6:5) to find (שכח, three times in 6:5, twice in 6:6) some fault to use against him. Then in verses 8 and 12–14, seek (בעה) is used in the sense of praying or seeking a petition from royalty or a deity. This use of the same word with a slight difference of meaning is an example of antanaclasis. Thus there is pronounced contrast between how Daniel prays to his God while his enemies seek his destruction. The irony is emphasized further by the fact that counselors try to find (שכח) a fault in Daniel in verse 5 but instead find him praying to God in verse 12. Then in verses 23 and 24 Daniel is found innocent and no harm is found on him. This process of seeking and finding results once again is an ironic contrast between the enemies and Daniel. Another wordplay in this chapter is based upon the usage of the word law (דת) to describe the law of God (6:6) and the law of the Medes and Persians (6:9, 13, 16). The officials attempt to indict Daniel, who is following the divine law of his God, by recourse to their own human law, creating another ironic contrast. This use of a single term that carries two meanings is a technique called sylepsis.

Wordplay and Ideology

The extensive use of Aramaic wordplay demonstrates the text's satirical use of the official language of the court to win an ideological battle with the king. The Aramaic language is manipulated in such a way that it mocks and ridicules the king. His very language is used against him. In this way, the use of Aramaic is itself an act of satire and an integral part of the menippean structure of Dan 1–6. There is something deliciously wicked and witty in turning the king's official language on him. When the king appears on the scene in full force with direct speech, his advisors begin to betray him in the language of power. This technique enhances the effect of the public versus hidden transcript first revealed in Dan 1.

The presence of wordplays in both Hebrew and Aramaic also helps resolve another aspect of the language conundrum of Dan 1–6. The wordplays are one of the most important indices that neither the Hebrew nor Aramaic portions of Dan 1–6 were translated out of an original in the other language. Most wordplays do not translate well. It is extremely difficult to emulate in the receptor text any acrostics, alliteration, anagrammatical wordplays, antanaclasis, homonym wordplays, onomatopoeia, paronomasia, puns, and rhyming that appears in a source text. Such phenomena literally get lost in translation. Although Aramaic and Hebrew are cognate languages with great similarities, it remains impossible to translate the large number of wordplays in Dan 1–6 effectively across the two languages. It is for this reason as well that translation theories regarding the presence of the two major languages in Daniel fail. The Aramaic in Daniel is another aspect of its satirical drive.

The appearance of the few Greek words in Dan 3 highlights the internationality of the macaronic effect. The listing of several of the instruments in Greek indicates that the author has many languages at his command. He could have written in any of the three languages. Furthermore, it is no accident that the musical instruments are in Greek. Just as the three Judeans will not "sing" to a Greek tune, readers need not either. The light application of Greek words is a reminder of the social location of Dan 1–6 and the socio-ideological nature of this literature. The Aramaic text with its few Greek inserts is a highly complex creation designed to judge king and empire. This manifestation of heteroglossia underscores how language can be employed to destabilize and delegitimize control (Bakhtin 1981a:263–75). According to Ferdinand Deist, such humor is a particularly effective way for common people to define their identity and to subvert the violence of power (423).

IMPLICATIONS FOR DANIEL 7–12

Although Dan 1–6 is the focus of this study, one obvious question remains: Why does the Aramaic of the book of Daniel not disappear when the royal court tales disappear from the text at the end of Dan 6? If the only point of the Aramaic is to lampoon the king, then the job is done at Dan 6:29. One possible answer to the problem is simply to suggest that this early piece of macaronic literature is as imprecise as Ezra is in its application of multilanguaged dialogism. That could be right. It is also possible, however, that the carryover is deliberate and serves its own narratological and ideological functions. A brief investigation of the structure of the entire book is helpful.

It is interesting to note that from a language point of view the book has a dual, 1:5 construction; with the exception of Dan 2:1–4a, which disrupts the schema just slightly, the Daniel narratives begin with one Hebrew chapter that is followed by five Aramaic chapters. The Daniel visions begin with one Aramaic chapter that is followed by five Hebrew chapters. This structural pattern may be calculated. It reflects a twinning, or doubling, of form in the two parts of the book. In Daniel, form is just as important as content in conveying its ideological message.

Furthermore, the first six chapters of Daniel are "earthbound." Although a number of other-worldly visions occur, the setting of the chapters are fixed on earth in the royal court, in the royal domicile, in the royal banquet hall, the slaves' quarters, on the executioner's block, on the plain of Dura, and so forth. The space is terrestrial and the language is predominantly Aramaic, the official language of the literary court and the popular language of the intended audience for whom the text is written. In Dan 7–12, however, the space is other-worldly because heavenly visions dominate the text. Hebrew in this period is already a language that is associated with sacredness and is less well known among the people, although not entirely so. Arnaud Séran-dour, it may be recalled, argues that Hebrew represents a local and sacred idiom in this period while Aramaic signifies the official international and political language of profane use. If this is correct, then the use of Hebrew to represent the other-worldly visions would carry its own ideological message. Daniel 2–6 uses Aramaic to bring judgment upon earthly empires. Daniel 8–12 uses Hebrew to bring judgment upon the descriptions of empire in the heavenly vision.

Obviously, this structure is not perfect. Daniel 1 and 7 do not follow suit with respect to language and space. Perhaps Dan 1, as the book's introduc-tion, is intentionally written in the Hebrew as a *reversal* of the pattern of the other earthbound chapters. This underscores the importance of the language switch in Dan 2:4. If Dan 1–6 were composed entirely in Aramaic and Dan 7–12 entirely in Hebrew, one would not pay great attention to the change and probably never bother to question the underlying ideology of language use in the text. Daniel 7, on the other hand, is the introduction to the visionary part of the text and is a hinge chapter within the book. It has, in the concentric structure of Dan 2–7, many parallels with Dan 2. It would make sense for it to continue the argument of Daniel 2 in the same language. The language reversal in Dan 8 might well then jar the reader into noticing the switch to the sacred language. The overall effect is to cause the 1:5/1:5 doubled pattern of the book.

This twinning pattern plays out in content as well as structure between Dan 1–6 and 7–12. While it is beyond the scope of this study to do a careful analysis of Dan 7–12, note several of the mirroring devices between the two major sections of the book of Daniel. First, the date formulae of Dan 7–12 refer to Belshazzar (7:1; 8:1), Darius (9:1; 11:1), and Cyrus (10:1). Second, Daniel's Neo-Babylonian name, Belteshazzar, is mentioned in 10:1. Third, Daniel again eats no rich food, meat, or wine in 10:2. Fourth, precious metals and stone are part of the symbolism of the visions, as gold is mentioned alone in 12:5, gold and silver in 11:38, bronze in 10:6, and precious stones in 11:38. Fifth, the visions of Dan 7–12 are intensifications of their counter-parts in the earlier part of the book. The four beasts (7:2–14) and the ram and the goat (8:2–14) are extremely arresting images. Sixth, Daniel now acts very much like the kings with regard to oracular visions. Daniel is the one

with the terrifying visions that he does not understand and that need interpreting. The interpretations are provided to Daniel by heavenly figures and
provoke extreme reaction. For instance, Daniel has "a dream and visions of
his head while he lay in bed" (7:2). He repeats that he "watched in the night
visions" (7:13). As to his fear, Daniel says, "my spirit was troubled within me
and the visions of my head terrified me" (7:15). Even after the dream is interpreted, Daniel states, "my thoughts greatly terrified me, and my face turned
pale" (7:28). Again, Daniel "became frightened and fell prostrate" in the face
of another vision (8:17). Daniel is overcome by the vision and lays sick (8:27).
His strength leaves him, and his complexion grows deathly pale in 10:8. The
great man of his vision says to Daniel, "Do not fear" (10:12, 19); still he shakes
(10:17). Daniel must approach an attendant to have his vision interpreted in
7:16. In Dan 8 Daniel tries to understand his vision (8:15). Someone stands
before Daniel "having the appearance of a man" (8:15). It is Gabriel, who
interprets this dream for Daniel, but even so Daniel still cannot understand
it (8:27). Gabriel gives Daniel "wisdom and understanding" in 9:22, which
he apparently maintains in 10:1. The "one in human form (who) touches
and strengthens Daniel" in 10:18 is also Gabriel. Unfortunately by 12:8, he
again has no understanding. Daniel seeks answers by prayer and fasting (9:3),
sharing behaviors with his prior self and Darius. Daniel says of one of his
interpreted visions: "the vision ... that has been told is true" like he once said
to Nebuchadnezzar (8:26). Seventh, kings are just as self-centered, prideful,
and vicious in Dan 7–12 as they were in 1–6. The text says that no one can be
rescued from the ram's power (8:4, 7), which is similar to the power of God
in Dan 1–6. The horn of the goat grew as high as the host of heaven (8:10),
much like the tree before it. The horn "acted arrogantly" and "took the regular burnt offering away from him and overthrew the place of the sanctuary"
(8:11; cf. 8:13), calling to mind the sacred vessels of Dan 1 and 5. In spite
of these acts, the horn "kept prospering," as did Nebuchadnezzar before his
judgment (8:12). Moreover, the text again reports that forces sent by a con-
temptible man will occupy and profane the temple and abolish the regular
burnt offering (11:31; 12:11). A kingdom will be divided and be uprooted in
11:4 like the statue of Dan 2. A branch from the root of the daughter of a king
will rise up in 11:7 like the trees branches in Dan 4. The king of the south is
moved with rage (11:11). A king and his rage simply cannot be parted. The
king will exalt himself and consider himself greater than any god, and he too
will prosper (11:36–37). Eighth, God is once again the court of last resort
(7:10). His throne is made of fiery flames (7:9), and a beast is put to death by
fire (7:11), which counteracts the fiery furnace of Dan 3. Judgment is given
for the holy ones of the Most High (7:22) much like in Dan 4. All peoples,
nations, and language serve the one who is like a human coming with the

clouds of heaven (7:14a); his dominion and kingship will never pass away or be destroyed (7:14b). Finally, the very best is saved for last. Daniel is rewarded at the end of days (12:13).

The two major sections of Daniel are not independent pieces. The switch from Aramaic back to Hebrew is original to the text. The 1:5/1:5 pattern is important to the overall message of judgment in the book. Consequently, the use of three languages in the book of Daniel must be appreciated as an essential feature of its dialogism and satiric artistry—*and* its menippean shape.

<h2 style="text-align:center">CONCLUSION</h2>

Daniel 1–6 uses inserted genres, multiple tones, multiple voices, multiple social languages within Aramaic, and multiple national languages, namely, Hebrew, Aramaic, and Greek, to create a dialogic piece. The loosely constructed narratives exhibit varying degrees of irony, parody, and humor. Each chapter can function as an autonomous tale (Holm: 155), but when the stories are edited and read together through the lens of menippean Satire, an overall organic unity emerges. There is a consistent and persistent message of judgment that weaves through the stories. The message disrupts controlling authorities and voices. It challenges easy claims to truth. It offers a hilariously subversive resistance to empire and any who support it. Each story creates memorable images independent of the others, but when they are read as a unit, the tone of judgment and satire becomes dominant and clear. Bakhtin's concept of heteroglossia/polyglossia provides an essential tool to uncover the parody that is the foremost characteristic of the stories of Dan 1–6, including a more satisfying explanation for the presence of multiple languages in this text.

THE APOCALYPTIC CHRONOTOPE

Michael E. Vines

It has been twenty-five years since the SBL Apocalypse Group published its survey of apocalyptic texts: *Apocalypse: The Morphology of a Genre* (Collins 1979c). In the introductory article of that volume, John Collins provided a serviceable description of apocalypse as a literary genre. However, in retrospect, Collins's definition of the genre seems overly formalistic. The purpose of this paper is to revisit the definition of apocalypse and see what additional insights a Bakhtinian approach can provide into the nature of the genre. By examining the rather peculiar way in which narrative time and space is construed within apocalypse, as well as the unique perspective of its form-shaping ideology, we should be able to refine the definition of the genre and better discern its particular value as a medium for expressing a theological perspective on human affairs.

It might be helpful to begin by considering the difficulties that attend to the problem of classification. In 1859, the famous naturalist Louis Agassiz noted that Carolus Linnaeus, the father of the modern system of biological classification, persisted in referring to *mammalia* as *quadrupedia* up through the tenth edition of his book *Systema naturae*. In commenting on this anomaly, Agassiz remarked that Linnaeus failed to include "the *Cetaceans*" with the mammals and continued to include them "among the Fishes" (211). Agassiz's criticism of Linnaeus illustrates the chief problem that confronts those who embark upon the task of classification: Which features are essential, and which are merely accidental? It is hard to fault Linnaeus for assuming that a whale is a type of fish. One might reasonably assume that a characteristic as obvious as the number of a creature's (visible!) appendages should surely be considered taxonomically essential. But, as we know, that proved not to be the case. The lesson is that when we undertake the task of classification, we can often be deceived into thinking that obvious characteristics are therefore essential.[1]

---

1. This problem is as old as Aristotle, who knew that valid definitions must be based on essential qualities (*Top.* 101b35–36, 102a14–16).

At its most basic level genre is about organizing literature into classes so that we can better understand the conventions that govern both the creation and interpretation of specific works. We proceed initially on the basis of induction. We collect specimens and then note their similarities and differences. However, at some point, we need a theoretical grid that will help us distinguish between accidence and essence. Without such a grid we are engaged in a merely "formalistic" comparison that runs the risk of becoming atomistic and reductionistic (and susceptible of classifying whales as fish!). It is here that Mikhail Bakhtin assists us. Bakhtin's theoretical investigations into the nature of literature and his related explorations of literary genre help us identify what is essential in literature and place our generic classifications on more stable ground.[2] For Bakhtin, genre is not about the presence or absence of particular literary forms (or linguistic devices). Genre is instead primarily about a work's meta-linguistic form: the formal structure of a work that transcends its linguistic devices. Bakhtin observes that the various linguistic devices in a literary work are always made to serve a more comprehensive authorial intention, what Bakhtin calls the work's "architectonic form" or its "form-shaping ideology."[3]

For Bakhtin, literature is primarily a mode of interpersonal communication.[4] Behind the individual literary work is an author who is trying to give expression to a particular way of viewing the world. The author's goal is to express this viewpoint in a persuasive way to a reader. Like any interpersonal communication, the relationship between the author and reader is a dynamic exchange between two thinking and perceiving subjects. Overly formalistic approaches to literature tend to overlook this somewhat obvious characteristic of literature and instead treat the literary work as a static object that can be successfully analyzed by breaking the work down into its constituent forms. This analytical approach is destructive of the underlying dynamism of literature as a mode of interpersonal communication.

According to Bakhtin, instead of "analyzing" literature we should try to discern the author's voice. We do that by looking for the overarching unity

---

2. For a more detailed discussion of Bakhtin's theory of genre, see Vines 2002:33–68.

3. Bakhtin seems to use the phrase "architectonic form" (1990:269–70) and "form-shaping ideology" (1984a:82–83) to specify the same concept. As for the problematic word ideology, the best definition of this term, as it is used by Bakhtin, is provided by V. N. Voloshinov [M. M. Bakhtin], who defines it as "the whole totality of the *reflexions* and *refractions in the human brain* of social and natural reality, as it is expressed and fixed by man in word, drawing, diagram or other form of *sign*" (1983:98 n. 5).

4. Bakhtin explores the interpersonal dimension of communication in detail in his essay "The Problem of Speech Genres" (1986:60–102).

of the literary work; the unity imposed upon it by the author's creative inten-tion. With respect to genre, the most important aspect of the author's creative intent is the way in which the author creates the world of the narrative. Although the author shapes the world of the narrative to match her creative vision, this created world is never completely idiosyncratic. Instead, within the broader literary environment specific patterns of "form-shaping ideol-ogy" coalesce around particular perspectives and themes. These patterns of ideological expression are what we call genre (Bakhtin 1981:288; Bakhtin and Medvedev: 129–30, 133, 134). At the risk of oversimplification, there are two main aspects of these patterns that we should notice: an internal aspect and an external aspect.

Internally, these patterns help an author create a context for the substan-tive content of the literary work. To use a simple example, when we wish to communicate a formal message to someone, we use the conventions of the "business letter." These conventions establish a context for the message which communicates seriousness and formality. In narrative literary works, the cre-ation of context is more complex, since the author is creating a whole world for the action of the narrative. By creatively using the conventions of genre, an author is able to construct an artificial context for the expression of a par-ticular point of view within the literary work. This context establishes the axiological possibilities for the action of the hero. The literary work is there-fore a kind of axiological or ideological experiment. The hero of the work, who generally embodies the values the author wishes to test, is placed in a world created by the author specifically to test the hero and the values repre-sented by the hero (Bakhtin 1984a:135; 1981:388–89). Since the author creates the world of the narrative, its temporal and spatial qualities can be manip-ulated to test the hero's values, or the values of other characters within the narrative, in very specific ways. This manipulation is not merely dimensional (the length of story time or the expanse of narrative geography). The author charges the time and space of the narrative with ethical qualities of mean-ing and significance. For Bakhtin, it is precisely the value-laden temporal and spatial quality of a work, or its chronotope, that is the primary indicator of its generic relationships (1981:84–85).

Externally, the use of a specific pattern or genre engages the author in an ongoing conversation about life, a conversation that may change and evolve over time. From this perspective, genre is not so much about taxonomy but about ongoing conversations over what Bakhtin called "great time" (1986:4; 1984a:106). Thus, as an act of human communication, Bakhtin claims that a literary work is inherently dialogic. To the extent that the author is conscious of this ongoing conversation and the surrounding cultural polyphony, its importance may be acknowledged within the world of the text. Thus, within the literary work, the narrative may be more or less dialogic to the degree that the author allows competing points of view to enter the world of the text. Works that tend to be unaware of, or foreclosed to, competing viewpoints are monologic, while those that intentionally orchestrate multiple viewpoints are dialogic (1984a:82–84, 88). Ancient works of literature, such as apocalyptic, are generally very monologic, the overtly dialogical work being a more modern literary form. However, even ancient works sometimes explore dialogism through the mimesis of dialogue within the narrative and through the incorporation of diverse subgenres (1981:50). However, these works remain essentially monologic, since the values of the author control the representation of the dialogic voices within the text and distort their perspective on life.

However, even monologic works are externally dialogic. The resources of language and genre that an author uses to express his intention belong not solely to the author but also to the surrounding culture in which the author is embedded. The use of these common cultural resources engage the author in a kind of dialogue with others who are using the same resources in similar ways. To be properly understood, a literary work should be situated within an ongoing dialogue with other works that share a similar form-shaping ideology or genre (Bakhtin 1984a:157). Therefore, if we wish to understand the importance of a particular literary work within a genre, we need to be engaged in what we might call a diachronic history of literature, not merely in its taxonomic classification.

Having established a theoretical framework for a Bakhtinian approach to the problem of genre, we are now in a position to examine what this perspective might contribute to the understanding of apocalypse as a literary genre. In contrast to Collins, we are interested not so much in the particular "forms" used in the apocalypse and their relative frequency but in the ideological framework that holds these forms together. Following Bakhtin's lead, we can probe the nature of apocalypse by organizing our observations under three headings: chronotope, author and hero, and dialogue.

CHRONOTOPE

The peculiar way in which time and space is constructed within apocalypse is one of the genre's most distinctive features. The time and space of apocalypse transcends the boundaries of this mundane world both dimensionally and axiologically. Dimensionally, the temporal and spatial boundaries of apocalypse are permeable and limitless. Vast expanses of time can be surveyed in both directions. Historical events can be reviewed and assessed and future events can be revealed and celebrated. The temporal boundaries of apocalypse are not limited by quotidian concerns. Nor is time bound by the biological extent of the hero's life. The normal temporal boundaries of human life are suspended to make room for revelation. At times, the suspension of time within the narrative is explicit, as in 2 En. 2, but elsewhere the revelation occurs without any indication of its temporal duration. Even when there are temporal indications within the text (e.g., 4 Ezra), these primarily serve to create time for spiritual preparation and do not indicate the total extent of time taken up by the revelation.

Similarly, the spatial dimension of apocalypse is permeable and unbounded. This is true whether the hero is taken on a heavenly journey or is given a heavenly vision. In either case, the hero is allowed to pass freely, either physically or mentally, between earth and heaven. From the vantage point afforded by the journey or revelation, the hero can survey all the realms of heaven and earth. Within this unbounded space, the hero sees the splendor of heaven, the horrors of hell, and the persistent misdeeds of humanity. The lofty perspective of apocalypse is strange and disorienting to the hero. The visions are filled with strange symbolic creatures, and the heavenly realm is populated with fantastic supernatural beings. The hero's confusion is dispelled by a divine companion who guides the hero on the otherworldly journey or explains the mysterious visions.

The significance of both the temporal and spatial unboundedness of apocalypse is that it affords a divine perspective on human activity. The purpose of apocalypse would therefore seem to be to gain a God's-eye view on human history and activity. If we ask why the apocalyptic authors created such a perspective, we need only look at what these texts imply about the state of human affairs. The meaning of human history has become opaque. The assumption that prevailed in Israel's epic literature (the Torah, the Deuteronomistic History, etc.), namely, that God's covenant love ensures the success and prosperity of God's people, no longer seems to hold.[5] Instead, the world has become a hostile place overrun by those who refuse to acknowledge the one sovereign God and, worse yet, who torment and persecute God's righteous followers. The possibility of justice in the present has disappeared. The apocalypse is therefore profoundly pessimistic about world events, human activity in general, and the terrestrial welfare of the righteous. Whatever hope

---

5. I am drawing here on Bakhtin's distinction between "epic" and "novelistic" literature. He describes the former as having three main constitutive features: "a national epic past," a "national tradition [that] serves as the source for the epic," and "an absolute epic distance [that] separates the epic world from contemporary reality," whereas the latter creates a "zone of maximal contact with the present" (1981:11, 13). I believe a similar distinction can be made between the literature of Torah and the apocalypse.

might be expressed in the world of the apocalypse must be projected into the eschatological future.

AUTHOR AND HERO

The role of the hero in the apocalypse is distinctive. In the first place, the hero is most often a righteous figure borrowed from Israel's epic past: figures such as Enoch, Abraham, Baruch, or Daniel. Presumably, these epic figures are incorporated into apocalypse because they are the only ones capable of being entrusted with such important truths. If, as we noted above, the present age of the apocalypse is utterly corrupt with little or no hope of being salvaged, then the only possible bearer of the divine message must come from the epic past. By using heroic figures from the past, the author of apocalypse betrays both his mistrust of the present, and implicitly celebrates the virtues of a bygone age. These heroes embody the values that once sustained God's people and guaranteed their blessing, but their day has passed. Now these heroes become the bearers of a message that asserts the sovereignty of God while it simulta- neously acknowledges the hopelessness of the human situation.

As the recipient of the apocalyptic message, the hero is almost completely passive. The hero of apocalyptic is not the deed-performing hero of Greek mythology whose actions affect the course of human events. The hero of the apocalypse is a completely passive vehicle of divine revelation. The hero is selected to be the bearer of revelation because of his exceeding virtue, but these virtues are never put to the test in the world of the apocalypse. Even in the Testament of Abraham, where Abraham shows himself to be a harsh judge of human failure, Abraham's actions are only a demonstration of his surpass- ing virtue and not a test of his fidelity to God (10:5–12). The passivity of the hero of apocalypse establishes an important distinction between apocalypse and prophecy. In biblical prophecy, the hero is expected to relate the con- tent of the divine revelation to a hostile audience. The virtue of the prophetic hero is measured by his faithfulness in speaking the "word of God" under these difficult circumstances. In apocalypse, the emphasis is on the splendor and complexity of the heavenly message, along with its proper interpretation, rather than on the action of the hero.

Rather than testing the hero, the author of apocalypse is more interested in testing the cosmos. "Creation" is therefore the character that is scrutinized by apocalypse. The author of apocalypse seems all too aware of the corrup- tion of the world. The question is: How does the creator intend to deal with this corruption? What will be done to right the inequities of society? Is the creator still in charge of the cosmos? The hero learns not only that the ter- restrial world is beset by corruption but that corruption also extends to the supernatural realm. Nevertheless, the hero also discovers that God has always been in control of the cosmos, even during times of great injustice and human unrighteousness. Furthermore, there is a divine plan to deal with disobedience, sin, and corruption. It is the disclosure of this plan that is the main content of the apocalypse, and its purpose is to display the majesty of God and to vindicate God's sovereignty and justice.

Dialogism

With respect to its internal dialogism, apocalypse supplements heavenly visions and journeys with the somewhat fantastic mechanism of otherworldly dialogue. The hero normally has a heavenly guide with whom he converses. However, the hero is usually passive in this regard as well. The hero sometimes argues with his divine guide on behalf of humanity, and will even prayerfully intercede for those who are in need. However, the action of the hero consists mainly in pressing his heavenly guide for explanations of the meaning of things. This provides the author with an opportunity to express his finalizing vision of this world and the world beyond. The apocalypse is therefore a profoundly monologic genre, since no dialogic response is allowed or even entertained within the discourse of apocalypse. The thoroughly negative assessment of human history offered within the apocalypse is unmitigated by any competing perspective. Thus, there is little or no sympathy in the way apocalyptic reads history and no rebuttals are allowed to counterbalance its harsh judgments.

An investigation of the apocalypse's external dialogic relations would take us well beyond the limitations of this paper. At best, all that we can do is to propose some prospective lines of inquiry. First, how is apocalyptic related to biblical prophecy? This question is not so much about whether or not the apocalypse is a transformation of biblical prophecy but more about an inquiry into the ideological connection between the two genres. Both types of literature are clearly revelatory and concerned with bringing a divine perspective to bear on the human condition. Yet they are at the same time clearly different in the way they convey this perspective. The prophetic chronotope is by turns both fantastic and realistic, both prosaic and poetic, while the apocalypse is more firmly rooted in the fantastic and the supernatural. The prophet speaks the "word of God" to his contemporaries, but the hero of apocalypse only witnesses and internalizes the revelation. The point of this difference seems to be that prophetic literature seems to hold that the present is still redeemable, if only people will reform themselves and follow the spirit and intent of God's laws, while the apocalypse despairs over the possibilities of reforming the present.

A second line of inquiry might explore historical and ideological developments within apocalypse. Collins is struck by the distinction between those apocalypses that are based upon mystical visions, which he labels Type I apocalypses, and those that involve heavenly journeys, which he calls Type II apocalypses (1979b:22). If this purely formal distinction is valid, we might be led to ask what historical or social changes were involved in this change within the genre. But from a Bakhtinian point of view the question is whether or not Type I and Type II apocalypses construe the chronotopic boundaries of apocalypse in different ways. It seems to me that they do not. The difference between the two types appears to be only formal, and therefore not such that it would indicate an essential difference within the genre.

CONCLUSION

In a more recent treatment of apocalypse, John Collins has claimed that "A worldview is not necessarily tied to any one literary form, and the apocalyptic worldview could find expression in other genres besides apocalypses" (1997:8). A Bakhtinian approach to the problem of genre suggests that this cannot be the case. The particular way in which a literary work construes the world is essential to its genre. This is not to deny that the apocalypse may be in conversation with other literary genres that construe the world in similar ways, but we should be able to point to something distinctive in the worldview, or chronotope, of the apocalypse if it is a distinct genre.

In this too brief survey of its chronotopic characteristics, we find that apocalypse is an essentially "finalizing" genre: an attempt to fix the axiological position of human activity and then measure it in relation to divine standards of justice. Within the world of the apocalypse there is no room for rebuttal or justification. Invariably, the cosmos is found to be deeply, if not fatally, flawed. Apocalypse is not interested in deliberating over the guilt or innocence of the cosmos. What it wants to explore is how the sovereign creator God intends to deal with a flawed creation. The past is filled with errors and the present appears irredeemable. What then will God do about the future? The hero of the apocalypse is invited to view the cosmic situation from God's point of view and learn the mysteries of God's hidden plan. This is true whether the hero gains this perspective by a mystical vision, or a heavenly journey. What the hero learns is that God is in control of the cosmos, and that there is a plan for dealing with human disobedience and corruption.

This, it seems to me, is a much more helpful way of looking at the essential nature of apocalypse. It is not that the formal approach is fundamentally wrong. It is rather that attention to literary devices does not go far enough in uncovering the essential unity of apocalypse as a literary genre. If we look at apocalypse through the lens of chronotope we begin to discern this essential unity. With greater clarity about the essential nature of apocalypse as a literary genre, we are in a much better position to engage in the kind of literary history that will help us understand its place in the development of literature and ideas.

Matthew's Genealogy as Eschatological Satire: Bakhtin Meets Form Criticism

Christopher C. Fuller

Introduction

In this essay I argue that the genealogy in Matt 1:1–17 is composed in a manner that invites the reader to engage the remainder of the First Gospel as an eschatological satire. I make this argument by positioning form-critical conclusions about the genealogy as the basis for a Bakhtinian reading of this text that focuses on its chronotopic qualities in partnership with a recurrent pattern of otherness.

Throughout his life Bakhtin addressed the role of memory in aesthetic activity. In his early philosophical essays it contributed to how one participated in the finalizing of another's life. He writes, "Memory of someone else's finished life (although anticipation of its end is possible as well) provides the golden key to the aesthetic consummation of a person" (1990:107). In his later literary studies he addressed memory and its relationship to genre. The concept through which Bakhtin expresses this relationship is the chronotope.

The chronotope is one of Bakhtin's most distinctive conceptions. It is also one of his most difficult, not least because he never provided an adequate definition of it. He describes it as "the intrinsic connectedness of temporal and spatial relationships that are expressed in literature" (1981:84). For Bakhtin, time and space within a literary narrative are inseparable. Chronotopes are "the organizing centers for the fundamental narrative events of the novel. The chronotope is the place where the knots of narrative are tied and untied. It can be said without qualification that to them belongs the meaning that shapes narrative" (250). Its primary function is to materialize time and space, which are fused within a given context. According to Morson and Emerson, "For a truly chronotopic imagination … time must be understood in its interconnection with specific space, and space must be understood as saturated with historical time" (1990:417).

What chronotopes do is infuse events within a narrative with significance beyond their ability to present straightforward information. In this way, they organize literary texts as worlds that exist independent of the text. That is, they create a context within which the reader participates in the text's dialogic relations. In addition, Jay Ladin writes, "Through the chronotope, abstract ideas (such as fate, or the absurdity of human existence) are translated within a text into sensual descriptions and ontological circumstances" (212).

Bakhtin argues that any and every literary language is chronotopic. He writes, "Language, as a treasure-house of images, is fundamentally chronotopic. Also chronotopic is the internal form of the word, that is, the mediating marker with whose help the root meanings of spatial categories are carried over into temporal relationships (in the broadest sense)" (1981: 251). Because language not only participates in the present construction of meaning but is also inhabited by the history of its prior use, the chronotope does not transcend history. Rather, it is enmeshed within history. It mediates the relationship between a narrative's literary discourses and the historical, biographical, and social contexts that intersect with them. The results, according to Alice Bach, are "fictional environments where historically specific constellations of power are made visible" (99).

Chronotopes can dialogically interact with one another. This kind of dialogue is not part of the world represented in the text but rather an interaction between this world and that of the author and the reader. This does not mean that there is not a distinction between the world of the text and the world around the text. However, this distinction does not preclude interaction between the author, text, and reader. Morson and Emerson rightly point out that failure to acknowledge the boundaries between the text's world and the reader's world invites a naïve realism or naïve reader reception (1990:428). On the other hand, in Bakhtin's view, adherence to a rigid, impermeable boundary is likely to result in "oversimplified, dogmatic hairsplitting" (1981:254). Near the end of his life Bakhtin advocated "benevolent demarcation, without border disputes" (1986:137).

In the zone between the world of the reader and the represented world of the text there is the creating world, where, "uninterrupted exchange goes on ... similar to the uninterrupted exchange of matter between living organisms and the environment that surrounds them" (Bakhtin 1981:254). The potential for meaning within this creating world is never finalized but is unceasingly excavated as different chronotopes emerge to readers within different contexts and different historical periods. Therefore, one's temporal, spatial, and cultural outsideness in relation to a work is necessary for creative understanding to thrive. According to Bakhtin, "The work and the world represented in it enter the real world and enrich it, and the real world enters the work and its world as part of the process of its creation, as well as part of its subsequent life, in a continual renewing of the work through the creative perception of listeners and readers" (254).

Single works, as well as the complete oeuvre of a single author, may contain a number of different chronotopes as well as complex interactions between them. The reader encounters them in the "external material being of the work and in its purely external composition" (Bakhtin 1981: 252). Bakhtin focuses his attention primarily on the chronotopic qualities of genre. Those chronotopes that Bakhtin identifies that bear on studies of the Gospels are the adventure novel of ordeal, the adventure novel of everyday life, and ancient biographies and autobiographies (99, 116).

Bakhtin does not propose impermeable criteria to identify these genres. He recognizes that genres grow and change through time. He writes that a genre "is always the same and yet not the same, always old and new simultaneously. Genre is reborn and renewed at every new stage in the development of literature and in every individual work of a given genre" (1984a:106). Genres are coalescences of "givenness" and "creation." They provide the "givenness," but final works are not constrained by it. The result is that they become something new through the act of composition or creation. Such a view comports well with the New Testament Gospels. They exhibit the qualities of biography but also possess "novelness" as well (Talbert; Aune; Burridge; Tolbert; Vines). Bakhtin's insights provide the opportunity to view the Gospels not entirely as one or the other genre nor as completely *sui generis* but at the crossroads of givenness and creation.

As important as the literary elements of each generic chronotope are to Bakhtin, he also examines the relationship between genre and memory. For him genres are more than an assembly of literary devices or linguistic elements; they are a form of thinking. They accumulate experience and, through repeated use, acquire a sedimented memory of their use through time. "Genres ... throughout the centuries of their life accumulate forms of seeing and interpreting particular aspects of the world" (Bakhtin 1986:5). Genres bring their own languages into the novel, and, consequently, they "stratify the linguistic unity of the novel and further intensify its speech diversity in fresh ways" (1981:321). Memory not only preserves the past but also enacts a creative transformation in the present. The accretion of lived experience collaborates with others' surplus to produce something new.

Bakhtin's argument that all language is chronotopic means that one may encounter chronotopes not only at the macro generic level but also within individual words themselves. Ladin rightly points that a word-by-word chronotopic analysis would be an arduous and, ultimately, self-defeating undertaking. It is necessary, however, to decide at what level such an undertaking is useful. He advocates examination of what he calls "local chronotopes." He provides four ways that one can determine their significance: (1) they are associated with the enactment of key scenes and events; (2) they repeat or explicitly use language that calls attention to time and space; (3) they fuse a particular quality of time and "well-delineated" space in a manner that is distinct from other space-times; and (4) they provide physical metaphors for abstract ideas (Ladin: 218–19). More important than the specific qualities of different local chronotopes is that their existence also argues for generic examination at the local level within a text as well as analysis of the dialogic relationships between local genres.

READING MATTHEW 1:1–17 "LIKE" BAKHTIN

Anyone familiar with Bakhtin's writings is aware that it is folly to propose his work as the foundation of a method to interpret the First Gospel. Rather, he serves as a guide by providing concepts that attune the reader to relationships within the text and between the text and the reader. Barbara Green refers to this process as reading a text with or "like" Bakhtin. In this manner of reading, "we do not try to peer beneath the frame to see more of the picture but try to see well what is represented on the verbal canvas" (Green 2000:70). This process pushes the reader to be more aware of and creative about the choices he or she makes and to be responsible for those choices. There is no passive acceptance, only active and answerable engagement with the plenitude of voices within the text. With this in mind, the search for meaning moves beyond conscious authorial intent. This approach is premised upon Bakhtin's description of what he called "creative understanding."

Creative understanding relies on the interpreter's surplus of vision, due to his or her position outside of the literary world of the text (e.g., one's own cultural experience), as a dialogic partner in the process of excavating potential meaning. According to Bakhtin, "*Creative understanding* does not renounce itself, its own place in time, its own culture; and it forgets nothing. In order to understand, it is immensely important for the person who understands to be *located outside* the object of his or her creative understanding—in time, in space, in culture" (1986:7). This conviction grows from Bakhtin's notion of unfinalizability and his belief that great literature has a surplus of meaning that exists as an as-yet-unencountered potential. With these insights in mind, what follows is a creative understanding of Matt 1:1–17 that results from reading it "like" Bakhtin.

Matthew opens his Gospel with "an account of the genealogy of Jesus the Messiah, the son of David, the son of Abraham" (1:1). He then records the genealogy of Jesus from Abraham through his birth to Mary. A series of thirty-eight begettings does not resonate well with many modern readers, but it does immediately establish the Evangelist's goals to excavate the Hebrew Bible for language that defines the life, ministry, death, and resurrection of Jesus. The Evangelist alerts the reader to this relationship with the first line that in its Greek form, Βίβλος γενέσεως, evokes not only the creation of the world in the book of Genesis but also the genealogies of the Hebrew Bible, especially in the Septuagint (Gen 2:4; 5:1). In this essay I do not speculate on how Matthew composed the genealogy or what sources the Evangelist drew from to compose it. Instead, I focus on the form of the genealogy and survey arguments for its function within Matthew's narrative. I then examine the chronotopic elements of Matthew's genealogy to argue that Matthew employs the genealogical genre as a form of parody.

Genealogies attest to a person's ancestral descent and to a sense of his or her connection to the past. They existed in oral form within the Near Eastern culture that nourished the composition of the Hebrew Bible. Thus, it is no surprise that genealogies emerge as a literary form within the Hebrew Bible. They appear ubiquitously in texts such as Genesis and Exodus, which tell the stories of the early history of the Israelites, or in literature from the period after the return from the Babylonian exile in 538 B.C.E. (1 and 2 Chronicles, Ezra, Nehemiah). Robert Wilson identifies two genealogical forms. The most common is the segmented genealogy, which shows the relationship of children to their parents (Gen 35:22–26; Num 26:5–51). This form possesses a vertical orientation that describes the relationship between two generations and a horizontal orientation that defines the relationship between siblings by tracing them to a common ancestor. The function of a segmented genealogy is not only to describe family relationships but also to express status, economic position, geographical location, or position within the cult.

The other form is the linear genealogy. Wilson defines these kinds of genealogies as "lists of names connecting an individual to an earlier ancestor by indicating the kinship relationships that tie all of the names together" (930). Genealogies that employ the linear form possess only a vertical dimension. Their singular function is to establish a person's claim to power, rank, or status as derived from an earlier ancestor.

In either their segmented or linear forms genealogies serve different social, political, or theological functions. The result is that different genealogies may be created for the same person depending upon their purpose. Genealogies may present the order of descendants from parent to child (1 Chr 9:39–44) or the reverse (9:14–16). Wilson notes that, while distinct forms can be identified, they can also be mixed together to create a hybrid form, as in 1 Chr 6 (930).

Marshall Johnson argues that in the postexilic period the colonized political status of the Jewish people and the diversity of cultures within which it
found itself resulted in two areas of genealogical focus: (1) the concern to
preserve the distinctive identity of Jewish culture (as documented in Ezra-
Nehemiah); and (2) speculation about the Messiah and his ancestry (see Pss.
Sol. 17; Johnson: 85). Ezra 2 tells of the Jews who returned to the Holy Land
and their ancestral connection to those taken into exile. The writer describes
that these descendants were verified by genealogical records and that those
who had no genealogical verification were culturally suspect and stripped of
their priestly status (2:62). The record of descendants is not a random list.
Rather, it establishes distinctions among the returning exiles: (1) Israelites,
priests, and Levites of direct descent (2:2–42); (2) temple and royal servants
(2:43–58); and (3) Israelites and priests without genealogies (2:59–63). Johnson also notices that there is little evidence from the period that demonstrates
the existence of genealogical records for the laity or of one's relationship to
any of the twelve tribes of Israel. These records most likely existed as oral tradition. Thus, among the functions of genealogies during the Second Temple
period were to protect cultural integrity and also to maintain cultic distinctions. These distinctions also defined a returning Israelite's relationship to a
physical space, the Second Temple, and the sociopolitical power symbolized
by it.

Johnson identifies within some strands of early rabbinic literature a reaction against the use of genealogies to establish cultural standing and social
rank (93–95). While one must always exercise caution with rabbinic literature
because of its later date of compilation and composition, Moody's insights
establish an emphasis on genealogical purity during the Second Temple
period and traces of a minority voice expressing dissatisfaction during this
same period.

Another object of ancestral speculation during the Second Temple period
was the Messiah. Johnson notes that, "whatever the ultimate antecedents of
the Messianic concept might be, speculation on the role and nature of the
eschatological Messiah reached its height in the postbiblical writings of Judaism" (116).

In 2 Sam 7:11–16 God provides assurance that the house of David will
rule Israel forever. The intersection of this and other passages from the
Hebrew Bible with the cessation of the Davidic kingdom after the destruction
of Jerusalem in 587 B.C.E. gave rise to the expectation among many Jews of
the Second Temple period that a descendant of David, God's "anointed one"
(messiah), would arise to expel Israel's enemies and rule over Israel as God
had promised. Some literature from this period assured Israel of God's promise to Israel (Sir 47:22) as well as categorically identifying the Messiah as a

descendant of David (4 Ezra 12:32; Pss. Sol. 17:4, 21). However, messianic
speculation did not focus only on the descendants of David. Other texts from
the period reveal an interest in a priestly Messiah derived also from the line
of Aaron (1QS 9:10; CD 12:23; 14:18; 19:10). This difference is evidence that
there was no uniform set of criteria for the Messiah within Judaism during
the Second Temple period.

Although it is neither Wilson's nor Johnson's intention to do so, their
examination of genealogies within biblical texts alerts the person who reads
with Bakhtin to the potential of the genealogical form to function as a local
chronotope within a biblical narrative. Their work demonstrates the use of
a familiar form that acquired a cultural memory through repeated use over
a long span of time. This form was not static but was adapted creatively to
transform Judaism's understanding of itself within changing cultural circumstances. Finally, the genealogy is a form that fuses time with space in order to
define cultural identity and sociopolitical power. As someone who employs
the genealogical form, Matthew harvests the potential of the chronotope to
provide a creative understanding of Jesus as Israel's Messiah.

The temporal nature of Matthew's genealogy is easily apparent. It begins
with Abraham as the great patriarch of the Jewish people and ends with the
advent of Jesus as the fulfillment of Israel's messianic hopes. Thus, the list
spans the course of salvation history from the foundation of Israel as a people,
to the monarchy under David's kingship, to the calamity of the deportation
to Babylon, to the restoration of the Davidic kingship with Jesus' birth. The
Evangelist clearly has Jesus in mind as a descendant of David and fulfillment
of the hopes for a Messiah from David's line.

The Evangelist also emphasizes the temporal importance of the genealogy by dividing it into three periods of fourteen generations. Scholars debate
the meaning of the number fourteen and the fact that the last period (1:12–
16) seems only to contain thirteen generations (Johnson: 189–208). However,
there is abundant evidence from the Hebrew Bible and Second Temple literature of the importance of numbers to emphasize the divine purpose with
which God created the world (e.g., Gen 1:1–2:4a) and the eschatological purpose with which God has guided Israel's history (e.g., Jubilees, 1 Enoch, 2 Bar.
53–74). Matthew's accent on the three groups of fourteen generations that
conclude with the Messiah clearly possess an eschatological thrust (Waetjen:
211–13).

Thus, Matthew's genealogy betrays a theological thrust that exceeds the
need for historical accuracy. One example is the absence of names within the
genealogy in order to preserve the 3 x 14 structure (Brown: 77–79). These
absences betray the Evangelist's selectivity in fashioning the genealogy (Carter
2000:53). As a genealogy that employs the words Βίβλος γενέσεως, it evokes

the Hebrew Bible as memory and form to establish the messianic credentials of Jesus. In this way Matt 1:1–17 possesses the qualities of a linear geneal-ogy within the Second Temple period to establish Jesus as the inheritor of God's promises to David as well as God's promises to Abraham (Gen 12:2–3; see Luz). By adopting phraseology and structure from the Hebrew Bible, the Evangelist is employing what filmmaker Pier Paolo Pasolini called "stylistic contamination" (Rumble: 3–15).

I have thus far not argued anything that is foreign to standard scholarship on Matthew's genealogy. However, a chronotopic focus emphasizes an element that Matthean scholars have ignored: the spatial character of the genealogy. As much as the names and their sequence evoke the direction of Israel's history toward the advent of the Messiah, they are also infused with Israel's travels as a people. The clearest example is the reference to the Babylonian deportation in Matt 1:11–12. However, several of the names also possess spatial significance. God commissions Abraham at the age of seventy-five to move his family to another land that will belong to him and his offspring (Gen 12:1–7). By God's command Judah and his brothers take their father and offspring into the land of Egypt (46:1–27). Amminadab and Nahshon participate in Israel's desert wan-derings after the exodus. Rahab evokes the Hebrews' entry into the Holy Land (Josh 1–3). It is through Ruth that the descendants of Judah settle in Bethle-hem, the birthplace of David (1 Sam 16:4), Jesus (Matt 2:1), and the king of the Jews, according to the chief priests and scribes in Matt 2:5. Finally, through David's leadership Jerusalem becomes the capital of the Israelite kingdom (2 Sam 5:6–9) and the location for the First and Second Temples. God declares that in both Jerusalem and the temple his name will dwell forever (2 Kgs 21:7).

Thus, in Matthew's genealogy time and space are fused within the con-text of Israel's salvation history. This history is expressed not only through the past that is inherent in the generational sequence of names but also through the importance of the land and temple as a part of Israel's history. Morson and Emerson observe, "In its primary sense, a chronotope is a way of under-standing experience; it is a specific form-shaping ideology for understanding the nature of events" (1990:367). Matthew's genealogy, as a local chronotope within the First Gospel, foregrounds the relationship between Israel's guid-ance by God as a people, its connection to the land and the temple, and Jesus as the Messianic "son of David." However, the effect of this chronotope is to subvert expectations.

Bakhtin argues that chronotopes bear, as do genres and utterances, the memory of their prior use whenever they are employed in other contexts. With this in mind, it is productive to consider how the chronotope of Matt 1:1–17 carries the memories of the genealogical form and how its use of this form contributes to the relationship between author, text, and reader.

Matthew's genealogy employs the traits of a linear genealogy in a time when ancestral lineage was important to maintain Judaism as a distinctive culture in relation to the foreign governments that had ruled over it before and since its return from the Babylonian exile. However, while the use of Βίβλος γενέσεως does identify Matt 1:1–17 within the tradition of genealogies from the Hebrew Bible, it also departs from that tradition in several ways. One way is in the naming of the genealogy itself. Genealogies in the Hebrew Bible normally identify themselves by the first name on the list (e.g., Gen 10:1), not the last (Gundry: 13). Yet the Evangelist clearly identifies Jesus, the last person in Matthew's genealogy, as the person who gives the genealogy its name.

Another manner with which Matthew departs from the genealogical form is by highlighting the subversion of primogeniture as the path through which Israel achieves its salvation (Carter 2000:58). Within ancient cultures the normal transfer of inheritance was from father to the first-born son. However, while Matthew's references to Isaac, Jacob, Judah, Perez, David, and Solomon acknowledge key figures in Israel's history, they also establish a pattern that God has chosen those who are normally outside of the line of succession to preserve Israel's fortunes.

Finally, there are the four women: Tamar (1:3a), Rahab (1:5a), Ruth (1:5b), and "the wife of Uriah" (i.e., Bathsheba [1:6b]). I have already noted that, while rare, women do appear in genealogies of the Hebrew Bible. However, scholars have noted that the manner with which the Evangelist includes the women in Matthew's genealogy breaks the formal pattern throughout the rest of the genealogy ("A was the father of B"; Harrington 1991:32; Davies and Allison: 184; Wainwright: 66–67; Carter 2000:58). In addition, while Tamar and Bathsheba do appear in one of Matthew's possible sources, 1 Chr 1–2, Ruth and Rahab do not appear in any genealogies of the Hebrew Bible.

There is no scholarly consensus about the role of the women in Matthew's genealogy. The following explanations have been offered to account for their inclusion. Some of the explanations are combinations or nuances of others. (1) They were sinners, and their inclusion points to Jesus' ministry to sinners and the outcast (Jerome: 8; Aquinas: 62). (2) There were irregularities in the sexual activity of each woman. This and the initiative each woman took to further God's plan points to Mary and the birth of Jesus (Stendahl: 94–105; Anderson 1983:9; Paul: 22–36; Hagner: 1; Harrington: 32; Brown 1993:42). (3) The irregular nature with which the sexual activity of each woman furthered salvation history provides a defense against those who argue that Jesus was of illegitimate birth (Davies: 65; Schaberg). (4) The four women were Gentiles or "foreigners" whose inclusion points to the universality of the salvation that Jesus will offer (Keener: 78–80; Senior:

38; Garland: 14–15; Stock: 4–25; Carter 1996:123; Luz: 100). (5) The women serve a dual role: their status as Gentiles points to the universality of Jesus' mission, and, despite their lowly status, they were used by God to further salvation history, thus connecting them to Mary (Bauer: 148–50). (6) Johnson argues that their inclusion reflects a polemic between the Pharisees who expected a Davidic Messiah and the Sadducees who expected a Levitical Messiah (176–79). (7) The women were Gentiles, and the natures of their sexual unions point to Mary and the birth of Jesus. Thus, their inclusion reminds the reader of the unexpected ways by which divine intervention has guided the salvation history of Israel (Schnackenburg: 17; Davies and Allison: 171; Patte: 19–20). (8) In a variation on the sinners argument, John Paul Heil argues that the women themselves were not sinners, but their presence draws the implied reader's attention to the sinful nature of the Davidic dynasty. Jesus' birth as the Messianic Son of David eliminates the dynasty's sinful history (Heil: 544–45). (9) The women represent the fashion with which God often fulfills divine promises by deviating from human expectations. Their presence prepares the way for Mary, the birth of Jesus, and the displacement of Joseph from the patriarchal line of descent (Waetjen: 216). (10) Elaine Wainwright contends that the women occupy positions that disrupt the andocentric thrust of the genealogy and remind the reader of the place of women in Israel's salvation history. The actions of these four particular women place them outside of the patriarchal structures within which they functioned and threatens to undermine those structures. The result is that they serve a purpose in the genealogy that critiques patriarchy and allows for the tension of absent feminine voices to come to the foreground (60–69). (11) Amy-Jill Levine argues that Tamar, Rahab, Ruth, and Bathsheba are examples of "higher righteousness." That is, as persons without power in male-dominated cultures, the women acted when the men in power failed to do so. They ignored social mores in order to advance Israel's destiny. They were also women outside of traditional domestic arrangements: unmarried, separated from their spouse, widowed, or prostitutes. This informs the reader that one need not be married to undertake righteous action (340–41).

Some of the explanations can be discounted entirely or as singular arguments. There is a near consensus that Matthew did not include the women because they were sinners. In fact, Heb 11:31 heralds Rahab's faithfulness (see also Jas 2:25), while Gen 38:28 acknowledges Tamar's righteousness, and Ruth 4:11 compares Ruth to Rachel and Leah. Other scholars correctly note that the genealogy includes many males who were sinners (Waetjen: 205–30; Davies: 170; Carter 2000:59). It should also be noted that it is difficult to make the connection to Mary, who is not described as a sinner.

Several scholars discount the argument that the four women provide a defense against the claim that Jesus was of illegitimate birth. They note that to foreground the sexual irregularities of the women provides little argument against controversies surrounding Jesus' birth. More likely, they were the impetus for those controversies (Johnson: 148; Harrington: 32; Levine: 340; Waetjen: 219).

Craig Keener does not discount sexual irregularity as a possible element to explain the presence of the four women. However, he does note that there are other more prominent women for whom this argument also holds true: Sarah, Rebecca, and Rachel. Therefore, this cannot provide the sole explanation for the presence of Tamar, Rahab, Ruth, and Bathsheba (Keener: 79).

Johnson argues that proponents of a priestly Messiah bolstered their claim by noting that David's lineage included Gentiles, particularly Ruth the Moabite. In Deut 23:3, God declares through Moses that even up to the tenth generation "no Moabite shall be admitted to the assembly of the LORD." Therefore, no descendant of David could be the Messiah. The Pharisees defended this attack by arguing that God's intervention in Israel's history frequently took unexpected turns. As appealing as this argument appears, Davies and Allison note that there is no evidence for Rahab in relation to such a disagreement among Second Temple Jewish groups (171). It also relies on rabbinic literature whose dating is uncertain.

Finally, while Rahab and Ruth were Gentiles, the cultural status of Tamar and Bathsheba is not clear. In 2 Sam 11:3 Bathsheba is identified as the daughter of Eliam, an Israelite from Giloh (23:34). However, Matt 1:6 describes Bathsheba as "the wife of Uriah," which alludes to her affiliation with a Hittite Gentile. The Hebrew Bible ascribes no cultural identification to Tamar. Postbiblical Jewish literature describes her as a Gentile (Philo, *Virt.* 220; Jub. 41:1; T. Jud. 10:1). In spite of their Gentile origins, some of these women were also recognized as proselytes to Judaism. For example, Tamar is celebrated for her virtue in turning to the worship of Israel's God (Philo, *Virt.* 220–222). In addition, it is difficult to discern their thematic relationship to Mary, who was not a Gentile.

While the arguments that the women were sinners or that the genealogy is a defense of Jesus' legitimacy can be dismissed, the other explanations offer credible, although in some cases incomplete, cases for their presence. Carter correctly warns against accepting only one argument at the expense of all others and, in so doing, cautions against a monologic reading of the role of the four women (2000:61). However, these scholarly conclusions do serve as reminders of Bakhtin's insight that genres are never static. Instead, they are renewed with each use. How Matthew renews the genealogical chronotope in the First Gospel comes into view when the credible arguments are allowed to work together to form a pattern greater than any single claim.

When the unusual presence of the women is partnered with the spotlight that is cast upon the unexpected manner with which Israel's heritage is passed from father to son, a pattern of otherness emerges. Wainwright's and Levine's insights are valuable in this respect, although they limit their attention to the women's cultural otherness. However, there are men whose patrilineal otherness also surfaces. Together the unexpected women and the unforeseen men invert the genre expectations of a linear genealogy within the Second Temple period. It is not by culturally defined notions of direct descent that Israel's Messiah arrives at the turning point of salvation history. Rather, God prepares Israel for its savior through a series of cultural and social irregularities. This pattern of unexpected events is prefigured by the unusual ascription of the genealogy to the last descendant rather than the first and confirmed by the emergence of Mary, whose surprising pregnancy threatens to cast her outside her own culture by bringing shame to Joseph and herself (Matt 1:19). Therefore, Matthew's genealogy establishes the other as a participant whose outsideness is necessary for Israel's salvation history. This other, who is outside of power, is set in tension with those who possess power. This tension between what is inside and what is outside manifests itself throughout the Gospel, such as in Jesus' disagreement with the Jewish leaders over purity issues (Matt 15:1–11; 23:25–26).

However, reading with Bakhtin argues that the genealogy does more than remind the reader of the unexpected ways that God has preserved Israel throughout its history. The friction that derives from the inversion of the genealogical form through the presence of the women and the subversion of primogeniture invites the reader to reevaluate other matters alluded to in the genealogy, such as the chronotopic relationships between salvation history, land, and temple. Not surprisingly, the Evangelist will portray Jesus throughout the remainder of the Gospel in conflict with the concepts of land and temple and their relationship to Israel as a people (Matt 4:8–10; 12:6; 20:1–16; 21:12, 28–46; 26:61; 27:40, 51). The chronotope as the bearer of narrative and cultural tension will also manifest itself throughout the Gospel. For example, in Matt 2 the Evangelist will describe Jerusalem "in the time of Herod the king" (2:1) as troubled by the birth of Jesus. This reaction foreshadows the conflict between David's city and David's descendant.

A chronotopic reading of Matthew's genealogy also suggests that the present also folds back to interpret the past. Wainwright's insights are helpful in this regard. She maintains that the argument that the women were "foreigners" or "irregular" in some manner reflects a "form of gender politics" in which women are either recognized only when they are problems or they are positioned as outsiders in a patriarchal world. Contrary to these solutions, Wainwright argues that the four women alert the reader to a break in the orderly pattern of salvation history; their disrupting presence calls attention to itself, provoking an acknowledgment of patriarchal literary forms within biblical narratives (65–67). Through chronotopic memory the genealogies of the past cannot now escape this scrutiny and the reader's queries about the general absence of women in them.

The generic inversion and interaction of conflicting spheres of cultural experience in the genealogy correspond with elements of what Bakhtin defines as the menippean satire. Bakhtin writes, "Very characteristic for the menippea are scandal scenes, eccentric behavior, inappropriate speeches and performances, that is, all sorts of violations of the generally accepted and customary course of events and the established norms of behavior and etiquette, including manners of speech" (1984a:147). Scandal, eccentricity, impropriety, and cultural contravention are all present in Matthew's genealogy when it is read "like" Bakhtin. The Evangelist will also employ them as elements of Jesus' ministry. Thus Matt 1:1–17 prepares the reader not only for theological themes that will echo throughout the remainder of the narrative but for Jesus' ministry as the satirical fulfillment of God's plan for Israel and the world. It is not satire that inspires laughter but an overturning of cultural and narrative expectations through the active participation of the reader.

Conclusion

Bakhtin's advocacy for creative understanding provides many opportunities for biblical studies, not least of which is an approach that accounts for more than the authorial intentions (real or implied) of texts. Reading with Bakhtin alerts the reader to the manner in which the author employs creative understanding in Matthew's genealogy in order to refashion its generic expectations.

Bakhtin's ideas are rich with potential because their focus on relationships requires answerability between readers, authors, texts, and histories. They do not preclude other methods of biblical criticism. Rather, they recontextualize these methods as appropriate within the sphere of dialogic exchange. For example, I argue elsewhere that composition criticism aids the reader in engaging the dialogic voices of the fulfillment citations in Matthew's infancy narrative (1:22–23; 2:5b–6, 15b, 17–18, 23b) and that narrative criticism provides the basis for a carnivalesque reading of the story of the Magi in Matt 2:1–12 (Fuller: 128–37, 153–61). At their most fundamental, Bakhtin's ideas provoke serious reconsideration of issues that span from the historical critical to postmodern methods such as genre and its relationship to meaning. R.

Branham correctly notes that the novelty of Bakhtin's terms is far less important than their power to provoke reconsideration of how texts are constructed
and the relationships they inscribe (1995:79).

With this in mind, in this essay I have applied the concept of the chronotope to the genre of the biblical genealogy. In a similar manner, Michael
Vines employs the chronotope to argue that the genre of the Gospel of Mark
is not a Greco-Roman biography (Vines). His work moves beyond formalist
typologies to considerations of how Mark's apocalyptic use of space and time
resonate with Hellenistic Jewish novels. Vines acknowledges that Bakhtin
provides a beginning to the rethinking of the matter of genre, not an end
(161–64). With this in mind, the challenge that Bakhtin offers is a reconsideration not only of what literary forms the Gospels employ but also *how* they
use these genres. In the following excerpt, Bakhtin addresses the use of quotation in Hellenistic literature, but his concluding question could easily apply
to the matter of genre:

> One of the more interesting stylistic problems during the Hellenistic period
> was the problem of quotation. The forms of direct, half-hidden and com-
> pletely hidden quoting were endlessly varied, as were the forms of framing
> quotations by a context, forms for intonational quotation marks, varying
> degrees of alienation or assimilation of another's quoted word. And here the
> problem frequently arises: is the author quoting with reverence or on the
> contrary with irony, with a smirk? (1981: 69)

If genre is both what is given and what is being created, perhaps the First
Evangelist is casting his own smirking glance at the genealogical forms from
which he draws influence.

Bakhtin's Dialogism and the Corrective Rhetoric of the Johannine Misunderstanding Dialogue: Exposing Seven Crises in the Johannine Situation

Paul N. Anderson

One of the most fascinating thinkers and literary theorists within the last century is the late Russian form critic Mikhail Bakhtin, whose theory of dialogism seeks to account for several levels of dialectical tension and interplay in great literature.[1] On one level, Bakhtin observes the "heteroglossic" character of language. Between its centrifugal uses in popularistic culture and the centripetal actions of philologists and grammarians attempting to standardize meanings and associations, living language is always in a state of flux. On another level, Bakhtin suggests that discourse is always "polyphonic." Because meanings reverberate with and against each other upon their utterance, transmission, and reception, the making of meaning is itself a dialogical reality. On a third level, when ironic misunderstanding is used in novelistic prose, Bakhtin asserts this feature is always rhetorical:

> The device of "not understanding"—deliberate on the part of the author, simpleminded and naive on the part of the protagonists—always takes on

---

1. Note, for instance, the three levels of dialogue regarding John 6 (Anderson 1996:167–251). Here we have the Evangelist's dialogue with his tradition, a literary set of dialogues with his audience and other traditions, and the dialectical situation of Johannine Christianity itself, as it engaged several crises within its own developing history. On the level of historical memory and narrative, or even the narrator's engagement with a story's hero, Bakhtin's works on "Art and Answerability" (1990:1–3) and "Author and Hero in Aesthetic Activity" (1990:4–256) are relevant; on the literary and rhetorical level, Bakhtin's work with the dialogic imagination is especially applicable (1981); on matters of sociological dialectic, as culture itself moves from order to fluency and back again, Bakhtin's School Papers are especially insightful (Voloshinov 1983).

great organizing potential when an exposure of vulgar conventionality is involved. Conventions thus exposed—in everyday life, mores, politics, art and so on—are usually portrayed from the point of view of a man who neither participates in nor understands them. (1981:164)[2]

While the Fourth Gospel is not as novelistic as the prose of Cervantes and Dostoevsky, the humiliation of the Word, the suffering Son of Man, the rejection of Jesus by religious leaders, disappointments of the crowd, backsliding and scandalized disciples, the ironic trial before Pilate, and the paradoxical glorification of the cross all expose the false conventionalities of the world precisely because Jesus as protagonist is portrayed as the ironic "fool." His mission is an utter failure in human terms, and yet precisely because of Jesus' forfeiture of this-worldly success, the tables are diametrically turned. In the nonreceptive judgings of Jesus in John, the unbelieving world finds *itself* judged, as Jesus, the agent of God, stands opposed to everything that is false. As in Plato's allegory of the cave, the one who beheld the truth of daylight had to be silenced and killed, lest shadows and their conventions be exposed— evoking accountability on more levels than one.[3] The paradoxical failure of the protagonist thus exposes the failings of the conventionally minded. In John, Jesus not only reveals truth and light; he *is* that which he reveals. Again, Bakhtin writes, "Stupidity (incomprehension) in the novel is always polemical: it interacts dialogically with an intelligence (a lofty pseudo intelligence) with which it polemicizes and whose mask it tears away" (1984:403).

This being the case, however, nowhere is the rhetorical effect of misunderstanding more pronounced than when it is combined with the failure to understand the protagonist on behalf of his discussants. This is especially true when the miscomprehending person or group is "privileged," or "authoritative" (using Bakhtin's words), and such characters are ironically exposed as lacking and inadequate by the protagonist. Whenever this occurs in narrative, not only does that particular individual or group stand corrected, but

---

2. On heteroglossia, see Morson and Emerson 1990:142–45, 306–65.

3. Anderson (1996:194–97). Note these parallels between the characters in Plato's allegory of the cave in book 7 of the *Republic* and the Johannine audience: (1) humans are surrounded by darkness, yet what they believe to be reality is not; (2) the revealer of truth brings "good news" as to their captivity and the limited character of their knowledge; (3) rather than warming to the light of truth, they reject it and kill the witness; (4) despite their failure to believe the truth (about the truth), future audiences are invoked not to repeat such a mistake; (5) the killed witness (Socrates/Jesus) is understood to be the rejected revealer, yet the story bears pointed significance for the later targets of Plato's/the Fourth Evangelist's audiences. Thus, misunderstanding of the protagonist in the allegory/narrative is aimed rhetorically at the narrators' contemporary targets.

so do the persons and groups in the audience they represent. In this and other ways, the Fourth Gospel's portrayal of Jesus' misunderstanding discussants is highly parallel to Plato's sketching of Socrates' naïve students and his non-comprehending audiences. In both the Platonic and Johannine dialogues a later writer portrays the truthful teacher who exposes the foolishness of conventionalities—even those of otherwise privileged society members—and in refuting the misunderstanding discussants each author also addresses contemporary issues and targeted members of his own situation.

Applying Bakhtin's views regarding the polemical effects of exposing monologism, the present essay will consider the corrective function of the Johannine narrative within its first-century context. The thesis of this paper is therefore that misunderstanding in the Johannine dialogue is characteristically used rhetorically by the Evangelist as a specific corrective for particular sectors of his audience. Depending on the oral and written renderings of each dialogue, preliminary targets in the Johannine audience may be inferred with varying degrees of plausibility. Some masks are torn away close to the finalization of the Fourth Gospel, around the end of the first century c.e., while others reflect somewhat cooled debates within Johannine Christianity by the time of John's completion. Whatever the case, Bakhtin's theory of dialogism points the way forward, and earlier correctives continue to impact later audiences in ways beyond the author's original imaginings.

First, however, a comment as to the applicability of Bakhtin's work to first-century rhetorical criticism is in order. While some might object that his work with Cervantes and the modern novel makes his work irrelevant for working with first-century Gospel narrative, they have wrongly confined Bakhtin (monologically) to an overly narrow set of interests, when his work was wide-ranging. Bakhtin bases his theory in part on Socratic practice and sees it not as simply another literary theory but as epistemologically central to effective quests for truth. In that sense, to confine Bakhtin to literary criticism alone misjudges his contribution.[4] He worked with philology, ontology, epistemology, art, and historiography as well as novelistic discourse.[5] Even

---

4. Ironically, despite the fact that Bakhtin operated as a literary form critic, to limit his contribution to literary analysis alone fails to appreciate the deeply epistemological, sociological, psychological, and anthropological character of his work. If anything, his work should be considered from the standpoint of what I call cognitive-critical analysis (Anderson 1996:137–251; 2004:127–48; and Anderson, Ellens, and Fowler 2004:247–76). On Bakhtin and psychology, see Morson and Emerson 1990:172–230; on existence as dialogue, see Holquist 1990:14–39; on the dialogic self, see Jackson 1987.

5. On philology and the ontological character of language, see Voloshinov 1983, Morson and Emerson 1990:123–71; and Holquist 1990:40–66; on art and novelistic

in his literary analysis Bakhtin works analytically on the philosophy of the act, develops extensively the hermeneutical implications of time and chronotope (time/place presentations) in narrative, and elaborates on the rhetorical function of discourse in the novel.[6] These are not simply means of conveying content heuristically; they possess the capacity also of getting at the character of truth and its representations, engaging directly the making of meaning existentially. Likewise, the Fourth Evangelist clearly operates Socratically and portrays Jesus as engaging his discussants in dialectical explorations of truth.

Another fact is that John's forward-moving and cyclical-repetitive style betrays the epistemological origin of the Evangelist's unitive-and-disunitive Christology, which is well considered the most fascinating aspect of the Johannine witness. Rather than reflecting a literary dialogue between literary sources having high/low Christologies, or ones having embellished/existential valuations of signs, John's is a basically unitive theology held in dialectical tension within the thinking of the Evangelist. Tellingly, both C. K. Barrett and Mikhail Bakhtin cite the *same passage* from *Theatetus* (189–190) as a key to understanding the relation between inward and outward dialogue in Greek classical literature (Barrett 1972:49–50; Voloshinov 1983:134). In one of the most significant nonmonographic treatments of John's distinctive Christology, "The Dialectical Theology of St. John," Barrett comments upon the epistemological origin of John's dialectical presentation of Jesus' ministry:

> For myself I suspect that the roots are to be found if not in Socratic theory at least in the Socratic practice. In Socratic dialogue—concepts are looked at first from one side then from another, definitions are proposed, attacked, defended, abandoned, or improved, opposite points of view are canvassed and sometimes at least, combined. And the process of thought itself is conceived as fundamentally unspoken dialogue.
> Socrates. "Do you mean by 'thinking' the same which I mean?"
> Theatetus. "What is that?"
> Socrates. "I mean the conversation which the soul holds with herself in considering anything." (Barrett 1972:49–50)

---

discourse, see Patterson 1985; Shevtsova 1992; and Holquist 1990:67–106; on the disjunctive and prescient relation between novel and history, see Singer 1988 and Holquist 1990:107–48; on intertextuality and polyphony, see Durey 1991 and Morson and Emerson 1990:231–68.

6. Bakhtin's treatment of a philosophy of the act (Bakhtin 1993) considers the moral and interpersonal implications of aesthetic activity; his time and chronotope analysis (1981:84–258) considers spatial and temporal relationships in narrative; and his treatment of discourse in the novel (1981:258–422) shows the relation between verbal art and the content of narrative.

The point is that Socratic dialectic probably served as a literary and historical precedent, if not a pattern, for the shaping of the Johannine witness, and this is also one of the models employed by Bakhtin in constructing his theory of how discourse functions in narrative literature. As a contrast to the fool being the protagonist in the modern European novel, however, in Greek biography and in John it is the misunderstanding of the protagonist's discussants that is used most pervasively and effectively. In sketching the misunderstanding of individuals and groups in John, the Evangelist exposes and corrects conventional and false notions within his immediate audience(s). This corrective action not only suggests some of the rhetorical interests of the Fourth Evangelist but also functions to identify varying targets within different strata of the Gospel in ways that corroborate particular crises and issues within Johannine Christianity. As Wayne Meeks has said,

> More precisely, there must have been a continuing dialectic between the group's historical experience and the symbolic world which served both to explain that experience and to motivate and form the reaction of group members to the experience. (Meeks 1986:145)

In these ways the dialectical thinking of the Evangelist constructs a set of literary dialogues with varying audiences within the Johannine situation, whereby they are brought into an imaginary dialogue with Jesus. As the unfolding narrative is engaged by its audiences, positive responses to the protagonist point the way forward as favorable examples, whereas miscomprehending responses to Jesus challenge similar tendencies and patterns in the audience. Even the presentation of the corrected discussant, whereby an originally flawed understanding of Jesus comes around to "getting it right" and becoming a loyal follower of Jesus (the Samaritan woman, Nicodemus, Peter, Mary Magdalene, some of the Ἰουδαῖοι, etc.) shows the way forward. Initial misunderstanding need not be the end of the journey; rehabilitation by the truth is always a possibility! Consider, therefore, the character of the Johannine dialectical situation.

THE DIALECTICAL JOHANNINE SITUATION.

While a full demonstration of Johannine history cannot be developed here, when one considers the sorts of misunderstanding represented in John, as well as the corrective teaching of Jesus and the commentary of the Evangelist, several crises in the Johannine situation may indeed be inferred from the narrative. J. Louis Martyn (2003:27–143) described well the two levels of history in John's narrative depicting a set of dialectical relations with the leadership of the local synagogue community, yet this particular set of dialogues was not the only one within the Johannine situation. Religious communities rarely enjoy the luxury of fighting on only one front for an extended period of time, and it is likely that several crises confronted Johannine Christians over three decades within their Asia Minor settings, rather than just one crisis or another coming from a singular direction. These were living communities struggling on many fronts, often at the same time, and certainly multiple groups and issues were engaged over the relatively long period of time within which the Fourth Gospel was being composed and edited. It may even be that, while the Johannine writings emerged from a particular region or setting, they may have been intended for broader distribution instead of a local one, only.[7]

Interestingly enough, several sources of information corroborate one's assessment of the dialectical Johannine situation. These constructs are developed independently elsewhere, but they also have implications for each other. They include: (1) a two-edition theory of John's composition based upon the composition theory of Barnabas Lindars (which identifies as later, supplementary material the Prologue; chs. 6, 15–17, and 21; and the Beloved Disciple and eyewitness motifs as having been added to an earlier edition, exposing Jewish/Johannine and Roman/Christian tensions as central to the first-edition material and antidocetic correctives and ecclesiological concerns as central to the final-edition material);[8] (2) parallel developments in the Johannine Epistles and the letters of Ignatius (at least five of these crises/issues are sketched in one or both of these sets of writings); (3) similar concerns represented in the Johannine Apocalypse (while Revelation appears to be the work of another hand, it nevertheless has at least some Johannine connection, and several of these crises may be inferred behind its writing); (4) comparison/contrasts with Synoptic traditions (dialogues between the first edition of John and Mark betray corrective tensions regarding valuations of Jesus' miracles, and dialogues between John's supplementary material and the Matthean tradition betray corrective tensions regarding ecclesiology); and (5) corroborations within the dialogues of John 6 (at least five crises may be

---

7. This is the argument by Richard Bauckham 1998: the Gospels were intended for general reception, rather than internal use alone. He corroborates his thesis by showing the crafting of John for readers of Mark.

8. Of all the composition theories available, a modification of Lindars's theory (1981:46–54) continues to be the most plausible. Adding to that view, to the first edition of John (80–85 C.E.) supplementary material was added (100 C.E.) by the editor, whom I believe to have been the author of the Johannine Epistles (85–95 C.E.), completed after the death of the Beloved Disciple (see the outline in Anderson 2006:193–95; this outline is similar to table 2.5 on page 64).

inferred in the "history and theology" two-level drama, conveyed by John 6 and the dialogical character of the Johannine bread of life discourse).[9] In longitudinal perspective, the Johannine tradition appears to have developed through three major phases with two crises in each. A seventh crisis (ongoing dialogues with other Gospel traditions) appears to have spanned all three periods, and my two-edition theory of John's composition—emerging within the Johannine dialectical situation—is as follows:[10]

An Outline of the Johannine Situation in Longitudinal Perspective

Period 1: The Palestinian period, developing tradition (ca. 30–70 C.E.)

    Crisis A   Dealing with north/south tensions (Galileans/Judeans)

    Crisis B   Reaching followers of John the Baptist

    The oral Johannine tradition develops.

Period 2: The Asia Minor period I, the forging of community (ca. 70–85 C.E.)

    Crisis A   Engaging local Jewish family and friends

    Crisis B   Dealing with the local Roman presence

    The first edition of the Johannine Gospel is prepared.

Period 3: The Asia Minor period II, dialogues between communities (ca. 85–100 C.E.)

    Crisis A   Engaging docetizing Gentile Christians and their teachings

    Crisis B   Engaging Christian institutionalizing tendencies (Diotrephes and his kin)

---

9. What Martyn achieved with John 9 I have sought to replicate with John 6 (Anderson 1997:24–57). Here, though, at least five crises within the Johannine situation can be inferred, not simply one: (1) the crisis of the meaning of Jesus' signs (in dialogue with the prevalent Synoptic valuation of the signs miraculous value instead of their existential implications; (2) tensions with Jewish leaders concerning the "bread" of Moses (Torah) versus the bread availed by Jesus; (3) more subtly, the presence of Roman imperialism is palpable in the political realism of John 6; (4) the "bread" of suffering, especially a challenge to docetizing Christians; and (5) Petrine hierarchical struggles introduced by the likes of Diotrephes and his kin (3 John 9–10). These "crises" were largely sequential but somewhat overlapping.

10. Most of these crises are actually alluded to by Raymond Brown 2003, although the arrangement is somewhat different (see the fuller outline in Anderson 2006:196–99).

Crisis C   Engaging dialectically Christian presentations of Jesus and his ministry (actually reflecting a running dialogue over all three periods)

The Epistles are written by the Johannine Elder, who then finalizes and circulates the testimony of the Beloved Disciple after his death. 100 C.E.

In addition to earlier north-south tensions with Jerusalem-based religious authorities and debates with followers of John the Baptist, at least five other distinct crises may thus be identified within the middle-late Johannine situation. These crises are also corroborated by other literature and are illuminated by an incisive analysis of the Johannine misunderstanding motif. While their developments were somewhat overlapping, these crises include: (1) tensions between northern Palestinian (Galilean, Samaritan, or both) spirituality and southern Judean (Jerusalocentric) religious conventions; (2) debates with followers of John the Baptist seeking to point them to Jesus as the authentic Messiah; (3) debates with local Jewish communities regarding the messianic agency of Jesus; (4) enduring hardships related to the local Roman presence and its increasing requirement of public emperor laud; (5) bolstering group solidarity, especially for Gentile and docetizing Christians, in the face of Roman occupation under Domitian; (6) counters to rising institutionalism in the late first-century church; and (7) a desire to correct prevalent (either Markan or Synoptic) valuations of the miraculous ministry of Jesus (this set of dialogues may have spanned most of the others chronologically).[11] Each of these threats is addressed rhetorically in the Johannine text by exposing individuals and groups as failing to understand particular aspects of the teaching and ministry of Jesus. Furthermore, the notions being corrected in each of these crises are first exhibited in the words and actions of the discussants, and the authentic way forward is then declared by the Johannine Jesus. All of this is conveyed, however, by means of the rhetorical function of the Johannine misunderstanding dialogue.

---

11. While John 6 was added later and thus represents some later features, the Johannine countering of Markan/Synoptic views of miracles was somewhat early in the development of Gospel traditions rather than later only. Other themes, such as eschatology and ecclesiology, for instance, enjoyed a later engagement with the Markan traditions.

The Rhetorical Function of the
Johannine Misunderstanding Dialogue.

The Gospel of John progresses by means of two dialogical modes, which are also set off by the presentation of the words and actions of the characters within the narrative. The prevalent mode is a revelational one. Virtually all of John portrays Jesus' mission as effecting the saving/revealing initiative as an expression of God's love, offered for the redemption of humanity (John 3:15–17). God speaks to humanity through the Scriptures, John the Baptist, the words and works of Jesus, the ministry of the Paraclete, the testimony of Jesus' followers and the voice from heaven (twice), the fulfilled words of Jesus and Caiaphas, the written Gospel itself, and, finally, the Word made flesh.[12] Indeed, the saving initiative of God or God's agencies calls forth a believing response on the part of humanity, and this is the *Leitmotif* of the entire Gospel (20:31). As Sandra Schneiders says:

> The central concern of the Fourth Gospel is the saving revelation which takes place in Jesus. This revelation, however, must be understood as a dia-logical process of Jesus' self-manifestation as the one being continuously sent by the Father (7:16–18) who is thereby encountered in Jesus (10:30; 14:9–11) and the response of belief on the part of the disciple (17:8).[13]

As well as drawing people to God (and indeed no one *can* come to the Father except he or she be drawn; 6:44, 65) this divine-human dialectic also challenges religious norms and authorities, exposing their human origin and thus their final bankruptcy. Furthermore, it scandalizes what Bakhtin calls the privileged language and symbols of religious and political authorities, declaring them less than ultimate and exposing their limitations. Not only are privileged *groups* such as the Ἰουδαῖοι (representing religious authorities), "the crowd" (representing popular conventionality), and "the disciples" (representing Jesus' followers, would-be or otherwise) challenged, but such privileged *individuals* as Nicodemus, Pilate, and even Peter are deftly lampooned by the Evangelist. But in doing so, the primary function is not simply the portrayal

---

12. Primary examples of scenarios denoting the divine-human, revelational mode of discourse include: 1:1–18 (the Word of God receives an uneven reception in the world); 5:5–15 (Jesus liberates the paralytic); 10:22–39 (Jesus reveals himself to the Judeans); 11:17–45 (Jesus ministers to Martha/Mary and others); 12:20–50 (the culmination of Jesus' ministry); 17:1–26 (Jesus prays for his disciple); 20:10–18 (Jesus reveals himself to Mary Magdalene).

13. Schneiders 1982:39. Note, however, that several scholars have also applied Bakhtinian dialogism to the character of theology: Newsom 1996 and Classens 2003.

of a person or group who suffers from simple-minded conventionality. Rather, particular individuals and groups in the Evangelist's audience are here being targeted and drawn into an imaginary dialogue with the Johannine Jesus, a dialogical bout that the Evangelist intends Jesus to win.

Note how the presentation changes when the narrative shifts into a rhetorical and corrective mode. First, the initiative shifts from God's saving initiative and agency to a human actant denoting creaturely origin and flawed conventionality. Here the theological motif of "of-ness" in John, explaining why some accept and reject God's truth revealed in Jesus, is typified by the subtle detail of initiative. Whenever a person or group takes the initiative and comes speaking to Jesus, making a bold claim or lodging a challenging question, this feature inevitably betrays human incomprehension to be corrected by the Johannine Jesus. A few exceptions exist (such as the mother of Jesus in John 2, although a misunderstanding may be corrected there as well regarding Jesus' "hour"), but note that even Jesus' disciples resist asking him questions, lest their miscomprehension be exposed, according to the narrator. Then, the misunderstanding dialogue is presented with any assortment of the following features:

The Form of the Johannine Misunderstanding Dialogue

(1)   The setting is usually described.

(2)   Individuals or groups come to Jesus, asking a question or making a statement that reveals, either subtly or explicitly, a telling clue to the discussants' inadequate notions.

(3)   Jesus responds, making some corrective remark about the true character of the kingdom of God, his mission, the Father's work, authentic spirituality, and the like.

(4)   The discussants (usually) make further comments that betray their continued lack of understanding more clearly, building the ironic tension in the narrative.

(5)   Jesus' final response (often) launches into a discourse clarifying the spiritual meaning of the topic at hand, usually a Christocentric elaboration upon the "true" character of the kingdom, Jesus' mission, God's work, life in the Spirit, and so forth.

(6)   The result is usually described along with a transition into the next scenario.

(7)   Sometimes a resurfacing of the discussant(s) later in the narrative reveals their inclination toward the truth: some have begun to walk in it, thus becoming examples of corrected, while others continue as pejorative examples of miscomprehension.

In Bakhtinian terms, when lofty pseudo-authorities are taken on either by the knowing "fool" or the protagonist within a narrative, conventional understandings, thus exposed, are thereby countered in the interest of more transcendent realities, such as virtue, authenticity, and truth. Not only is the figure's stance tried and judged, but according to Bakhtin regarding Dostoevsky, "His novels are sharply etched novels of trial" (in "Discourse in the Novel," 1981:391). Interestingly, the scene of "the Grand Inquisitor" in *The Brothers Karamazov* not only builds on the temptation narrative in the Q tradition, but it also contrasts the bondage of power-dependence to the Johannine motifs of the truth that sets humanity free (John 8:32) and the life-producing bread that comes down from heaven (6:32–33). In that sense, the "hagiographic" tradition used by Dostoevsky, as analyzed by Bakhtin, is rooted in the Gospels' presentations of Jesus. In the Johannine text it is precisely the lofty, self-assured discussants that represent what Bakhtin calls "the First Stylistic Line," whereby discussants "approach heteroglossia from above, as if they *descended* onto it" (1981:400).[14] They inevitably are set straight by Jesus within a rhetorical mode of discourse. When the initiative shifts, however, to Jesus or another of God's agents, however (Moses, John the Baptist, the Word or Light of God), this inevitably poses a revelational mode of discourse. Consider, for instance, Jesus' trial before Pilate as a fitting example of the rhetorical misunderstanding dialogue in John.

(1) First, the setting is described chronotopically (John 18:28–32): having come from Caiaphas to the Praetorium early in the morning, Pilate objects to Jesus being tried in a Roman court, but he is finally maneuvered into trying Jesus by the Jewish leaders. (2) Pilate then seizes the initiative and asks Jesus if he is "the king of the Jews" (18:33). (3) Jesus responds to Pilate, inquiring if the question is Pilate's own or if he is reacting to the influences of others (18:34). Here the issue of "kingship" begins to take on multiple levels of meaning, contrasting Pilate's conventional understanding of power with Jesus' transcendent assertions about authority. (4) Pilate rejects Jesus' inference regarding his interest in Jesus' kingship and unwittingly acknowledges that he is subservient to the agendas of others (18:35), exposing his ironic status as "the impotent potentate." (5) Jesus' climactic response clarifies the spiritual meaning of the topic at hand: he indeed is a king, and his "kingdom" is one of truth (18:36–37); all who are on the side of truth hear him. (6) Pilate's miscomprehension is then portrayed undeniably: "What is truth?" (18:38). This results in a transi-

---

14. Not only does the Johannine Revealer challenge all that is of human origin with the scandal of the Divine Initiative, but this affront to the self-assured wiles of the *cosmos* is exposed in the initiative-taking presentation of misunderstanding discussants (Anderson 1996:221–24; 1997:17–24).

tion into the next scenario, where Pilate goes back and questions the Jewish leaders, seeking the release of Jesus. Despite his juxtaposition of the release of Jesus with the release of the scoundrel Barabbas, the crowd rejects the loaded offer. The irony intensifies as Pilate claims to possess the power to set Jesus free or to put him to death, but then he spends the next half chapter (18:39–19:16) begging the crowd to let him let Jesus go. Also ironic is the crowd's act of blasphemy ("We have no king but Caesar!") committed in order to ensure the elimination of Jesus as one charged with blasphemy. (7) Finally, Pilate is shown to have some inclination toward the truth, as he lets stand what he has written about Jesus: "He *was* the king of the Jews" (19:17–22). As a rhetorical mode of discourse, however, Jesus' dialogue with Pilate did not simply exhaust its targeting with those who lived in political proximity to the Jerusalem Praetorium. In the end, this challenge to political power by the authority of truth would have continued to confront Roman hegemony throughout the development of the Johannine tradition, emboldening all who would speak truth to power and who would empower the truth.

The Johannine misunderstanding dialogue thus functions to expose conventional "stupidity," or miscomprehension, so as to draw the attention back polyphonically to the saving/revealing initiative of God presented in the mission and reception of Jesus. The questions/comments, assumptions, actions, and identities of the human actants and discussants in John are thus designed to represent the same in the experience of the reader. With one's notionalities thus exposed as inadequate and corrected by God's representative agent, the reader is thereby drawn into a crisis existentially: whether to continue holding on to unenlightened perspectives, or whether to forsake the shadows for the light of the truth. The narration of the result following the responses of Jesus' discussants also helps the reader along. Where the word of Jesus is rejected, the narrator clarifies the bankruptcy of the act in terms of outcomes; conversely, when the word of Jesus is received, the positivity of outcomes points the enlightened way forward. In Bakhtinian terms, the Evangelist performs a heteroglossic task:

> Heteroglossia, once incorporated into the novel (whatever the forms for its incorporation), is *another's speech in another's language*, serving to express authorial intentions but in a refracted way. Such speech continues a special type of *double-voiced discourse*. It serves two speakers at the same time and expresses simultaneously two different intentions: the direct intention of the character who is speaking, and the refracted intention of the author. (1981:324)

As well as being important to consider as a heuristic device, conveying reflectedly the theological intention of the Evangelist, the Johannine misunderstanding dialogue also casts into sharp relief several crises in the Johannine situation that deserve particular consideration.

SEVEN CRISES WITHIN THE JOHANNINE SITUATION
AND THEIR DIALOGICAL ENGAGEMENT BY THE NARRATOR

While these crises are largely sequential, they also varied in terms of duration and character. Put otherwise, they may have overlapped to some degree, and at times the Johannine community may have been struggling on more that one front at once. Some of these crises may even have spanned the entire range of the others, and in that sense some were more chronic and ongoing than acute and short-lived. For instance, the Johannine critique of Synoptic-type thaumaturgy (there is no evidence of a signs Gospel underlying John[15]) may have continued for several decades, even reflecting a difference stemming back to the early stages of Gospel traditions. Also, the effect of one crisis may have evoked the next. Consider likewise the interrelationships between each of these four sequential-yet-overlapping crises in the Asia Minor situation. The crisis with the synagogue may have precipitated the crisis with Roman authorities as expelled followers of "the Nazarene" were deprived of the Jewish monotheistic dispensation, excusing them from having to worship the emperor. Therefore, expulsion from local synagogues created the crisis of facing into the growing expectation of emperor laud during the reign of Domitian. In turn, Gentile Christians may have been unconvinced about the contradiction between Jesus being the eternal Lord and worshiping Caesar as the political Lord, leading to a defense of assimilation by means of arguing a docetic Christology. These and other schismatic tendencies, then, were countered by organizing hierarchies and ecclesiological structures in the name of apostolic authority, but not all apostolic communities or leaders felt comfortable with such innovations. Hence, the Johannine corrective to rising institutionalism in the late first-century church was a response to a particular crisis, but this crisis was precipitated by several others. While some scholars consider only one or two of these crises, the polyphonic character of the multiplicity of issues in the evolving Johannine audience—extending over seven decades—deserves to be considered in literary and socioreligious perspective.

(1) The debates between Jesus and the Ἰουδαῖοι provide a series of sustained engagements between the Galilean prophet and Jerusalocentric

---

15. See Anderson 1996:48–165. For fuller treatments of John's dialogical autonomy, see Anderson 2001a; 2001b; 2002; and 2004.

authorities.[16] While some of the Ἰουδαῖοι come to believe in Jesus, for the most part they are presented as rejecting Jesus and his mission on religious and scriptural grounds. These figures are wrongly thought of as "the Jews," since Jesus, the Beloved Disciple, and all of his followers in John are *deeply Jewish*. Despite the fact that John has been a leading biblical text contributing to anti-Semitism, the Johannine presentation of the Ἰουδαῖοι is anything but anti-Semitic. If anything, it claims to showcase the radically authentic Semitic Messiah, who ironically came unto his own people but was rejected by their religious leaders. From the Johannine perspective, however, spiritually authentic Judeans and Israelites received him.

Among the presentations of the Ἰουδαῖοι in John, at least twenty-two of the seventy references explicitly connect these leaders with Jerusalem or Judea. While debates with the leaders of local synagogue leaders (crisis 3, below) may be inferred in other parts of John (9:22; 12:42; 16:2), north-south tensions between the Galilean prophet and Judean religious authorities present themselves clearly in other parts of John.[17] Following the Jerusalem-based authorities' questioning of John the Baptist as to whether or not he was the Christ, Elijah, or the Prophet (1:19–28), Jesus performs a prophetic sign in Jerusalem temple itself. The Judean leaders even demonstrate their lofty miscomprehension in asking for a sign to legitimate his temple demonstration (2:18). Jesus points to his future resurrection—building up "this temple" in three days, after it had been destroyed—as a culminative sign, which they mistakenly assume is a temple-reconstruction project (2:19–21). The narrator here clarifies the true reference as being a prediction of Jesus' victory over death in the light of the disciples' eventual postresurrection awareness (2:22).

The pinnacle of the north-south impasse is found in John 5 and 7, where the healing of the paralytic on the Sabbath leads to a heated debate over Jesus'

---

16. Regarding the northern-southern tensions (Judean/Jerusalocentric versus Galilean/Samaritan socioreligious dialectic) consider the following dialogues: 1:47–51 (Jesus and Nathanael); 2:13–25 (Jesus and the dove sellers/Judean cultic leaders); 4:4–42 (Jesus and the Samaritan woman/Samaritans); 5:16–47 (Jesus and the Jerusalem leaders); 7:25–44 (the people of Jerusalem: Pharisees/Judeans and Jesus); 7:45–52 (the temple guards, chief priests, Pharisees, and Nicodemus); 18:19–24 (the high priest and Jesus). See also Anderson 1996:194–251; Brown 2003:157–72.

17. Again, the disjunctive error is to assume that tensions with Jewish leaders after the fall of Jerusalem eclipsed earlier tensions with southern, Judean leaders from an earlier Galilean perspective. In both of these Jewish-Johannine sets of dialectical relations, the religious leaders are presented as speaking with what Bakhtin would call "authoritative discourse" (1981:341–55), seeming internally compelling except for its ironic dethronement by the Johannine Jesus, who is presented as fulfilling the very authoritative Jewish ideals being propounded by his discussants.

origin and authenticity. Here the Jerusalem-centered Ἰουδαῖοι get it wrong on many levels. First, they blame the paralytic for carrying his mat, next they fault Jesus for healing someone on the Sabbath, and then they seek to kill Jesus for claiming to do the works of his Father (5:10–18). Indeed, the mention of the desire to kill Jesus in John 5 seems abrupt if it is assumed that this was his first visit. Apparently, the request for a sign in 2:18 made no difference to these Judean leaders. Their interests are exposed as political and power-based rather than spiritual and truth-based, and the extensive discussion of Jesus' authentic mission as one having being sent from the Father (Deut 18:15–22) builds steadily throughout the rest of John 5. Climactically, Jesus declares that, despite their searching the Scriptures for divine life, these religious leaders fail to acknowledge the life-producing agency of Jesus, to whom the Scriptures witness (5:39–40). With greater specificity, Jesus then declares that it was of him that Moses wrote (5:46).

The debate with the Jerusalem leaders continues, then, in John 7, as John 6 appears to have been inserted between chapters 5 and 7 during a later augmenting of the first edition. References to John 5 are clear, in that the Judean leaders' desire to kill Jesus is described as the basis for Jesus' reluctance to return to Jerusalem openly (7:1–10, 25), and the debate over the healing of the paralytic on the Sabbath continues (7:19–24). Jesus calls for righteous judgment rather than judging superficially (7:25), and the northern critique of Jerusalocentric religious hegemony continues to build in several ways over the rest of the chapter. First, several Ἱεροσολυμιτῶν (Jerusalemites) speculate that the reason Jesus speaks openly without challenge is that the religious leaders wanting to kill him really believe he is the Christ. They second-guess themselves, though, by stating that no one will know where the Christ is from, but the origin of Jesus is indeed known (7:25–27). Here the "whence" subject (πόθεν) is developed ironically. The Jerusalemites assume they know Jesus' "origin" because they see him as a northerner (ἐκ τῆς Γαλιλαίας), when the real issue (a righteous judgment) is his divine agency as having been sent from the Father (7:16–18, 28–29, 33).

Upon Jesus' declaration in the temple on the main day of the feast (7:37–39), several members of the Jerusalem crowd declare Jesus an authentic prophet, and others declare him to be the Christ. The miscomprehending Jerusalemites, however, declare it impossible for him to be the Christ because they claim to know that the Christ is not supposed to come from Galilee but from the seed of David and from Bethlehem (7:40–43). The religious leaders therefore fail to recognize the authenticity of Jesus' mission because they look for a Davidic and Judean Messiah rather than the Mosaic prophet typology Jesus fulfills prolifically. When the servants of the chief priests and Pharisees hesitate at arresting Jesus, their masters rebuke them by pointing to the unbelief of their own company (7:44–48). When Nicodemus comes to their defense, claiming the law's requirement of a fair trial before judgment is exacted, these religious leaders question whether he too is from Galilee—the ultimate Judean insult. The Jerusalocentric leaders then unwittingly expose the epitome of their miscomprehension: despite missing the multiplicity of ways Jesus fulfills the prophet-like-Moses prediction of Deut 18:15–22 (see Anderson 1999), they hold to the more superficial understanding of messianic expectation, limiting it to a region rather than having seen the signs or acknowledged the fulfilled and fulfilling words of Jesus (John 7:50–52).

The north-south tensions are vindicated by the reception of Jesus by the woman at the well and the Samaritans. Not only does she come to believe in Jesus, but many others come to believe in Jesus on the basis of her testimony and because they themselves have perceived Jesus authentically. Their believing reception, parallel to the belief of disciples at the Cana wedding and the Roman official at Capernaum, shows a marked contrast to the religious certainty-and-blindness of the Judean leaders. Finally, however, the issue is not a factor of a north-south divide, with the northerners having preeminence. In response to the Samaritan woman's question, while the way forward is not to worship in Jerusalem, neither is it to be found by worshiping in a northern site such as Mount Gerizim. Rather, because God is Spirit rather than geographically limiting, authentic worship will ever be in spirit and in truth. The Father actively seeks those who worship in this way (John 4:24).

(2) The outreach to followers of John the Baptist is effected by the early Johannine narrative in several ways.[18] First, John points centrally to Jesus as the first of the witnesses and declares Jesus' primacy over himself. Indeed, Jesus' baptism and ministry not only had precedence over his own, but John declares that Jesus *was* before him, as well—a theme eventually picked up in the Prologue. In Bakhtinian terms, the presentation of the heroic Baptist as an interlocutor of "ennobled discourse" (Morson and Emerson 1990:353–55; Bakhtin 1981:381–85) elevates the status of Jesus by means of his paradoxically self-deprecating witness. John claims to be the voice of the one crying in the wilderness, "Prepare the way of the Lord!" Second, the Baptist likewise declares the negative ἐγὼ οὐκ εἰμὶ (1:20, 21, 27; 3:28) as a counterbalance to the positive ἐγώ εἰμι of the Johannine Jesus (without a nominative, 4:26; 6:20; 8:24, 28, 58; 13:13, 19; 18:5, 6, 8, 37). When John's followers ask their master

---

18. Regarding the tensions related to the followers of John the Baptist versus Jesus as messianic hero, consider the following dialogues: 1:19–34 (John and Jerusalem authorities); 1:35–43 (Jesus and John's disciples); 2:1–11 (Jesus' mother and Jesus); 3:22–36 (a Judean questioner of John); 4:27, 31–38 (Jesus' disciples and Jesus); 4:46–54 (the royal official and Jesus). Raymond Brown also acknowledges this dialectical relationship (2003:153–57).

if Jesus is the Messiah or whether they should wait for another, his answer is clear. Jesus is the bridegroom; John is merely the friend of the bridegroom. Third, the presentation of two groups of John's disciples shows the way forward for potential readers dialogically. The first of the Baptist's disciples were pointed to Jesus (1:35–51) with the declaration: "Behold the lamb of God who takes away the sin of the world!" The first two followed Jesus and even brought two more to Jesus: Andrew and Peter. This shows the way forward as a positive example. Jesus is worth following, and even the followers of the Baptist (and perhaps even the Fourth Evangelist himself) become his disciples.

The second group of the Baptist's followers displays miscomprehension at the outset. They had been debating matters of purification with an unnamed Judean, but out of that argument they came complaining to John about Jesus and the fact that more people were going over to Jesus than following the Baptist. At this miscomprehension, John sets the record straight with finality. Not only is Jesus the Messiah that John is not, but Jesus must become greater and John less (3:30). While the response of the Baptist's second group of adherents is not narrated, the message for the hearer/reader is clear. Any would-be followers of John the Baptist would honor their hero supremely by turning to the one he came to point out: Jesus, the authentic Messiah. Thus, by both positive and negative narrative construction, followers of the Baptist are invited to join the primate of the Johannine witnesses in pointing to and following Jesus as the authentic Messiah/Christ (see Anderson 2000:10–13). He is the ultimate "hero" to which his heroic predecessor points.

(3) The debate with the local synagogue, probably transcending the 70s and 80s, is the most broadly covered crisis reflected in John's narrative.[19] Virtually all the dialogues with the Jewish leaders illustrate this series of dialectical tensions, and the works of Brown (2003), Martyn, and Rensberger cast valuable light on them. The individual discussant who typifies this debate most clearly, however, is *Nicodemus*, who comes to Jesus by night— probably reflecting fear of the Jewish leadership, notional inadequacy (being "in the dark"), or both. Notice, however, his privileged status ("a Pharisee … a leader of the Jews … a teacher of Israel") and thus the ironic punch of his misunderstanding. In the ensuing dialogue, the concerns of crypto-Chris-

---

19. Regarding the tensions with local Jewish leaders and Jewish Christians in the Asia Minor setting, consider the following dialogues: 3:1–21 (Nicodemus and Jesus); 6:30–59 (the crowd/the Jews and Jesus); 7:11–24 (the Jews and Jesus); 8:12–58 (Jesus and the Judeans/believing Jews/Pharisees); 9:8–34 (the man born blind/his associates and the Pharisees/Jewish leaders); 9:35–10:21 (Jesus and the man born blind/Pharisees). This threat coincides with the first antichristic threat in the Johannine Epistles (1 John 2:18– 25); see Anderson 1997:32–40; Brown 2003:172–75.

tians (what Raymond Brown calls Christian believers who remained behind
in the synagogue after the expulsion of known Christians) are exposed and
their masks torn off by the Johannine Jesus. Nicodemus starts off on the right
foot, acknowledging (unlike the crowd of John 6) the significance of Jesus'
signs: "Rabbi, we know you are a teacher who has come from God, for no
one could do such signs … except God be with him" (3:2). However, when
Jesus agrees and says, "It is not enough to be sent from above, you must be
born from above" (3:3), Nicodemus misunderstands. He thinks Jesus means
a second physical birth. At this point Jesus clarifies that being born of water
is not enough. One must also be born from above (ἄνωθεν)—born of the
Spirit—to enter the kingdom of God. (3:5) Put pointedly toward crypto-
Christians, water purification or even baptism may be a start, but unless one
is willing to set one's sails to the wind of the Spirit and risk socioreligious
rejection, one has not apprehended the dynamic activity of God's reign (3:1–
21). Therein lies the reality and the scandal of the transcendent kingdom.

Likewise, debates between Jesus and the Jewish leadership reflect
numerous issues that contemporary Johannine Christians must have faced.
Obstacles to "the world" recognizing the saving presence of God in the mission of Jesus include an over-reverence for the temple, Sabbath laws, the
Scriptures and Torah, Moses and Abraham, Davidic messiahship, Judean
(versus Galilean) roots, Jewish (versus Gentile) heritage, and even monothe-
ism proper. The key corrective text is 6:32: "It is not Moses who *gave…*, but
my Father who *gives you the true bread from heaven.*" But this is no mere exegetical triumph, where the midrashic mastery of Jesus wins the day. Rather,
it involves the overturning of exegesis proper, lest it eclipse the recognition
of the one to whom the Scriptures point. In short, retrospective exegesis is
displaced by realizing eschatology. The telling assessment of these flaws,
however, is their bondage to *conventionalism.* Concluding the signs section
of the Fourth Gospel, the Evangelist declares:

> Nonetheless, however, even many of the Jewish leaders believed in him,
> but because of the Pharisees they did not confess openly, lest they should
> become synagogue outcasts (ἀποσυνάγωγοι γένωνται). For they loved the
> praise of humans more than the glory of God. (John 12:42–43)

As a privileged authority, receiving its legitimation from above, Bakhtin
undoubtedly would have picked up on the ironic portrayal of Jewish leadership
as idolatrous in its religious zealotry. Its motivational scaffolding is definitely
base—from below. Theirs is a spiritual monologism that, although perhaps
well-meaning, certainly in a distortional way has displaced divine-human
encounter with creaturely instrumentalities. Bakhtin's analysis of chronotope

(time-place setting) in the Greek biographical rhetorical novel applies to the Johannine misunderstanding dialogue extremely well. The "public square" settings for these Jewish dialogues with Jesus includes the temple area in Jerusalem, the synagogue in Capernaum, Solomon's colonnade, various feasts in Jerusalem, and the trials before Jesus' death. By scandalizing the scandalized, the Evangelist deconstructs the socioreligious hegemony of his community's setting and bolsters the faith of its Jewish Christian members.

(4) A fourth crisis for Johannine Christianity involved the stepping up of the Roman expectation that all subjects of the empire would demonstrate loyalty to Caesar by means of requiring public emperor laud.[20] Even in the first-edition material, probably completed in the early-to-mid 80s, we see the stage being set for the Johannine appeal in the ironic portrayal of Pilate as misunderstanding the character of authority and truth. As the case study above shows (pp. 143–44), indeed Jesus *is* a king, but his kingdom is one of truth. This is a kingdom not maintained through human force, which is why Jesus' disciples do not fight. Pilate's question "What is truth?" is a flat-out acknowledgement that Pilate has no say about, or even access to, Jesus' kingdom. (18:28–40) Here the tables are turned, whereby the man on trial is actually the ruler, and the Roman regent is portrayed as gazing upon the true kingdom from the outside. On the transcendent plane, Pilate is not yet even a dot, but on the human plane he fares little better.

Appealing to his privileged position of authority, Pilate attempts to slap down the insubordinate Jesus: "Do you not know I have the power to kill you or release you?" he threatens. Jesus responds in a double entendre, "Indeed, you would have no authority were it not given you by my Father who is in heaven." In the following scenario, Pilate's mask is torn off as he is portrayed as being held hostage by the crowd. He is reduced to political impotence, begging the crowd to allow him to release Jesus, a blatant and highly ironic denial of his previous claims to authority (19:1–16). Finally, the crowd reduces itself to blasphemous emperor laud in their desire to rid the land of the one accused of blasphemy. "We have no king but Caesar!" they chant. In the light of appeals to emperor worship in the early 80s, this rendering of Jesus' trial

---

20. Regarding Roman hegemonic demands of emperor worship as experienced by beneficiaries of the *pax Romana* consider the following dialogues: 6:5–15 (Jesus and several disciples/the crowd); 14:1–31 (Jesus and disciples: Thomas, Philip, other Judas); 18:1–9 (Jesus and soldiers); 18:28–19:16 (Pilate and Jesus). During the reign of Domitian (see Cassidy 1991) from 81 to 96 C.E., even Domitian's Roman counterparts were commanded to worship him as "Lord and God"; against this backdrop, Thomas's confession before Jesus, "My Lord and my God!" would have been seen as an explicit defiance of Roman hegemony (Anderson 1996:221–31).

must have had a tremendously powerful effect on the Johannine audience. Roman demands in later generations could not be taken as seriously, given the memory of Pilate's miscomprehension of truth, the transcendent kingdom of God, and dethroned political authority.

(5) A fifth crisis alluded to in the Johannine situation involved an anti-docetic corrective that was levied against denials of Jesus' humanity among the Gentile Christian population of Asia Minor in the 80s and 90s.[21] Lindars insightfully points out that virtually all the antidocetic motifs in John are included in the supplementary material added to an earlier edition of the text. This fact, combined with the docetizing antichrists of 1 John 4:1–3 and 2 John 7, representing a different schismatic threat than the synagogue-returning antichrists of 1 John 2:18–25, suggests a later and different schismatic threat, and such a tandem sequence may also be inferred from the letters of Igna-tius. The Jewish threat preceded the docetic threat in late first-century Asia Minor Christianity. What was really at stake, however, in the docetizing ten-dencies of Gentile Christians was not the threat of bad theology proper, but the implications of bad theology in terms of praxis. While Romans probably never sought out Christians to persecute as a pastime, the reign of Domi-tian with its emperor-laud requirements brought with it at least occasional, if not repeated, testings of Christian solidarity with their Lord and the commu-nity of faith. Pliny's correspondence with Trajan some two decades later (*Ep.* 10.96-97) makes this pattern clear.

What Schnelle, Borgen, and others who have illuminated the Johan-nine antidocetic thrust for us have understated, however, is the connection between the docetist's refusal to acknowledge the humanity and suffering of Jesus and the reluctance to suffer for Christ at the hand of the Romans. Put simply, "If Jesus the Son of God did not suffer on the cross, neither should it be expected of the Christian convert." Gentiles in Asia Minor would have had a long history of assimilation with respect to governing groups' requirements, and this new Christian teaching, that to offer emperor laud was blasphemous, must have had a higher price tag than they had anticipated. The reluctance to suffer for their new-found faith, in combination with a Greek dualistic under-standing of Jesus as the divine (and therefore, supra-human) Son of God, must have spurred on the docetizing advance. If docetic Christian leaders

---

21. Regarding tensions with docetizing Gentile Christian teachers and community members in the Asia Minor setting, consider the following dialogues: 6:60–66 (Jesus' disciples and Jesus); 7:1–10 (Jesus' brothers and Jesus); 16:17–33 (Jesus' disciples and Jesus); 21:18–22 (Peter and Jesus). This crisis also coincides with the second antichristic threat of the Johannine Epistles (1 John 4:1–3; 2 John 7; see Anderson 1997:41–50; Brown 2003:175–80).

who had themselves assimilated (at least externally) to Roman emperor laud traveled among the churches teaching this "new gospel," this would explain why the antichristic docetists of the Johannine Epistles were regarded as "false prophets" and "deceivers" who had gone out into the world bringing a false teaching with them. The point I want to make is that John's antidocetic motifs converge with appeals for solidarity with Jesus and his community in the face of suffering, and this particular crisis is illuminated again by the Johannine misunderstanding dialogue.

The intramural Johannine audience is then addressed by the rhetorical use of the disciples' scandalization and noncomprehending abandonment of Jesus in John 6, part of the supplementary material. Like Amos's oracles against the nations, the most severe judgment is reserved for the final group addressed: in Amos's case, Israel; in the narrative of John 6, the disciples of Jesus. The masks of the crowd and the Jews have already been yanked away, but now the penetrating words of Jesus are served to Jesus' disciples. Their noncomprehension is portrayed both ironically and tragically. Ironically, after hearing Jesus say, "Unless you eat my flesh and drink my blood, you have no life in yourselves," the disciples themselves are now scandalized. What has been debated by scholars as a eucharistic requirement or interpolation is actually an expansion upon 6:51c, "The bread that I offer is my *flesh*, which I shall give for the life of the world." While eucharistic imagery is involved, the hortatory message is about the cross and disciples' willingness to shoulder it. To ingest the flesh and blood of Jesus is to be willing to suffer with him in the face of persecution, and that clear message is the source of the disciples' scandalization. Corporate solidarity with Jesus and his community in the face of Roman persecution was the central issue addressed by Ignatius and the Fourth Evangelist, not participation in cultic theophagy. Interpreters have often missed this distinction. Irony may even be built into the debate, as the question of the Jews in 6:52 appears to launch a predictable cannibalism-versus-Eucharist debate. The Johannine audience must have swallowed hard, though, when it came to realize Jesus is not simply defending a Christian practice against a typical Jewish objection but is calling for the radical willingness to suffer for their Lord in the face of Roman persecution (see Anderson 1996:110–36, 194–220). *That* was the "hard word" to swallow, figuratively and otherwise.

The second shoe falls hard with 6:66. Even some of Jesus' disciples abandon him and walk with him no longer. Here the Evangelist has constructed a masterful scenario of rhetorical biography. On an *Einmalig* (Martyn's term suggesting a "once upon a time" reference to the past as a means of engaging the present situation) level, Meeks (1967) is right. There is ample reason to assume Galilean messianic hopes did include king-like-Moses ideologies, and some of Jesus' "followers" must have turned away upon his distancing himself from nationalistic triumphalism. These events, mirrored in John 6:14 and 66, are brought to bear upon the immediate situation of the Johannine audience around the time John 6 was finalized (probably in the 90s). On the rhetorical level of their delivery, these events pose the existential question powerfully: "Will you also abandon the Lord, as those noncomprehending Galileans in days of old, or will you be faithful to the end?"

(6) The sixth crisis betrayed by Johannine misunderstanding motif involved an ecclesial corrective to rising institutionalism in the late first-century church.[22] The primary discussant portrayed as not understanding servant leadership in John, of course, is Peter. Furthermore, Peter is juxtaposed to the Beloved Disciple in ways that embellish Peter's noncomprehension, while the Beloved Disciple clearly shows the exemplary way forward. In the light of 3 John, where "Diotrephes, who loves to be first," has been excluding Johannine Christians and excommunicating any who would take them in, we see a likely motivator for this intramural corrective. While emerging hierarchical forms of leadership likely functioned smoothly in many settings, all it takes is one case where judgments are not meted graciously for one to object to such an innovation—which is precisely what the Fourth Evangelist does. He appeals to the original intentionality of Jesus to lead his church by means of the Holy Spirit. In John 20:21–23, the Johannine equivalent to Matt 16:17–19, Jesus breathes upon (inspires) believers and declares, "Receive the Holy Spirit." Then he "apostolizes" them ("As the Father has sent me, so send I you") and gives *them* (plural) the priestly responsibility to be forgivers of sins. Furthermore, as a contrast to entrusting Peter with instrumental keys to the kingdom of heaven, he entrusts the Beloved Disciple with his mother, a relational symbol of ecclesial coinage, rather than an instrumental one. But notice how the foundation for this constructive work is set by the deconstructive portrayal of Peter as failing to comprehend servant leadership.

First, Peter refuses to allow the mission of Jesus to falter and declares him to be the "Holy One of God," who will vanquish God's enemies by his triumphal might and exalt the elect on his right and left. Jesus rejects this understanding and declares: "I have not *chosen you the Twelve* [as in elected

---

22. I am indebted here to the work of Käsemann 1968 and others for the ecclesial implications of the juxtaposition of Peter and the Beloved Disciple in John. Regarding tensions with institutionalizing (Petrine) Christian leadership, consider the following dialogues: 6:67–71 (Jesus and the twelve/Peter); 13:1–20 (Simon Peter and Jesus); 13:21–30 (Jesus and disciples/Beloved Disciple/Judas); 13:31–38 (Jesus and Peter); 21:1–14 (Jesus and the disciples); 21:15–17 (Jesus and Peter). For dialectical engagements with rising institutionalism within Christianity, especially responding to Diotrephes and his kin (3 John 9–10), see Anderson 1991; 1996:221–51; 1997:50–57; Brown 2003:180–83.

you, the Twelve, to surface triumphantly], and one of you is a devil." The Greek, οὐκ ἐγὼ ὑμᾶς τοὺς δώδεκα ἐξελεξάμην..., is normally translated as a question, "Have I not chosen you the Twelve...?" but the declarative is certainly possible, and it even works better if by "election" is implied the sparing of hardship or loss. This also would explain Jesus' sharp response to Peter's otherwise orthodox-sounding confession. By confessing Jesus as the triumphant "Holy One of God"—even the one feared by the demoniac in Mark 1:24—Peter is portrayed as misunderstanding the sacrificial character of Jesus' ministry.

A second misunderstanding dialogue between Peter and Jesus involved Jesus' washing of Peter's feet. Peter fails to comprehend the action and lampoons himself by requesting a full bath, as though water-cleansing were the issue instead of servanthood. After Peter's misdirected enthusiasm, Jesus lectures the group as to the character of loving servanthood. But the concluding comment must have had a corrective sting in it for aspiring hierarchical leaders in the late first-century audience, claiming Petrine authority as did Ignatius a decade or so later: "Truly, truly, I tell you, a slave is *not* greater than his master..."; so far so good, but now for the corrective sting: "nor is the apostle [ἀπόστολος] greater than the one sending him." Parallel to Matt 16:17, a blessing is given in the next verse, John 13:17, but the macarism is not bestowed for making an inspired confession; rather, it is promised for obeying the servant-leadership injunctions of Jesus.

The third misunderstanding dialogue between Peter and Jesus takes place in John 21 after the resurrection. As well as being a priestly go-between at the Last Supper, the Beloved Disciple again is the one who points out the Lord to Peter. Unencumbered by reflective pause, Peter jumps into the water and comes to Jesus quickly. There on the shore, Jesus restores Peter around a charcoal fire, giving him the opportunity to make a threefold confession after having uttered a threefold denial (also around a charcoal fire, obviously an act of reconstructive therapy). But the reinstatement is not free from ambiguity. Despite Brown's showing of the nearly synonymous interchangeability of ἀγάπη and φίλος love, Peter is portrayed here as failing to understand Jesus' injunctions to love and tend the flock in an ἀγάπη manner. He is even hurt (ἐλυπήθη) that Jesus pressed the question three times, and this deserves to be understood as a corrective to the ascending institution associated with Peter's memory rather than a personal one alone. Put ideologically, the issue of leadership continuity was redefined by the Evangelist in terms of Christocracy: the effective means by which the risen Christ continues to lead the church. While he does not abolish institutions proper, he juxtaposes Jesus' original intention to lead the church though the Paraclete, available to all believers, over and against an emerging structural model associated with Peter. This motif comes even clearer when the disciples as a group are portrayed as failing to understand Jesus in John 16:17–18.

Central to the supplementary material added to the Fourth Gospel's first edition, probably in the 90s, is the teaching of Jesus on the Paraclete. Having already been introduced in the first edition of the Gospel, this theme becomes all the more significant as the last of the apostolic generation fades off the scene. Whereas the Matthean tradition addressed this crisis by posing an institutional answer to the problem, the Johannine tradition posed a Spirit-based approach. The disciples are portrayed as being absolutely confused regarding Jesus' teaching, and here we have the only explicit declaration of discussant noncomprehension in John (16:17–18, paraphrased):

> Therefore, some of his disciples said to one another, "What is this he's telling us: 'In a little while you won't see me any more?' And, 'Again, in a little while you will see me?' And, 'Because I am going to the Father?'" Therefore, they said, "This "little while" stuff he's talking about *leaves us absolutely clueless!*"

From a Bakhtinian perspective, here we have the use of the second stylistic line, where heteorglossia is now introduced from below. Their here-para-phrased declaration of miscomprehension is designed to pique internal dialogue in the understanding/experience of the hearer/reader. The reporting of cognitive dissonance evokes the same for the audience, and intentionally so. Jesus thus clarifies their misunderstanding in chapter 16 by offering his last will and testament in chapter 17, and Käsemann is right. We have an outline of Johannine ecclesiology in the great prayer of Jesus, which punctuates the Paraclete passages in the previous three chapters. In response to the disciples' failure to understand not only his absence but also his eschatological presence in the church, the Johannine Jesus offers not simply an ecclesiological lecture but an intercessory prayer. But the outline of that prayer offers the constructive sequel to the deconstructive misunderstanding motif. The Christocratic presence of Jesus will guide believers faithfully within the gathered community, and they will not be abandoned as orphans having to devise their own schemes to get by. *Then* will their knowing be complete.

(7) Engagements with parallel Synoptic traditions can be inferred during the early, middle, and later stages of the Johannine historical situation.[23] Here it is listed seventh among the crises, not as a factor of sequence, but as a reflec-

---

23. Regarding dialogical engagements with Synoptic emphases and interpretations of Jesus' ministry, consider the following dialogues: 6:25–30 (the crowd and Jesus); 9:1–7 (Jesus' disciples and Jesus); 11:1–16 (Jesus and some of his disciples); 12:4–7 (Judas and Jesus); 20:24–29 (Jesus and Thomas); 21:18–25 (Jesus and Peter). On Johannine dialecti-

tion that it spans the other six. One of the earlier tensions with the Markan traditions involved the prizing of outward wonders, which is supplanted in John by the revelational and soteriological significance of Jesus' miracles. Thomas comes to Jesus declaring that he will not believe without an external sign. While Jesus does not rebuke him for his interest and even grants it ("Put your finger here…, and put your hand into my side" [20:27]), he also declares its inferiority to sightless trust. "Blessed are those who have not seen," declares the Johannine Jesus, "and yet believe." At this, the externalist becomes an authentic believer, as Thomas confesses, "My Lord and my God!" But does he do so because he has heard Jesus or because he has experienced a penultimate rather than the ultimate source of blessing? The Evangelist leaves it ambiguous, exposing Thomas's desire for external evidence as incomplete and portraying Jesus as both rejecting his interest while at the same time granting it. Such is the dialectical presentation of Thomas in John.

The misunderstanding crowd serves as a group whose conventional desires for more barley loaves are challenged by the Johannine Jesus in John 6. In Bakhtinian terms, prevalent Christian perceptions of Jesus are engaged dialectically in the "everyday-life" presentation of the misguided crowd. After first of all misconstruing Jesus' messiahship, wanting to rush him off for a hasty coronation, they come again asking, "Rabbi, when did you get here?" implying the hidden question: "When is the next feeding?" Jesus recognizes full well their agenda and responds prophetically: "You seek me *not* because you saw the signs but because you ate the loaves and were satisfied!" The corrective is obvious. Jesus fed the multitude with real bread, but he did not intend to be construed as a source of physical bread alone. His saving/revealing mission was conveyed through the sign, but the primary valuation of the miracle should have been that which it signified: Jesus' being sent from the Father as the eschatological, representative envoy. Not only are the thaumaturgic aspirations of the misunderstanding crowd challenged by Jesus, but in Jesus' response the preliminary target is also suggested. "Ate and were satisfied" is the result of *all five Synoptic feeding accounts*, and not only is it missing from the Johannine rendition, but Jesus is portrayed in John as rejecting that outcome as missing the entire point of his semiotic ministry. Rather than a backwater signs source being engaged existentially, we probably have the prevalent Christian valuation of Jesus' miracles, assuming it is represented or influenced by the unanimous Synoptic accounts, being corrected by the Johannine Jesus. It is hard to overstate the implications of this corrective.

---

cal engagements with Markan presentations of Jesus' ministry, see Anderson 1997:24–32; 2001a; 2001b; 2002; Brown 2003:90–114.

While the crowd is not a privileged sort of authority, descending from above, it still represents popular conventionality—certainly an emerging sort of authority—that is being corrected. The implication of such a move is that it betrays at least a particular controversy within the Johannine situation—although perhaps beyond it—wherein the valuation of Jesus' miracles was contested. The misunderstanding of the crowd exposes thaumaturgic conventionality within the middle to late first-century Christian setting, and the Johannine Jesus sets the record straight.

Finally, the narrator sets the reader straight eschatologically, as a corrective to the Markan Gospels' emphasis that the Son of Man would return before the apostles had all died. John's Jesus declares explicitly that Jesus was misunderstood to say the Beloved Disciple would not die (implying that he has died by the time the Fourth Gospel is finalized). Rather, he only said to Peter, "What is it to you if he lives until I come again....you follow me!" (21:18–23). In that sense, the other Gospel traditions are complemented, augmented, and corrected by the Johannine witness dialectically. Because of the Fourth Gospel, Jesus can now be viewed in bi-optic perspective.[24] In Bakhtinian terms, the Johannine evangel not only comments upon polyphonic readings of Jesus; it *contributes* to them.

CONCLUSION

In sum, Mikhail Bakhtin offers a systematic literary theory that accentuates interesting features in the Johannine Gospel. Furthermore, by employing a rhetorical/critical analysis of the Johannine misunderstanding motif, one's knowledge of the Evangelist's specific meanings can be narrowed to a more clearly defined set of contextual correctives—right? According to Bakhtin, wrong. First, he would say that the Holy Writ is its own authority from on high. It is simply to be listened to and heard, not analyzed and explained. Second, Bakhtin would say that no theory of language or literature can be systematically adequate entirely, precisely because of the dialogical character of truth and the human means by which we apprehend and express it. According to Clark and Holquist:

---

24. Such is the thesis of *The Fourth Gospel and the Quest for Jesus*, with twenty-four particular elements of historical plausibility from Synoptic and Johannine sources, made in favor of a more nuanced approach in part 4 (Anderson 2006:127–73). Historiography is itself an artistic venture, every bit as much as fiction (Anderson 2001b), as reality and artistry answer back and forth within the dialectic of subjective memory and human experience.

Dialogism is Bakhtin's attempt to think his way out of ... all-pervasive monologism. Dialogism is not intended to be merely another theory of literature or even another philosophy of language, but it is an account of relations between people and between persons and things that cuts across religious, political and aesthetic boundaries. ... *Dialogism liberates precisely because it insists that we are involved in the making of meaning.* (Clark and Holquist: 348)

Finally, while Bakhtin might agree with some of the connections between Jesus' misunderstanding discussants in John and the Evangelist's addressing of seven acute, largely sequential-yet-overlapping crises in his situation, Bakhtin would consider those intentional meanings preliminary, but never final. He would not, however, disconnect the original author-hero relationship from evolving author-audience dialectical engagements; like art and answerability, one set of realities answers back and forth in the experience and cognition of the narrator, until past is connected with present in a further dialogical work of artistry. Further, knowledge within one disciplinary approach informs one's investigations within another. More universally and existentially, as we find *ourselves* drawn into an imaginary dialogue with the Johannine Jesus, the reader finds one's own conventions exposed and corrected in the place of the crowd, Nicodemus, Thomas, the Jews, Peter, and the disciples. With these words, Bakhtin closed the last article he ever wrote:

There is neither a first word nor a last word. The contexts of dialogue are without limit. They extend into the deepest past and the most distant future. Even meanings born in dialogues of the remotest past will never be finally grasped once and for all, for they will always be renewed in later dialogue. At any present moment of the dialogue there are great masses of forgotten meanings, but these will be recalled again at a given moment in the dialogue's later course when it will be given new life. For nothing is absolutely dead: every meaning will someday have its homecoming festival. (Clark and Holquist: 350)

Liberation Story or Apocalypse? Reading Biblical Allusion and Bakhtin Theory in Toni Morrison's *Beloved*

Bula Maddison

What does it mean, in a novel rich in biblical allusion, when a "Grandma"—who has some marks of a progenitor, including a twisted hip—dies of a broken heart? Or when a monstrous, devouring spirit is exorcised—at three o'clock on a Friday afternoon? Or when a man who ferries freed and escaping slaves across the Ohio River rejects the name Joshua—and later wonders if that was the right thing to do?

Allusion and Bakhtin's Theory: *Double-Voiced Discourse*

To read *Beloved* with attention to biblical allusion and Bakhtin's theory is to apprehend the workings of the dialogism so foundational to his thought: from what he calls the *internal dialogism of the word* to what he considers to be the profoundly *dialogical* nature of language and truth. Bedrock for Bakhtin is the internal dialogism of the word. The word does not come from the dictionary, Bakhtin holds, but from the mouths of others (Bakhtin 1981:294). It comes saturated with its history, laden with the "intentions of others." Its meaning is shaped on the fly, so to speak, not only by its source but by its destination: "Forming itself in an atmosphere of the already spoken, the word is at the same time determined by that which has not yet been said but which is … anticipated by the answering word. Such is the situation in any living dialogue" (280). Because meaning is continually being reshaped in this way, words do not have fixed boundaries. To use Bakhtin's language, "words do not coincide with themselves" (Todorov 1984:52).

What Bakhtin calls *double-voiced discourse* is language that can be seen to play with the word's internal dialogism, language in which a speaker intentionally and visibly uses another's words, language in which quotation marks can be heard (Morson and Emerson 1990:146). Double-voiced discourse can be found in ordinary, "extraliterary" language—in double entendre, for example, or in the speaker who makes ironic use of another's words. Such speech can be heard to contain a small conversation between two voices in a single utterance, the speaker both recapitulating and commenting on the other's words as she or he revoices them.

Bakhtin never takes up the topic of literary allusion. Yet allusion is precisely one voice heard to speak in another, language in which quotation marks can be heard. The Bible joins *Beloved* in a character who takes slaves across a river, and the reader expects him to be like the biblical Joshua in some way; an ancestor who has a twisted hip will somehow be like Jacob. Somewhat as in ironic speech, an allusion stages a conversation between two voices: What will (and will not) be the likeness? Morrison's allusions are perhaps more than usually "dialogical" in that often they function to problematize the very likeness they establish. If an ancestor in a novel is like the biblical Jacob, the man who became a nation, what might the novel's future hold if the ancestor dies of a broken heart? If a man Joshua who ferries slaves across the river unnames himself, what does that mean about the crossing? If a monster "dies" at three o'clock on a Friday afternoon, does that mean she is coming back?

One theorist of allusion describes literary allusion as a "marker" in a text pointing to an antecedent text and thereby invoking "intertextual patterning" between the two texts as the reader ponders the meaning(s) implied in the relationship (Ben-Porat 1976:107–8). This notion of intertextual patterning aligns well with Bakhtin's notion of the inherent dialogism in the word itself: the word without fixed semantic boundaries, the word that does not coincide with itself—the Jacob or the Joshua who is and is not Jacob or Joshua.

CONVERSATION BETWEEN LANGUAGES: *DIALOGIZED HETEROGLOSSIA*

Dialogism is writ large in Bakhtin's vision of the universe of language as a cacophony of endless conversation between languages or language-worlds, of contention among belief systems. This Bakhtin calls *heteroglossia,* and he considers it to be the fundamental condition of language.

> At any given moment of its historical existence, language … represents the co-existence of socio-ideological contradictions between the present and the past, between differing epochs of the past, between different socio-ideological groups in the present, between tendencies, schools, circles, and so forth. (1981: 291)

The job of the novel is to *represent* the vitality, the many-voicedness, the contention inherent in everyday language, what Bakhtin calls "extraliterary" or "living" language. "The prose artist elevates the social heteroglossia … into an image that has finished contours…; he creates artistically calculated nuances on all the fundamental voices and tones of … heteroglossia" (278–79). Bakhtin sums up the move from nature to art in these words:

> As distinct from the opaque mixing of languages in living utterances, [the novel] is *an artistically organized system for bringing different languages in contact with one another,* a system for having as its goal the illumination of one language by means of another. (361)

While the double-voicing in literary allusion exhibits the internal dialogism of the word, dialogism in heteroglossia—*dialogized heteroglossia* is Bakhtin's term—occurs when languages are brought to *"interanimate"*: when the perspectives and values in one language world must contend with the perspectives and values of another (295–96).

Beloved exhibits this "interanimation," this "illumination of one language by means of another," in novelistic language I would describe as a *hybrid* of language worlds. Just as the allusions in the language of the novel stage a conversation with an antecedent biblical text, so too does the language-world of the novel orchestrate a conversation in which, I propose, four or more languages or *belief systems* are revised and shaped and reshaped as they contend. In Bakhtinian terms, it would be appropriate to describe these languages or belief systems as *genres,* genre being not only a shape in which a language is ordered but the lens through which that language views the world (288–89).

The novel's intertextuality with the African American slave narrative is widely recognized in the critical literature (e.g., Christian 1997a:43–44). The pivotal event in the novel is the murder of a "crawling-already" baby by her mother, Sethe, an escaped slave, in order to save the child from capture and return to slavery. Morrison drew that story from the sensational historical narrative of a runaway slave named Margaret Garner, who tried to kill both herself and her children in order to prevent their return to slavery (39). Likewise, the critical literature widely acknowledges the importance in the novel of the spirit world of African cosmology (43–44). The ghost-character Beloved is unsurprising in that world—whether as a baby-haunt of the house at 124 Bluestone Road in Cincinnati or as transformed into a very corporeal young woman, a ghost who eats and sleeps, even gets pregnant. I would add a constituent genre that is not remarked on in the literature, perhaps because it is so obvious. That is the love story conventional in the modern novel: here, in the story of ex-slaves Sethe and Paul D, a woman and a man meet, make love, encounter obstacles, and overcome them in order to be reunited at last in the end.

The central source in my reading of the novel is the Bible as it is appropriated by African America (see Peach: 115, 116). The central text in that

Bible is what I would describe as an African American mythic origin story in the biblical exodus and conquest (see Gilroy: 207). African American Christianity writes the story of blacks' freedom from slavery in America onto the biblical story of the escape from slavery in Egypt and the journey to freedom in the land that had been promised, generations before, to Abraham and his progeny. The story continues in the New Testament, where God's family is refigured in the followers of Jesus and freedom as eternal life in the kingdom of God. Intersecting with the biblical exodus/conquest, and also important in the novel, is what I call the watery creation story, the typological story of Christian baptism, in which the person (or the nation, or the cosmos) is (re)born from the water. Following on the novel's epigraph in Romans, allusions in the novel establish multiple points of contact with the Bible, with the effect of drawing it into the novel as one among its constituent genres.[1] I propose that by means of biblical allusions and the conversation between the Bible and other constituent genres, the novel orchestrates a question about the exodus/conquest: Is it a liberation story—or an apocalypse?

THE EXODUS/CONQUEST IN AFRICAN AMERICA

The African American liberation story is movingly told in the poetry of spirituals and gospel song, where the Promised Land is sometimes freedom from captivity, in the north, other times freedom from toil, in heaven, oftentimes ambiguous (Ramey: 351). Songs like "Go Down, Moses" celebrate Moses' confrontation with Pharaoh, "way down in Egypt land," and Moses' ringing ultimatum, "Tell old Pharaoh, Let my people go." "Didn't Old Pharaoh Get Lost" recalls Pharaoh's army vanquished at the Red Sea. "Roll, Jordan, Roll" extols the power of the mighty river of imagination where the crossing is to eternal life: "I want to go to heaven when I die to see old Jordan roll." Perhaps most haunting in the American imagination, and immortalized by Marian Anderson, is the yearning for rest in "Deep River": "I want to go to that gospel place, that promised land, where all is peace." The conflation of the journey story of the ancestors with the story of Jesus' journey to Jerusalem and the cross is made vivid in "Ride On, Moses": "Ride on Moses, ride on King Jesus, I want to go to heaven in the morning."

The African American imagination maps the story onto the U.S. landscape, the Jordan refigured in the Ohio River, which separated slave states

---

1. The discussion here is largely limited to the exodus/conquest, but the novel's allusions encompass the Gospels and include the Song of Solomon as well. For a fuller treatment, see Maddison 2005: 73–104.

from free. In *Beloved*, Morrison establishes a number of points of contact with that reading of the biblical story. Among major characters I might describe as biblical hybrids, I have already mentioned Grandma Baby Suggs, the first of this family to cross the river from slavery, who recalls Jacob with her twisted hip, and also the man Stamp Paid, who ferries freed or escaping slaves across the Ohio, who used to be named Joshua. I would add here the shy girl Denver, who offers the hint of a new Moses: she is safely born to a runaway slave woman from a leaky old boat in the river, and thanks to the help of a white girl. But something is missing from the lineup of the landscapes:

ancestors (Jacob)	"Grandma" Baby Suggs (twisted hip)
Moses	Denver (born from the river)
Red Sea	[_____]
Joshua	Stamp Paid (ferries across the Ohio; formerly named Joshua)
Jordan	Ohio (freedom on the other side)

Spiritual and gospel song loves to celebrate Moses' victory at the Red Sea, but what has been forgotten in the poetry of the song is the American sea-crossing. In the African American story, while the Ohio River aligns nicely with the Jordan and the crossing into the Promised Land, the American sea-crossing is the Atlantic, the Middle Passage. That journey ends in slavery, not freedom; the dead at the bottom of the sea are not the enslaving Egyptians but the enslaved Africans who died in the crossing. These are the "Sixty Million and more" to whom Morrison dedicates her novel.

In *Beloved*, Morrison mobilizes the power of the biblical imagery to turn the story back on itself. She insists on the horror of the Middle Passage, where the Africans' crossing reverses the journey from slavery to freedom. This journey ends with Africans made captive and sold captive in the new land at the cost not only of their personal freedom but of their human identity as it was constituted in both language and connections to family and ancestors. Morrison accedes to locating the river-crossing at the Ohio, the boundary between slave and free states, but uses that *topos* to assert her proposal that neither escape nor emancipation brought freedom to African Americans; they remain captive in their identity as the objects of white subjectivity and remain oppressed by their repressed cultural memory of the Middle Passage (e.g., see Krumholz: 108).

The late scholar Barbara Christian has said it was not until the novel *Beloved* that Morrison brought herself to deal with the Middle Passage (1994). *Beloved* is about the Middle Passage, Christian says:

> That event is the dividing line between being African and being African American.... It is [a] four-hundred-year holocaust... Yet for reasons having as much to do with the inability on the part of America to acknowledge that it is capable of having generated such a holocaust, as well as with the horror that such a memory calls up for African Americans themselves, the Middle Passage has practically disappeared from American cultural memory... What did, what does that wrenching mean, not only then, but now? That is the question quivering throughout this novel. Have African American, How could African Americans, How are African Americans recovering from this monumental collective psychic rupture? (1997b:366)

Christian asserts, "No one in my family ... ever talked about that transition from Africa to the New World. Some elders even tried to deny that we came from Africa and had been slaves" (367). Christian describes *Beloved* as a healing ceremony for the African American people, a process of recovering ancestors so that they can be put to rest:

> Ancestral spirits must be nurtured and fed, or they will be angry or, at the least, sad.... If ancestors are not consistently fed or have not resolved a major conflict, especially the manner of their death, they are tormented and may return to the realm we characterize as that of the living, sometimes in the form of an apparently new born baby. So often I have heard someone in the Caribbean say, "This one is an old one and has come back because she needs to clear up something big." (366)

Christian reads the novel as leading the African-American reader to confront that most deeply repressed of cultural memories, what she calls the American holocaust.

THE EXODUS/CONQUEST *DIALOGIZED* IN THE NOVEL

Given the prevalence of river imagery in the African American imagination, the allusion to the Jordan seems clear when several characters—first Baby Suggs, then Sethe's three older children, then Sethe herself with the newborn baby—complete their escape from the plantation Sweet Home when they are ferried across the river to the "free" state of Ohio. There is a glancing textual marker as well in the man whose name used to be Joshua. The biblical Joshua was originally named Hoshea, "salvation." Moses changed Hoshea's name to Joshua, "The Lord saves" (Num 13:16). Morrison's Joshua reverses that renaming in "unnaming himself"

> when he handed over his wife to his master's son. Handed her over in the sense that he did not kill anybody, thereby himself, because his wife

demanded he stay alive. Otherwise, she reasoned, where and to whom could she return when the boy was through? With that gift, he decided that he didn't owe anybody anything. (184–85)

In other words, the novel appears to suggest, he did not owe his salvation to the Lord; he was paid up in his own coin. With Joshua's unnaming, the novel asks a question about the river-crossing as rebirth to freedom. Part 2 of the novel suggests an answer to that question when it casts the spirit-character Beloved as a slavemaster who cruelly rules over her mother, Sethe, and sister, Denver, on the "free" side of the river, in the house at 124 Bluestone Road in Cincinnati (Harris: 337).

The Ohio is starkly contrasted with the Jordan in a sort of antitalisman Stamp Paid carries in his pocket, a scrap of red ribbon he has worried to a rag (Morrison: 184). It came from the river:

> He caught sight of something red on [the river's] bottom. Reaching for it, he thought it was a cardinal feather stuck to his boat. He tugged and what came loose in his hand was a red ribbon knotted around a curl of wet woolly hair, clinging still to its bit of scalp. He untied the ribbon and put it in his pocket, dropped the curl in the weeds. (180)

The water monster, the beast, lives in this river: "Desperately thirsty for black blood, without which it could not live, the dragon swam the Ohio at will" (66).

The river fails as boundary between slavery and freedom on an apocalyptic morning when "four horsemen" ride up to 124: men from Sweet Home come to reclaim Sethe and her children under the terms of the Fugitive Slave Act. Sethe is just reassembling her children in the house of her mother-in-law, beginning to make a life. This world comes to an abrupt end when Sethe spies the horsemen, then gathers her children and rushes to the tool shed. Before Stamp Paid can intervene, she has cut the throat of her "crawling-already" baby with a hand saw to save her from capture.

Eighteen years later, when the novel opens, the house is haunted by the angry baby-spirit of that child, who never got named until the word "Beloved" was chiseled on her tombstone. When the baby spirit is banished from the house, she returns personified as an enigmatic young woman who seems to have been born from the water: the chapter where her mysterious appearance begins to be sketched opens with the words, "A fully dressed woman walked out of the water" (50). When Sethe first lays eyes on this whatever-it-is, her bladder fills to bursting: "She never made it to the outhouse.... The water she voided was endless. Like a horse, she thought.... But there was no stopping water breaking from a breaking womb" (51).

This is the daughter Sethe killed, the baby-ghost grown up, as the reader and Sethe and the younger daughter, Denver, slowly and painfully discover. The ghost possesses the new, struggling little family with a death-grip. But other possibilities emerge for the origins of this Beloved as well, and they are never resolved. She is the baby-ghost, certainly, but a passage late in the novel also situates her consciousness in the hold of a slave ship:

> All of it is now it is always now there will never be a time when I am not crouching and watching others who are crouching too I am always crouching the man on my face is dead his face is not mine his mouth smells sweet but his eyes are locked some who eat nasty themselves I do not eat. (210)

In this way, the spirit-child named on a tombstone and on the spine of a book gives a name to lost ancestry whose names are unknown or forgotten, the "Sixty Million and more" of the novel's dedication. The ancestor-ghost Beloved, "the fully dressed woman [who] walked out of the water," is born from the water of the Middle Passage.

I cannot say that the alignment of the Middle Passage with the Red Sea is specifically marked in the novel—unless one would want to trace the relation of the un-Joshua to Moses and follow Moses back to the Red Sea. Or, perhaps one might cite the novel's resetting of the infant Moses' rebirth in the Nile, discussed below, as a signpost that points to the Red Sea crossing, the event prefigured in the little rebirth story. But these associations seem notable in their indirection. Nor is the Middle Passage ever explicitly named in the novel. Perhaps it is suitable to Morrison's healing purposes that the reader must construct the Middle Passage from the highly impressionistic views in the hold of the slave ship, as in the passage I quoted above. Then the horrible reversal in the alignment with the Red Sea grows slowly, imperceptibly—irrefusably—in the imagination. That process leads the reader to confront the American sea-crossing and recognize in the character Beloved the restless anger of its unnamed, unmourned sixty million dead.

The hope for this family also was born from the water, born *in* the water. Sethe is pregnant with the girl Denver when she escapes from Sweet Home, and when the baby starts to come she is starving and has lain down to die, her bare feet swollen beyond walking, beyond recognition. A white girl finds her, a runaway from debt slavery, nearly starving herself. Together the two women accomplish the birthing, which takes place in a leaky old boat with one oar on the shore of the Ohio. "The strong hands went to work…, none too soon, for river water, seeping through any hole it chose, was spreading over Sethe's hips" (84). The scene recalls the rebirthing of the infant Moses from the Nile by the collaboration between slave and free women, the Hebrew mother and daughter and Pharaoh's daughter and her servant girl (Exod 2:1–11). In the end, Pharaoh's daughter "called his name Moses, … because I drew him out of the water" (2:10). In Morrison's story, the white girl goes on her way, leaving mother and infant daughter by the shore of the river and saying in her good-bye, "She's never gonna know who I am. You gonna tell her? Who brought her into this here world? … You better tell her…. Say Miss Amy Denver" (85). Sethe gives the new daughter an American name, Denver, for the stranger, the white girl, as a testament to one woman helping another.

When the novel begins to draw toward its conclusion, it is the shy girl Denver who ventures out of the house of horrors 124 has become, where Sethe and Denver are enslaved, even devoured, by the monster Beloved:

> The flesh between [Sethe's] forefinger and thumb was thin as china silk [while Beloved] whined for sweets although she was getting bigger, plumper by the day. Everything was gone now except two laying hens, and somebody would soon have to decide whether an egg every now and then was worth more than two fried chickens. (239)

Denver knows that if they are not to starve, she must do something. "It was she who had to step off the edge of the world," "leave the yard" (239, 241). Baby Suggs is long dead now, but Denver hears her Grandma Baby laugh, "clear as anything," and tell her, "Go on out the yard. Go on" (244). The community that was lost in the aftermath of the murder of the crawling-already baby is slowly restored now (see, e.g., Higgins: 103). When Denver asks for help, food begins to pour in from the community: she finds a sack of beans one day on a stump near the edge of the yard, "another time a plate of cold rabbit meat. One morning a basket of eggs sat there. As she lifted it, a slip of paper fluttered down…. 'M. Lucille Williams' was written in big crooked letters" (249). And in the end, it will be the community of women who invade the yard to exorcise the "devil-child," Beloved (256ff., 261).

TIME AND SPACE IN THE NOVEL: *DIALOGIZED CHRONOTOPE*

The effect of the hybrid genre of the novel can be well apprehended in the way time is represented. Barbara Christian comments that "Morrison's use of the folk concept of 'rememory' [is] common to many African and African diasporic peoples," recalling that it was a term her own mother used (1997a:42). Rememory is best understood "in the context of a cosmology in which time is not linear," Christian explains. Rather, "the future, in the Western sense, is absent, because the present is always an unfolding of the past. Thus every 'future' is already contained in what Westerners call the 'past'" (45). By way of illustration, Christian cites a passage from the novel in which the girl Denver "reminds us of the dangerous effects of disremembering: 'I'm afraid the thing that happened that made it all right for my mother to kill my sister could happen again.... Whatever it is, it comes from outside this house, outside the yard, and it can come right on in the yard if it wants to'" (45). Christian does not remark on it, but a further observation can be made from Denver's language of rememory: that is the spatialization of time in her notion that "it [the thing that could happen again] comes from outside this house, outside this yard." In the cosmology Denver describes, time and space are inextricable.

Alongside Bakhtin's work in discourse theory, encompassed in the previous discussion here about double-voicing in language and genre, rests his theory of *chronotope* (*chronos/topos*), an approach to understanding the representation of the interrelationships of time and space. He considered that "chronotopes ... provide the basis for distinguishing generic types; they lie at the heart of specific varieties of the novel genre" (250–51). Of course, situations and events of extraliterary life also can be understood chronotopically: one might call to mind the very different space/times in such "living life" situations as agricultural labor, sexual intercourse, or the assembly line (Morson and Emerson: 368). Similarly Bakhtin catalogues typical literary chronotopes: the chronotope "on the road," where "time flows into space," for example, and the chronotope of "the provincial town," where "time ... has no advancing historical movement; it moves rather in narrow circles ... of the day, of the week" (243–48). From a perspective in Bakhtin's theory, the African time of "rememory" constitutes a chronotope in the novel.

Lynne Pearce, writing about chronotope in the novel, calls attention to the following long passage early in the novel where Sethe talks with Denver about rememory:

> "Some things go. Pass on. Some things just stay. I used to think it was my rememory. You know. Some things you forget. Other things you never do. But it's not. Places, places are still there. If a house burns down, it's gone, but the place—the picture of it—stays, and not just in my rememory, but out there in the world. What I remember is a picture floating around out there outside my head. I mean, even if I don't think it, even if I die, the picture of what I did, or knew, or saw is still out there. Right in the place where it happened."
>
> "Can other people see it?" asked Denver.
>
> "Oh, yes, yes, yes. Someday you will be walking down that road and you hear something or see something going on. So clear. And you think it's you thinking it up. A thought picture. But no. It's when you bump into a rememory that belongs to somebody else. Where I was before I came here, that place is real. It's never going away. Even if the whole farm—every tree and blade of grass of it does. The picture is still there and what's more, if

you go there—you who never was there—if you go there and stand in the place where it was, it will happen again; it will be there for you, waiting for you. So, Denver, you can't never go there. Never. Because even though it's all over—over and done with—it's going to be there always waiting for you. That's how come I had to get all my children out. No matter what."

Denver picked at her finger nails. "If it's still there, waiting, that must mean that nothing ever dies."

Sethe looked right in Denver's face. "Nothing ever does," she said. (Pearce: 186)

Hence, as Pearce observes, at any moment, "time ... can ... reach out and grab you." And the events that threaten in this past that can present itself again are "for the most part unspeakable" (186).

Just as Bakhtin sees double-voicing in language and genre, so too can chronotope be hybrid; a novel brings chronotopes into interaction that is dialogical:

Chronotopes are mutually inclusive, they co-exist, they may be interwoven with, replace or oppose one another, contradict one another or find themselves in ever more complex interrelationships.... The general characteristic of these interactions is that they are *dialogical*. (252)

Bakhtin offers an example in the novel *Don Quixote*, which he describes as a "hybridization of the 'alien, miraculous world' chronotope of chivalric romances with the 'high road winding through one's native land' chronotope that is typical of the picaresque novel" (1981:165).

In bringing together the constituent genres of *Beloved*, Morrison sets the cyclical time of African and African American "rememory" alongside a more conventional (or Western) chronological notion of time that marches forward as the clock ticks and the calendar pages turn, a notion of time that the other three sources share. Such is the time of the love story of Sethe and Paul D, who meet, make love, encounter obstacles, overcome the obstacles, and are reunited in the end. Such is the time of the Bible as it is conventionally understood. The story moves forward as the promise unfolds, from creation to the ancestor stories with the promise to Abraham, to the exodus and the conquest of the Promised Land, to the exile and reentry into the land, and on into New Testament, where time is expected to continue ticking forward for as long as it takes until the Second Coming (albeit a promise that the storyline endlessly defers). And such is the time of the slave narrative, which appropriates the biblical exodus story with its anticipation of freedom in the end. All three of these sources participate in what Paul Gilroy calls "the politics of fulfillment: the notion that a future society will be able

to realize the social and political promise that present society has left unac-
complished, [a politics that] reflect[s] the foundational semantic position of
the Bible" (36–37).

In the genres participating in "the politics of fulfillment," the promise is
fulfilled in space: west of the Jordan in the Bible's Promised Land, in the north
of the slave narratives, across the Ohio in Cincinnati in the novel's love story.
In these Western chronotopes, time moves forward toward a future space
where hope is fulfilled. Slavery stays behind, in Egypt, in the south, closed off
from the future in a time that is past. But in the novel's African chronotope
of rememory, time and space are stuck together in an endless present where
the unspeakable past can happen again, where the plantation Sweet Home is
"never going away." The two chronotopes contend in the novel.

Morrison twines two of the constituent genres together in the novel's pivotal event, when the four horsemen ride up to 124. With the figure of the
horsemen, Morrison renders the story she retells from the historical slave
narrative of Margaret Garner a biblical apocalypse when Sethe cuts the throat
of the baby. But from a third perspective, that of the novel's African spirit
world, it is an apocalypse that can happen again, as Denver's reflection has
shown: although Denver does not know this, it was in fact the arrival of the
four horsemen that "made it all right" for her mother to kill her sister, the
event Denver fears might happen again.

Josef Pesch has proposed *Beloved* to be a "postapocalyptic novel": "Postapocalyptic literature tells us that [the final] catastrophe might not have been
really final.… The apocalypse has happened before the narration sets in"
(141). Such is the case in *Beloved*, as Pesch observes: "The specific apocalypse
of *Beloved* has happened eighteen years before the novel begins, when the
four horsemen arrive" (145). When the time of African cosmology is aligned
with the biblical apocalypse, the story goes on even after the final disaster.
You can run smack into Sweet Home at any time; you never know when the
four horsemen might ride up to your yard. Pesch is persuasive, but I would
modify his proposal to suggest that postapocalyptic is one of two contending representations of time, one of two chronotopes in the novel. The other
is the conventional chronotope of the modern novel—common to the Bible
as conventionally read, the slave narrative, and the stereotypical modern love
story—all characterized by what Paul Gilroy calls the politics of fulfillment.
The novel represents that contending possibility in what appears to be the
lived-happily-ever-after ending of the love story—and among the ambiguities
of the novel's conclusion as well.

CONCLUSION IN *POLYPHONY*

If a novel is fully to accomplish what Bakhtin regards to be its mimetic work, it must represent the dialogical nature of truth itself. Consonant with the dialogism internal to the word and the dialogical contention in the universe of language, the truth cannot be held in a single perspective for Bakhtin but only can be apprehended in competing points of view. He likens such a novelistic consciousness to the consciousness of Galileo:

> The novel is the expression of a Galilean perception of language, one that denies the absolutism of a single and unitary language—that is, it refuses to acknowledge its own language as the sole verbal and semantic center of the ideological world. (1981:366)

This Bakhtin considers to be the *form-shaping ideology* of the novel. He calls it *polyphony.*

The novel's contending chronotopes align with contending possibilities for the conclusion of the exodus/conquest story as it is appropriated in African America. I have suggested above that Morrison has designed the architecture of her novel to confront that story and to insist on the Middle Passage as the American analogue to the biblical Red Sea. The American sea-crossing ended in slavery and death. Nor does the subsequent river-crossing yield freedom in this novel, where Sethe and Beloved are shown to remain enslaved in Ohio, on the "free" side of the river. There they are haunted by repressed memories of the unspeakable and unspoken past, especially the past of the Middle Passage as it is represented in the monster Beloved has become. Yet with Denver, Morrison has given us a new, American Moses. Is there a role for Moses in this story after all? And near the novel's conclusion, Morrison gives water-imagery of baptism in Sethe's experience of the exorcism: she "trembled like the baptized" in the women's wave of sound (Morrison: 261). Is there the possibility for Sethe's rebirth to freedom at last? In this context, one recalls the interior speech with which Stamp Paid reveals his former name to be Joshua: he is *wondering* whether he had been right to reject the biblical name. So ... could the exodus/conquest story be the right story after all? Could it be that freedom can be found on the "free" side of the river?

The corporeal Beloved, the ghost slavemaster who has been fattening herself at the expense of her mother and her sister, mysteriously vanishes in the exorcism. Nobody seems to know exactly what happened. "One point of agreement is: first they saw [her] and then they didn't" (267). Any appearance of closure is immediately mitigated, however: "Later, a little boy put it out how he had been looking for bait back of 124, down by the stream, and saw, cutting through the woods, a naked woman with fish for hair" (267).

Does the typological baptism story include the possibility for the monster's rebirth from the water? Like the death of Jesus, the exorcism takes place at three o'clock on a Friday afternoon (Mark 15:33–39 and parallels). Does this imply the possibility for the monster's resurrection after three days? And in the time of rememory as it shapes the genre of postapocalyptic, when/where would "three days" be?

The novel reflects the conflicting possibilities in the ambiguous language twice repeated on the closing page: "It was not a story to pass on"; and "This is not a story to pass on." The expression plays on the meaning of "pass on" (see, e.g., Hove: 260). On the surface of the language, one reads "It was not a story to pass *on*," not a story to retell but a story to forget. Yet the novel has been about the importance of remembering. Underneath "it was not a story to pass *on*," one might detect the opposite: "It was not a story to *pass* on"; it is not a story to pass [by], but a story to tell. In this way, the novel's conclusion holds open the tension between the desire to forget and the need to remember. The novel's dialogization—from the double-voiced language of allusion to the contention among genres and chronotopes—ends in polyphony. The conversation instigated by the novel continues off the last page, held open—dialogized—by two meanings in one utterance, "not a story to pass on." Will Beloved's story be forgotten, or will it be remembered? In this crux rests a larger question of the novel: Is there a freedom story for blacks in America?

All these questions take me back to the novel's epigraph: "I will call them my people, which were not my people; and her beloved, which was not beloved" (Rom 9:25). Given the novel's dedication to the "Sixty Million and more" and the novel's irresolution, one reading of the epigraph yields this question: Can black Americans recover and name their sixty million dead? That is, can they acknowledge the painful truth of their past and thereby free themselves from it at last? To take into account the context of the epigraph in Romans and the context of its source text in Hosea—each concerned with the possibility for building or rebuilding community between two peoples—yields a different question: Can black *and white* Americans acknowledge the horrors of our common past, the unspeakables that the novel has finally spoken—and thus be reconciled at last? Can the novel itself—now an established part of the American literary canon and a staple of the undergraduate curriculum—begin to constitute in the American imagination the museum of the American holocaust, the museum that America has failed to build? From a perspective in Bakhtin's thought, one might say that the novel holds open the hope for a long and painful conversation that black America and white America must have if we are to recover from the unspeakable past we share.

Response—Beyond Formalism:
Genre and the Analysis of Biblical Texts

Keith Bodner

The five essays that I am responding to in this very fine collection have at least three things in common. First, each of these papers—in different ways—appropriate the critical work of M. M. Bakhtin with effective results. It is often said that Bakhtin represents not merely a way of categorizing a given text but rather a way of seeing the world and imagining the literary work, and these essays show the value of this kind of interface for biblical studies. Second, each of these essays evince an interest in moving beyond *formalism*. This is not meant to be a reductive statement, for many elements of formalist criticism still retain a high degree of analytic currency. Yet these essays illustrate the value of taking a given *genre* seriously, in ways that transcend many earlier methodologies in the stable of biblical studies. Third, each of these essays deploy eminently useful examples to build the case, and it is the various examples that form the core of my response to each individual paper.

A number of years ago, at an otherwise sedate scholarly meeting, Christine Mitchell and I gave consecutive papers on Solomon's accession. She focused on the account in Chronicles, while I looked at the Kings material. This is not worth mentioning except for the fact that we were both—like the two sons of Rimmon in 2 Sam 4—publicly impaled on a source-critical gibbet by our *de rigueur* respondent. However, Christine quickly recovered from the amputation, and argued eloquently in defense of the Chronicler as a literary artist and theologian who needs to be heard on his own merits. Such an argument is further enhanced with her essay in the present volume, as she points to a degree of sophistication on the Chronicler's part that I think will eventually win the day.

A case in point is Mitchell's discussion of King Asa in 2 Chr 13:23–15:15 (MT). As she states, this is a stretch of narrative that has limited parallels to the Deuteronomistic History, and thus the interpreter is in a good position to make surmises about theological intent and literary craft. If one takes seriously Mitchell's argument that "a genre expresses a certain worldview," then her discussion of the Judges intertext with the King Asa narrative is a powerful example. This story takes place fairly soon (within a half-generation) after the dissolution of the united kingdom, with north and south precariously close to civil war. That the reign of Asa should feature a host of allusions to Judges—both words and situations, as Mitchell delineates—indicates something of narrative importance.

The net effect of the Chronicler's allusion to Judges, as Mitchell proposes, is that Asa becomes a type of "new Gideon." The comparison is striking. Like Gideon, Asa prevails against a number of enemies, both foreign and domestic. Furthermore, there is some ambivalence later in the career of Asa, just as there is in Gideon, who suffers a poor run of form late in life (shifting from idol-breaker to idol-maker, as one commentator puts it). Admittedly, this is a brief example, but I think it is well-chosen, and Mitchell's conclusion is worth pondering: "Through the heteroglossic text of Chronicles, the genre of Judges (the larger Deuteronomic History as well?) is shifted into something else: perhaps theology?" Glancing at the previous chapter (2 Chr 13), it is tempting to answer in the affirmative and note that a similar kind of premonarchic heteroglossia can be discerned in the preceding chapter as well. I will loosely translate 2 Chr 13:4–9 as follows:

> And Abijah arose on the top of Mount Zemaraim (which is the hill country of Ephraim), and he said, "Hear me, O Jeroboam and all Israel! Don't you know that the LORD God of Israel has given kingship to David over Israel forever, to him and to his sons a covenant of salt? And Jeroboam son of Nebat—servant of Solomon, son of David—arose and rebelled against his master. Empty fellows [אנשים רקים] and sons of Belial have gathered around him, and they fortified themselves against Rehoboam son of Solomon, but Rehoboam was just a lad, tender of heart, and he could not strengthen himself before them. But now, you are thinking of strengthening yourselves before the kingship of the LORD in the hand of David's sons, for you are a huge crowd and you have golden calves that Jeroboam made for you to be gods. Haven't you banished the priests of the LORD—the sons of Aaron and the Levites—and made for yourselves priests like the peoples of the lands? Anyone who comes to fill his hand with a young bull of the herd and seven rams can become a priest to no-god!"

If there are allusions to the Gideon narrative of Judges in the Asa account of 2 Chronicles, then surely this scene—with an orator perched atop a hill, calling out to an assembled group—is evocative of Jotham's speech in Judg 9. Just as Jotham loudly warns his compatriots about the folly of alignment with Abimelech and his "empty fellows" (נשים רקים), so Abijah declares to

Jeroboam and all Israel that setting themselves in opposition to the Davidic throne and Aaronic priesthood is likewise fated to fail. Of course, there are some significant differences (Jotham resorts to a "fable" technique, whereas Abijah uses direct language), but such variation certainly does not blunt the force of the allusion. The remainder of Abijah's speech follows the same line of reasoning, but his words do not prevail. Jeroboam sets an "ambush" (מארב) in 2 Chr 13:13, just as Abimelech set an ambush (מארב) in Judg 9:35, and both suffer staggering defeats that are attributed to divine intervention.

There is a case to be made, therefore, that 2 Chr 13–15 has a number of connections with Judg 6–9. In dialogue with other commentators, Mitchell does not downplay this interplay with the Deuteronomistic History: "I would suggest, rather," she says, "that the Chronicler is deliberately reflecting on the book of Judges and the prophetic texts and trying to draw parallels between the reign of Asa and the period of the judges (perhaps Asa as a new Gideon?)." If Asa is a new Gideon, then his son Abijah bears a marked resemblance to Gideon's son Jotham. A corollary effect of the Judges intertext is that it becomes a rather powerful way of illustrating that Jeroboam is a new Abimelech—and since the latter functions as the antitype of a true king in the Deuteronomistic History, the comparison is not flattering for the upstart Jeroboam in Chronicles. By invoking the Judges material, the Chronicler reinvests the freight of theological meaning from the preexilic text to the postexilic world, with some artistic literary gains as well. Such subtle analysis as that of Christine Mitchell can only enhance the resurgence that Chronicles scholarship is witnessing in our day.

Along with Robert Polzin, Barbara Green is a scholar who has done a great deal to encourage and facilitate the conversation between Bakhtin and biblical studies. Her three recent books (*Mikhail Bakhtin and Biblical Scholarship: An Introduction*; *King Saul's Asking*; and *How Are the Mighty Fallen: A Dialogical Study of King Saul in 1 Samuel*) are ample illustration, providing both an excellent foundation and provocative readings of the biblical text. In general terms, Green approaches 1 Samuel as part of a larger narrative complex, the "Deuteronomistic History" that encompasses the books from Joshua to 2 Kings. To be sure, the notion of a somewhat unified Deuteronomistic History has been much discussed and lately doubted, but Green underscores the heuristic value of understanding the construct, and her sense of provenance has a certain appeal that transfers into her readings of the narrative.

Green's opening comments on dialogism forms a nice segue into her discussion of a biblical character who is primarily sketched in terms of relationships. By means of verbal exchanges, our perceptions of a character shifts: "The genuinely dialogic requires two or more distinct speakers, each with a voice, a set of experiences, distinct placement, attitudes and outlooks on the world." In some ways this is similar to the reader's dialogic relation to the literary work, and as the work unfolds, the reader gets progressively "educated," one could say. Furthermore, Green's discussion of utterance is important for her discussion of 1 Sam 20. The utterance is more than just what a character says; it is how the character's speech intersects with the rest of the narrative, "its relational and malleable nature," as Green calls it. In this section of the paper Green reiterates a point she makes elsewhere: "with Bakhtin, we need to make the sometimes difficult distinction between character psychology (which is *not* our concern, not available to us) and the language that we as interpreters manage in our own centers of consciousness (which *is* of urgent concern). In a word, the Jonathan, Saul, and David that we—you and I—are reading is primarily our own and needs to be owned as such. We have 'the same' text before us, the same discourse, but how we construe it will vary as we each take it up."

Of the myriad of characters in the Deuteronomistic History, Jonathan surely is one of the harder ones to figure out. 1 Sam 20 itself is a long and difficult chapter, fraught with clandestine conversation that takes place in an ambiance of danger. On one level, the chapter takes places at a moment in the story whereby it foreshadows (and acts as a transition to) the long period where David is a fugitive in the wilderness. On another level, the discourse is strained and does not elicit a great deal of attention from commentators. Yet Barbara Green argues that this chapter is a vital component of a character's education. Why does Jonathan need to be educated, and why do I—as a reader—need to be educated about Jonathan's education? Perhaps the education of Jonathan mirrors the education of the reader. Far from a flat and static character, Jonathan becomes indispensable to the reader's education.

It is curious that both David *and* Saul are trying to persuade Jonathan to accept their view of the situation—imposing their viewpoint. Jonathan thus becomes a *site* whereby the two rivals, both of whom have a claim on Jonathan's loyalty, further their own claims. If this is the case, then it is striking that Jonathan twice procures an oath from David in the chapter, once before his encounter with Saul and again afterward. One wonders if Jonathan— while appearing to acquiesce to both Saul and David—actually resists both. He rejects Saul's demands but distances himself from David as well by securing the oath(s). As Green points out, there is a movement in Jonathan's first speeches to David. Jonathan begins with a flat rejection ("Never!") of David's allegation that Saul harbors murderous designs but follows this with a less-emphatic question: "Why would he [Saul] hide this from me?" For Green, this opens the door for both David's rhetorical advances and Jonathan's education: "By asking that question, Jonathan admits the possibility that David's charge may be true." There is still a lot of dialogue to come after this question, and it takes a long time to finally negotiate the banquet subterfuge. Once the two of them march out to the field, however, it is striking that *only Jonathan speaks in the field*. David is not afforded any direct speech. Of the many words Jonathan utters in the field, the climax would appear to be 20:13b–17:

> "And may the LORD be with you just as he was with my father. If I live, may you act with the loyalty of the LORD toward me, or if I die, do not ever cut off your loyalty toward my house, not even when the LORD cuts off all of David's enemies from the face of the earth. And so Jonathan has cut a deal with the house of David, and may the LORD seek it from the hand of David's enemies." And again Jonathan made David swear an oath out of his love for him, for he loved him as his own soul.

By any measure, there is a dramatic shift from Jonathan's denial of Saul's motive to this carefully worded oath. After reading Green's essay, it seems harder to accept that Jonathan's securing of an oath is entirely without pre-meditation. Even more poignantly, Jonathan gets David to swear the oath *before* Saul flies into a rage (in 20:30ff.), and thus before he "knows" Saul's disposition for sure, he has a long-term deal with the house of David. From his first sustained appearance in the narrative, Jonathan has looked like an Ichabod figure, one from whose family the glory of the Lord has departed. While he is loyal to his father, we also see them at odds: first in chapter 14 and now here, especially when he talks about "the enemies of David," a camp that surely includes Saul (as Green suggests). It is not implausible, then, that Saul is being sketched as a threat to the survival of Jonathan's house, and the author of the sketch is Jonathan himself.

When Jonathan arrives at the banquet, the issue of the survival of his (royal?) house is fresh in the reader's mind. As Saul mutters to himself at the banquet, he ruminates on matters of "uncleanness," but he must sense a more palpable threat: If the son of Jesse accedes to the throne of Israel, will he leave a rival house intact? As Green remarks, "In one of his most candid reflections, Saul tells Jonathan that he knows that the son is choosing Jesse's son over against his own lineage (and his mother's nakedness)." Ever since the book of Genesis, Benjamin's survival has been precarious, and given the recent antagonism between Judah and Benjamin in Judg 20, one might say that Saul has biblical history on his side. Consequently, when Jonathan says that David is going to "his city" for a "clan fest," Saul is understandably annoyed, and this rage (by means of the spear aimed at the cranium) also becomes part of Jonathan's education.

Although a number of readers have wondered if Jonathan's reiteration of the oath in 20:42 is redundant ("Jonathan said to David, 'Go in peace, because both of us have sworn an oath in the name of the LORD, saying, "May the

LORD be between me and you, and between my descendants and yours forever" ' "), such an utterance is entirely consistent with a character who has
been maneuvering for the survival of his house throughout this long chapter.
It is possible, therefore, that Jonathan's education is instructive for an exilic/
postexilic generation. As Green intones, "My conviction is that the story of
Saul and his 'sons' (Jonathan and David in the present story) was recomposed
to be meaningful in the moment when the prospect of postexilic royal leadership was possible but not ultimately chosen." The lesson of Jonathan might be
that the best hope for the future is to bind oneself with the hope of David and
to be allied with a house of enduring promise.

The title of Judy Fentress-Williams's essay takes its cue, as far as I am
aware, from the earthy world of real estate. The idea is that property with a
prime location is worth more than property on the periphery. Such a theory
only works, of course, if there is a buyer who is of that mindset. For Fentress-
Williams, Gen 38 is intentionally placed in an area where an alert reader can
discern the value of its site for the development of meaning in the narrative.

So positioned, Gen 38 forms a dialogue with surrounding material, and
as Fentress-Williams argues, a primary way such dialogue is transacted is
through wordplay, motif, and theme. As Fentress-Williams points out, a key
motif in this complex is *clothing*, since garments (in the story) are used to
convey "status, position, favor, or role" and also have "the power to conceal
or reveal identity." Clothing can also be used as an instrument of deception.
One can immediately discern the value of this observation, not just in terms
of Gen 38 but also within the larger contours of the book of Genesis. When
Fentress-Williams discusses the "deceptive" use of clothing in Gen 38, one
straightaway recalls a makeshift garment earlier in the story:

> Now Rebekah was listening when Isaac spoke to Esau, his son. And Esau
> went out to the field to hunt game, in order to bring it. But Rebekah said to
> Jacob, her son, saying, "Behold, I heard your father speaking to Esau your
> brother, saying, 'Bring me game, and make for me savory food, that I may
> eat, and that my soul may bless you in the presence of the LORD before I
> die.' So now my son, listen to my voice, to what I am commanding you.
> Please go to the flock, and get for me from there two choice kids of the
> goats [גדיי העזים], that I may make them into savory food for your father,
> just as he loves. Then you can bring it to your father to eat, in order that
> he may bless you before he dies." … And Rebekah took clothes of Esau, her
> older son, the most desirable ones that were with her in the house, and she
> clothed Jacob, her younger son. (Gen 27: 5–10, 15)

Fentress-Williams would no doubt agree that clothing in Gen 27 is used
both to conceal and deceive. The fraudulent use of clothing first of all conceals

the real identity of Jacob as both a smooth-skinned man *and* the younger son. Further, the "goat" (גדיי העזים) clothing is used to fool the father and procure the desired blessing. In this scene, the role of Rebekah is a curious one. As the architect of the deception, she may appear in a dubious light, although the reader concedes that she does have the weight of the oracle of chapter 25 on her side: "Two nations are in your womb.... the elder will serve the younger." As Fentress-Williams notes, "The Tamar/Judah story alerts the reader to the fact that those things that appear to stand between the promises of God and the fulfillment of those promises are illusions." We can see, therefore, that Gen 38 does not appear in a vacuum but reaccentuates key images from earlier in the story. Jacob uses clothing and goat-stuff to deceive his father, and then later in chapter 37 we see the sons of Jacob deceive him with clothing and goat-stuff.

Genesis 37 represents, as Robert Alter and others have noted, a kind of *measure-for-measure* moment in the life of Jacob. After clothing his dreaming son Joseph in a lavish coat, Jacob is deceived by his other sons as to the fate of Joseph. It is striking that the brothers—led by their new spokesperson, Judah—rip the honored garment off their brother and dip it in the blood of a young goat (שׂעיר עזים). As in Gen 27, there is concealment and deception. Just as Jacob conceals his identity to deceive his father through clothing and a young goat, so now he is on the other end of a not-dissimilar deception. The motives are different—Jacob (and his mother) are motivated by the blessing, whereas the brothers are primarily driven by jealously—but the outcome has a number of parallels. Lest one think that such deceptions are finished in the first book of the Hebrew Bible, there is one more cameo appearance by a young goat in chapter 38. As Fentress-Williams discusses at length, the central (male) character in this story is Judah. Having pitched his tent with Hirah the Adullamite and married Bath-shua, various circumstances befall Judah whereby he eventually solicits Tamar, his daughter-in-law, with the promise of a young goat in return for her services. The end result, as Fentress-Williams comments, is an "eye-opening" experience for Judah at the entrance to Enaim. The presence of a young goat (גדיי-עזים) serves to lift the scales off the reader's eyes as well, since now Judah is deceived by means of clothing (and the young goat is involved), just as he deceived his own father in a comparable way.

Although E. A. Speiser and company assert that Gen 38 has little connection with the surrounding material, it seems to me that Judy Fentress-Williams has built compellingly on other literary-oriented studies and contributed to an antithetical argument. It is thus hard to resist her plea that, not only does the Judah/Tamar narrative function as an interpretive lens that helps one to understanding the larger Joseph story, but the "play within a play" idea will assist in reading later biblical narratives as well. After all, Gen 38 is not the last time that parental deception by means of clothing and a young goat occur. As one fast forwards to 1 Sam 19, we notice Saul's daughter Michal deceive her father through clothing and a net of goat's hair (כביר העזים), and I do not think it is a stretch to see the same kind of motifs in operation here. On the contrary, I would submit that Fentress-Williams's insights can be extended to the stories of *royal* dysfunctional families as well.

Carleen Mandolfo is a longtime member of the Society of Biblical Literature "Bakhtin circle," and her publications display a critical awareness of the Bakhtin interface with biblical studies. This particular paper—on Lamentations and the lament psalms in the Hebrew Bible—provides a useful reminder of the idea that prayer in the Hebrew Bible is a dialogic enterprise: a word that presupposes another word, or an audience, or a response. In other words, biblical prayer is not merely an internal discourse pertaining to self-actualization or entering into another state of being (although such may be included) but is predicated on an *other* who is dialogically connected. This paper, as I understand it, calls for a more relational approach to interpreting biblical poetry.

After rereading this essay, I was increasingly impressed with the DV (the "didactic voice," as Mandolfo calls it). This voice is far more elastic and dynamic than I may have thought. Previously, I might have categorized the DV as rather staid and "traditional," sort of like a poetic surrogate for someone like the prophet Samuel. However, I am now open to the idea that the DV is wide-ranging and creative as it gives utterance to the speaker/lamenter in the context of dialogue. On the one hand, as Mandolfo argues, "The function of the DV in the psalms seems to be to defend YHWH's goodness or justice, or, in a more pastoral sense it might be understood as offering reassurance to the supplicant." But, on the other hand, she continues: "What does it mean, theologically, when the voice traditionally representing the divine position, the voice of authority, speaks against its own interests and from the perspective of suffering humans?" To my mind, this is where Bakhtin can lend a hand by opening the door for further questions. If genre for Bakhtin is a way of organizing utterance—a frame for envisioning dialogue—then why are lament psalms composed this way? What is it about *this* genre that is compelling for prayer (in a way that narrative, which is ideal for Saul and David and Mephibosheth, would not quite work)?

For the discussion of Lamentations in the context of the "culture shock" of invasion and exile, Ps 22 is a powerful intertext. Since this poem itself generates ample dialogue within the wider biblical canon, Mandolfo points out numerous areas that merit careful thought. I will limit my comments to three areas of Ps 22, all of which stem from Mandolfo's reading.

First, despite their apparent familiarity, the opening words of the poem ("My God, my God") are actually quite rare in the Hebrew Bible. By commencing in this manner, the poet expresses a certain familiarity with God, and thus the hearer of the poem might be prepared for a number of creative variations of the typical lament genre. What interests me most in the opening section, however, are the words in verse 8 (English text), where the insults of passersby are quoted by the poet: "Roll over to the LORD! Let him rescue him. Let him deliver him, for he delights in him!" If Mandolfo is right—that the first hints of the DV occur as early as verse 3—then one might expect the DV at this particular place in the poem as well. But instead of a typical DV, the poet quotes the "voice" of his opponents, and their language could well be that of a conventional DV pastoral encouragement. In this context, the DV is "silenced," as it were, by the voices of mockery and sarcasm, thus heightening the supplicant's despair as expected words from the DV are confiscated by the jeering crowd.

Second, the pivotal line of the poem is probably verse 21b, since, as Mandolfo maintains, the rest of poem (for the most part) is the assumed DV. Line 21b, as a brief comparative survey will illustrate, can be translated in at least one different way. Instead of "from the horns of wild oxen rescue me," I am tempted to follow the lead of those translators who resist the path of emendation and render the line as, "and from the horns of the wild oxen you have answered me" (ומקרני רמים עניתני). After a long string of images that range from ravenous beasts to horrific personal injuries, the "answer" of line 21b is an unexpected interruption. Somewhere between the mouth of the lion and the horns of the ox, the lament is interrupted with an actual rescue, and even the awkward syntax suggests an element of surprise from the poet's point of view. The surprise answer certainly works as an effective point of transition to the rest of the poem, where the supplicant becomes a virtual DV. At the moment when hope seems most distant, the poet receives an answer just like his "ancestors" are described as being saved at the beginning of the psalm. The resultant situation created by this moment of stunning reversal must be one more example of what Ellen Davis describes as "exploding the limits" in this psalm.

Third, the psalm moves to a conclusion with spatial and temporal settings that are universal in scope and dimension. All the families of the earth, regardless of race or class, are included in the great assembly who experience of the kingdom of the Lord. Even the dead—those who have intimate experience with laments, I reckon—are included! The "present congregation" is quite a crowd, but the poet also looks to the distant future and describes a new generation who "will report his righteousness to people yet to be born, that it is finished!" The DV—that of the supplicant himself—represents the voice of one who has been dramatically rescued from the very horns of the wild beast, who has not been abandoned even though all hope was lost. As the psalm draws to a close, the DV has become a "dialogic voice" with a startling vision, and the expansion of the lament genre creates a new kind of consciousness in the reader. Through Mandolfo's essay, I think I grasped for a moment why this particular psalm generates such passion in the New Testament, and she has pointed out a line of inquiry that is worthy of future research.

After hearing David Valeta present a paper at an SBL Annual Meeting a few years ago, I was certain that I would never read the words in Daniel "O king, live forever" in quite the same way. Now, after reading this present essay on the use of language in Dan 1–6, terms such as "syllepsis" are part of my everyday vocabulary. I should also confess that in my younger days I never really got into the book of Daniel, probably because academic discussions of the book inevitably revolved around the rather sterile issue of its date of composition. While unstated, there was an implicit coercion as well: if one did not accept the obvious second-century dating, then one would always be somewhat naïve. Just bow down before the lute and zither of Achaemenid provenance, and the gold statue of the establishment would roll out the welcome mat.

My impression of this paper is that Valeta does well to move beyond the discussion of date and redaction by raising some very engaging questions about irony, parody, and humor in the book of Daniel. On that note, I was intrigued by his discussion of Dan 5 and how this chapter both interacts with surrounding material and contributes to the larger theme of the book with its own distinct contribution. For instance, in chapter 2 we have a king who demands an "interpretation" but does not trust his professional staff of interpreters, for fear they are "yes-people" and will only tell him what he wants to hear. In chapter 5, the situation is the parodic opposite, with a king who is desperate for any interpretation of the cryptic graffiti on the wall. As it turns out, the king has several layers of desperation, and the dire straights are nicely captured in the inimitable KJV:

> They drank wine, and praised the gods of gold, and of silver, of brass, of iron, of wood, and of stone. In the same hour came forth fingers of a man's hand, and wrote over against the candlestick upon the plaster of the wall of the king's palace: and the king saw the part of the hand that wrote. Then the king's countenance was changed, and his thoughts troubled him, so that the joints of his loins were loosed [וקטרי חרצה משתרין], and his knees smote one against another. (Dan 5:4–6)

"For all the high and mighty airs that kings exhibit," says Valeta, "they are still quite human with all the frailties that go with it." As Belshazzar's party moves into full swing, the "frailties" appear remote, as he and his inebriated colleagues drink "before a thousand" and then order the goblets from the house of God in Jerusalem to be brought forth. But it is at this hour that the frailties can be ascertained by both eye and nose. Not only does the color drain from the royal face when he sees the hand, but other (more alarming, perhaps) physiological anxieties are triggered, as the knots of the monarchial loins are loosened (וקטרי חרצה משתרין), and "his knees this way and that were knocking." So paralyzed, the king calls on the enchanters to interpret the writing, with the promise of lavish rewards, but the request is futile, as none can unravel the mystery. There follows a bit of a stalemate, until the surprising entrance onto the stage by a new character, the queen mother, who proceeds to make a long speech to the king of the loose loins,

> O king, live for ever: let not thy thoughts trouble thee, nor let thy counte-
> nance be changed: There is a man in thy kingdom, in whom is the spirit of
> the holy gods; and in the days of thy father light and understanding and
> wisdom, like the wisdom of the gods, was found in him; whom the king
> Nebuchadnezzar thy father, the king, I say, thy father, made master of the
> magicians, astrologers, Chaldeans, and soothsayers; Forasmuch as an excel-
> lent spirit, and knowledge, and understanding, interpreting of dreams, and
> shewing of hard sentences, and dissolving of doubts [ומשרא קטרין], were
> found in the same Daniel, whom the king named Belteshazzar: now let
> Daniel be called, and he will shew the interpretation. (Dan 5:10–12)

Throughout Dan 1–6, Valeta maintains, "the Aramaic language is being used in a creative and sarcastic manner." There certainly is such evidence in the queen mother's speech, but first one might wonder why this particular character is a principal carrier of wordplay in this stretch of narrative. Valeta cites the possibility that a female character is used to heighten the sarcasm of the scene, and such a notion is plausible when one considers that the queen mother is the figure who narrates past events to a drunk and soiled Belshaz-zar and provides lessons from recent history about antecedent monarchs who have listened to "a man of your kingdom." Not only does this character outline Daniel's *vita* to Belshazzar, but the queen mother also mentions the official name change, yet then calls him "Daniel" when encouraging the king to summon him. Daniel is the one, she claims, who will "dissolve doubts" (as the KJV renders the line). However, Valeta (noting the work of A. Wolters and S. Paul), points out a wordplay: the queen mother literally says that Daniel has skill in "loosening knots" (ומשרא קטרין), words that form the core of expression used above when the knots of the royal loins are loosened. Such a wordplay unquestionably comes across as satirical.

For the first time in the chapter, Belshazzar does a sensible thing by lis-tening to the maternal advice and calling forth Daniel. Yet in the ensuing interview the king does not look overly impressive. He begins by stating Daniel's pedigree as a child of captivity, then informs him that while the conjurers of the realm cannot solve this problem, Daniel is the one who can loosen his knots (וקטרין למשרא). So, Daniel is second choice over the wise men, yet it is the captive from Judah who is the only one who can read the Aramaic language. To be sure, it is Belshazzar who is looking rather ridiculous at this moment, with defiled royal garments and all. It is no wonder that Daniel tersely begins his reply by explaining that the king can keep his presents to himself. This carnivalesque moment is not only worthy of Rabelais but must contribute to the larger satirical vision of the Dan 1–6, and if chapter 5 represents Belshazzar's last night, then he exits the stage of this world in a rather embarrassing manner. One of the classic reasons for wordplay is to underscore a reversal of fortune, and the king's knotty problem is humbling in a most scatological manner. As David Valeta affirms, the resources of the Aramaic language are used for subversion and satire, and the day of judgment arrives in Belshazzar's court just as it visits other earthly empires that set themselves up against the Most High God.

Response—Using Bakhtin's *Lexicon Dialogicae* to Interpret Canon, Apocalyptic, New Testament, and Toni Morrison

Vernon K. Robbins

When Kenneth Burke wanted to define the principles underlying the appeal of literature in 1931, he discussed thirty-nine topics in a chapter entitled "*Lexicon Rhetoricae*" (1968:123–83). When Michael Holquist published M. M. Bakhtin's *The Dialogic Imagination* in 1981, he included a glossary with forty major topics, under which were many subtopics, to explain the way Bakhtin invests everyday words with special content to explain his theory of language and literature (1981:423–34). These topics and subtopics function as a *lexicon dialogicae* that reconfigures multiple aspects of the *lexicon rhetoricae* that emerged from the work of Burke and others during the twentieth century (Bizzell and Herzberg 1990:897–1266).

The contributors to this volume either discuss or refer in the introduction to nine topics or subtopics that appear in the 1981 glossary of Bakhtin's words (genre [428], monologic [monoglossia: 430], dialogic [dialogism: 426–27], voice [434], chronotope [425–26], polyphony [polyglossia: 431], unfinalizability [completed: 426], heteroglossia [428], and dialogization [427]). They also discuss a term not included in the glossary, carnivalesque, which Bakhtin did not feature in the four essays in *The Dialogic Imagination* but which played a major role in *Rabelais and His World* and *Problems of Dostoyevsky's Poetics*. By my count, the essays I have been asked to review (Buss, Newsom, Vines, Fuller, Anderson, and Maddison) in some manner or another refer to approximately twenty-five of the forty topics or subtopics in the glossary. The point is that they discuss more than half of Bakhtin's overall lexicon as it is displayed in *The Dialogic Imagination*.

One should readily grant that it would be cumbersome to create a Semeia Studies volume for people interested in biblical interpretation that contained all of the special terms Holquist included in the 1981 glossary to exhibit the nature of Bakhtin's dialogical, heteroglossic hermeneutical system. But if we cannot expect all of them to appear, how many should we expect in six essays on biblical canon, apocalyptic, New Testament, and Toni Morrison so they present a substantive Bakhtinian approach? We get, perhaps as one might expect, significantly different uses and highly varied applications of aspects of Bakhtin's approach to language and literature in these six essays. For the most part, the authors energize in one way or another an approach to biblical literature in which they, or some others in the field of biblical scholarship, have been engaged for a number of decades, or even for a century. The exception is the author of the essay on Toni Morrison's *Beloved*. Using the skills and resources available to a modern literary critic, the author of this essay makes this biblical scholar yearn for a time when biblical scholarship will be able to embed its remarkable knowledge in even more dynamic modes of analysis and interpretation than have been evolving during the last four decades. But now let us turn to the authors of these six essays by name.

Martin Buss, entitling his essay "Dialogue in and among Genres," uses Bakhtin's concepts of genre, voice, and dialogue as he discusses issues concerning the Hebrew Bible canon he has discussed in three earlier contexts: an essay on form criticism (1974); an essay on Hosea as a canonical problem (1996); and a chapter on "Implicit Recognition of Forms of Speech" in a chapter on "Biblical Patterns" in his book on *Biblical Form Criticism* (1999:27–30). When Buss introduces the term "genre" to the reader, he qualifies the term with "or speech type." His four assertions about genres in the Hebrew Bible either explicitly or implicitly lead to additional terms in the Bakhtinian *lexicon dialogicae*. Without referring to Bakhtin's distinction between "single-voiced discourse" (the dream of poets) and "double-voiced discourse" (the realm of the novel: 1981:324–31, 354, 434) or the "addressivity of the utterance" (1986:95–100), Buss asserts first that a genre can be identified on the basis of "the kind of address it embodies."

There are four kinds of address in particular, Buss suggests, that are helpful for analyzing genre in the Bible: (1) by God to humans; (2) by humans to God; (3) by humans to others about God; and (4) by humans to others without reference to God. This leads to a second assertion that the Hebrew Bible is largely arranged according to genres, namely, kinds of speech (see Buss 1999:27). Buss mentions five kinds: law, prophecy, narrative, proverb, and reflective discussion, which he introduces with a special eye on Job and Qoheleth. These five kinds, he suggests, tend to be gathered together either to create an entire writing or to form a particular section of a writing. In 1999 he also observed that "the vast majority of psalms" are gathered "in just one book" (27). It would have been highly appropriate for Buss to observe that Bakhtin perceived this kind of "gathering together" to be a centralizing force in any language or culture, which he considered to be a "centripetal influence," a participation in the "unitary language," that was caused by the rulers and high poetic genres of any era (1981:272–73, 425). A discussion of the centripetal forces and tendencies in every utterance leads naturally, in Bakhtin's thought, to a discussion of the centrifugal, stratifying forces in every utterance, namely, social and historical heteroglossia.

This leads naturally to Buss's third assertion, that there is variety within each genre. From Bakhtin's perspective, the variety functions as a decentralizing and dispersing force that creates "alternative 'degraded' genres down below" (1981:425). Explicit use of Bakhtin's concepts of centripetal and centrifugal forces within concrete utterances in a discussion of canon in the essay could have led, I suggest, to very interesting observations about the kinds of "extracanonical" literature that emerged during the third, second, and first centuries B.C.E. and the kinds of "degraded" genres (Gospels, letters, and apocalypse) that became central to the New Testament canon. It also would be interesting to know if Buss considers any of the genres in the Hebrew Bible to feature soliloquy, monologic discourse in Bakhtin's terminology. Jack Miles asserts that God talks to himself during the creation and again just after the flood, but from the call of Abraham onward, "every word he says is specifically addressed" (2001:41). Then, concerning the New Testament Miles asserts: "The Gospel of John reads at times like a book-length soliloquy with occasional digressions into conversation" (41). Does Buss see any genre in the Hebrew Bible that does not feature "dialogue"? It appears that the answer is no.

Buss's observation about variety in each genre leads him to a fourth assertion about the potential fruitfulness of dialogue between the Hebrew Bible and other bodies of tradition. Here one wonders if Buss remains in Bakhtin's conceptual domain of thinking about language and literature. Buss asserts that dialogue between traditions is likely to be most productive when similar genres are put in dialogue with one another through comparison. But is this what Bakhtin would say? Would Bakhtin focus instead on comparing any two utterances that are somehow similar, whether or not the interpreter perceives them to be "of a similar genre"? The point would be that any two utterances that an interpreter is somehow able to put in dialogue with one another may produce what Bakhtin called "interanimation" or "interillumination" (1981:429–30). Indeed, might Bakhtin have considered it to be more productive to compare discourses in different traditions on the basis of their chronotopes? It is obvious that Buss finds Bakhtin to be a fellow traveler in many respects as he investigates the Hebrew Bible canon with deep philosophical understandings of the nature of language, literature, and form. Perhaps deeper probing into Bakhtin's dialogical lexicon in the essay could have made the interesting observations about form and the Hebrew Bible canon even more accessible and usable to other interpreters, whether they be interpreters of the New Testament or the Qur'an, Hindu, or Buddhist literature, or any other kind of literature, sacred or otherwise.

As Buss's essay unfolds, it seems to be building on Bakhtin's concept of "everyday genre," as it is translated in the 1981 glossary: "what ordinary people live, and their means for communicating with each other" (428). This would seem to be the effect of Buss's emphasis on "life process," rather than on Gunkel's focus on "life situation," for identification of a genre. The emphasis on everyday life emerges in Buss's discussion of wisdom literature when he postulates that this genre was perhaps produced by religiously "lay" persons and "included many who were not highly specialized," in contrast to singers, priests, and prophets. A major issue here is the "dimension of life" Buss emphasizes as foundational for study of genres. Rather than focusing on "situations," he emphasizes that any one of three criteria—life process, content, or verbal form—can represent a genre. This means that anything like a greeting, conversation about the weather, death notice, or theology can be a genre. Perhaps Bakhtin's view of "zone," namely, "the locus for hearing a voice," which is "brought about *by* the voice" (1981:434), is related to Buss's assertions here. Bakhtin thought there were disputed zones, but never empty ones. Thus, people's intentions and speech must pass through zones dominated by other people "and are therefore refracted" (434). Is this what Buss is talking about when he says that culturally significant genres, each representing a dimension of life, "engage metaphorically in a dialogue with one another"? Metaphor, as it is currently understood, is "typically based on cross-domain correlations in our experience, which give rise to the perceived similarities between the two domains within the metaphor" (Lakoff and Johnson 2003:245). Is this what Buss means by genres engaging "metaphorically in a dialogue with one another"?

Holquist does not include "metaphor" in the 1981 Bakhtin glossary or index, nor does it appear in the index of *Speech Genres and Other Late Essays* or his books on formal method (1978), art (1990), or a philosophy of the act (1993). In fact, it may be the case that a major reason Bakhtin's *lexicon dialogicae* is not more prominent in current studies of language and literature is the absence of any significant focus on metaphor in the approach. Buss uses the term *metaphor*, but he does not clarify how he perceives "metaphorical dialogue" to function in this context, nor does he mention that he is reaching beyond Bakhtin's terms of interest when he introduces it into his discussion. Perhaps the reason is that Buss is more interested to assert that "dialogues exist metaphorically within genres," resulting in their not being "internally homogeneous," than to assert the effect of that metaphorical relationship. In the context of recognizing divergences within each genre, Buss suggests that his approach may stand close to Bahktin's carnival-like interpretation in *Rabelais and His World*, where there is an interplay between order and disorder. It seems to me that Buss does not develop this further simply because he thinks this is the nature of everyday life. Speech acts and therefore genres, in Buss's view, mix things together, because people engaged in life mix things together. In the process of mixing things together, however, humans give "form" to speech and therefore form to literature. This is indeed very close to Bakhtin's approach. If he were so inclined, Buss could, it seems to me, relate many more aspects of his approach to form, genre, and canon specifically to Bakhtin's *lexicon dialogicae* than he does in this essay. The issue here, of course, is the effectiveness of using Bakhtin's terminology. Perhaps it is best to appropriate and adapt the concepts of other interpreters rather than to use their specific terminology. This is certainly an issue with Burke's *lexicon rhetoricae* as well as Bahktin's *lexicon dialogicae*. It is understandable that Buss considers it more important to explain his approach in relation to the approach of Hermann Gunkel, who was a founder of form criticism in Hebrew Bible studies. Buss significantly tips his hat to Bakhtin in this essay, but he exercises notable restraint in the use of Bakhtin's terminology to explain his approach to form and canon in the Hebrew Bible.

When Carol Newsom discusses genre in her essay, she also exercises restraint in her use of Bakhtinian terminology. When she refers to "genre" at the beginning of her essay, she immediately refers to "genology," a term I have not found in writings attributed to Bakhtin. Observing that Gunkel and other form critics were interested in oral *Gattungen*, she rightly considers their approach to have some kind of intriguing relation to Bakhtin's reflection on "speech genres." As she moves her reflections to "apocalypse" in biblical studies, she introduces the phrase "metaphors and images" in her discussion of "members" of a genre and a genre's "boundaries." Citing the work of Jacques Derrida as helpful for thinking of genre in relation to a text's "rhetorical orientation," she introduces Adena Rosmarin's *The Power of Genre* (1985), which draws on art historian E. H. Gombrich's dictum that "all thinking is sorting, classifying," to assert that "the 'validity' of a genre category has to do with its potential for creating new critical insight rather than with its correspondence to the author's own sense of genre" (Newsom).

Observing that genre recognition involves some sort of "mental grouping of texts," Newsom appeals to Wittgenstein's notion of family resemblance as a bridge to Alastair Fowler's notion of kinds of literature (1982) and Jonathan Culler's notion of intertextuality (1975). In all of this, there is no further reference to Bakhtin. Rather, there is an implication that the issue of genre in relation to a text's rhetorical orientation leads directly from Bakhtin's approach to language and literature to these more recent studies. The goal of the forward movement of her essay is to arrive at the domain of present-day cognitive theory and to use insights into "prototypes" as they were studied in the 1970s by Eleanor Rosch (1975; 1978). At this point she takes the reader on an intriguing tour of references to "highly typical" and "less typical" apocalypses outside both the Hebrew Bible and New Testament canons, introducing an analogy with members and "quasi-members" of a club to characterize their relation to the "genre" apocalypse. Then, referring to the approach of Michael Sinding (2002), she observes a limit of this approach, since "prototype theory operates ahistorically." It is "extremely important," she asserts, that any theory of genre be able to incorporate "historical" information and insight into the genre that is the focus of the study. The case in point is apocalypses, which emerged sometime in the third century B.C.E. and reached their demise within Judaism in the aftermath of the Bar Kokhba revolt, even though they continued to be written in Christian circles.

Only after a rich tour through various theories and texts does Newsom's essay return to Bakhtin. It might be possible, she suggests, to recast Fowler's observation of "a process of continuous metamorphosis" within any literary genre in terms of Bakhtin's "notion of texts as utterances in dialogical relationship to one another." Calling attention to Bakhtin's perception of a "profound conservatism" within genres, she cites his dictum that "a genre is always the same and yet not the same, always old and new simultaneously" (Bakhtin 1984:106). Bahktin's approach, therefore, brings together the synchronic and diachronic elements of genre. In the end, Newsom concludes that Bakhtin is more suggestive than systematic in his reflections on genre. For this reason, recent cognitive theory, which works with "the mechanisms of mental creativity" and works systematically with "conceptual blending," is a necessary supplement to Bakhtin's work. Thus, throughout her essay Newsom prefers to build on insights in the Bakhtin corpus rather than to use terms beyond "speech genre" to discuss the "genology" of apocalypse. At the very end, she introduces the term "chronotope" and proposes that, while it "has mostly been explored in relation to narrative structures, there is no reason why it would not be fruitful for other types of literature." Thus, chronotope could be another useful concept to use for study of apocalypse, but Newsom leaves its application to the genre apocalypse for another time and place. This is a rich, creative, and highly productive essay, to be sure, focusing on the relation of Bakhtin's concept of "speech genre" to recent theories of genre and cognitive science. It leaves the reader with intriguing ideas about genre "prototypes" and the possibility of applying the concept of "chronotope" not only to novels but also to apocalypses.

Michael Vines picks up where Newsom ends, with an investigation of "The Apocalyptic Chronotope." As his essay proceeds, it discusses genre, chronotope, and architectonic form in Bakhtin's *lexicon dialogicae* and adds a new term, "form-shaping ideology," which appears to have been coined in the essays in *Mikhail Bakhtin: Creation of a Prosaics* (1990:367). The underlying premises of this essay reside in a blending of M. M. Bakhtin/P. N. Medvedev, *The Formal Method in Literary Scholarship* (1978) with M. M. Bakhtin, *Art and Answerability* (1990), neither of which Vines cited in the version sent to me for review. This means that, while the essay features "chronotope," which is highly important in *The Dialogic Imagination* (1981:84–258) and *Speech Genres and Other Late Essays* (1986:25–54), the philosophical underpinnings for the argument lie in two books that do not contain the word *chronotope* in their index. The approach Vines presents merges the sharply defined "critical sociological poetics" in *The Formal Method* with aspects of the two major sections of *Art and Answerability*: "Author and Hero in Aesthetic Activity" (4–256) and "Supplement: The Problem of Content, Material, and Form in Verbal Art" (257–325). In other words, rather than being guided by a definition of ideology as "simply an idea-system" that is "semiotic in the sense that it involves the concrete exchange of signs in society and in history" so that "[e]very speaker … is an ideologue and every utterance an ideologeme" (Bakhtin 1981:429), Vines's essay is guided by a critical sociological poetic that emphasizes "the distinctive features of the material, forms, and purposes of each area of ideological creation," whether that area is "art, science, ethics, or religion" (Bakhtin/Medvedev 1978:3). In the essay, Vines prefers the terminology in the "Supplement" (Bakhtin 1990:257–325), where the word "content" replaces the word "purposes."

Thus, when Vines refers to "architectonic form," his assertions relate to Bakhtin/Medvedev's comments about "the constructive unity of the work" that makes a work of art "a closed spatial body" (1978:45–46), but he uses the language of the work's "unification and organization of cognitive and ethical values" from *Art and Answerability* (1990:304). Arguing against "material aesthetics," Bakhtin/Medvedev asserted: "Architectonic forms are forms of the inner and bodily value of aesthetic man, they are forms of nature—as his environment, forms of the event in his individual-experiential, social, and historical dimensions, and so on" (1990:270). Here there is an argument for a bodily aesthetics as an alternative to material aesthetics, although I cannot find any place where the phrase "bodily aesthetics" actually appears to describe it. The argument does, it seems to me, bring the presentation very close to assertions by the conceptual metaphor theorist Mark Johnson in his book *The Body in the Mind* (1987). If so, this provides an important link between Bakhtin/Medvedev's work and some of the most exciting and potentially fruitful work in recent conceptual metaphor and conceptual integration (blending) theory (e.g., Fauconnier and Turner 2002; Lakoff and Johnson 2003:243–76).

When Vines introduces the phrase "form-shaping ideology," he is communicating Bakhtin/Medvedev's assertion that "the ideological horizon is constantly generating. And this generation, like all generation, is a dialectical process…. The artistic work … is penetrated by and absorbs some elements of the ideological environment and turns away other elements external to it" (1978:154). In this context, what Vines calls "an internal aspect" and "an external aspect" are translated as "intrinsic" and "extrinsic," with the assertion that "in the process of history, 'extrinsic' and 'intrinsic' dialectically change places, and, of course, do not remain unchanged as they do" (154). Vines's phrase "form-shaping ideology" substitutes "ideology" for Bakhtin's "author" when Bakhtin asserts that "An author is the uniquely active form-giving energy that is manifested not in a psychologically conceived consciousness, but in a durably valid cultural product, and his active, productive reaction is manifested in the structures it generates" (1990:8). Vines's depersonalization of the author into "form-shaping ideology" is a blending that overmaps the presentation in *Art and Answerability* with the philosophical argument in *The Formal Method*. The result is a Bakhtin that readers regularly do not see. We have not seen the Bakhtin Vines presents, because his "Bakhtin" is a blend of Medvedev and Bakhtin that gives priority to the philosophical hermeneutics in *The Formal Method* rather than the dialogical hermeneutics in *The Dialogic Imagination*.

When Vines introduces chronotope, the emphasis is related to Bakhtin/Medvedev's assertion: "The goal of the artistic structure of every historical genre is to merge the distances of space and time with the contemporary by the force of the all-penetrating social evaluation" (1978:158). Vines could have helped his readers by discussing the emphasis on "social evaluation" in *The Formal Method*. In that work, "social evaluation" is "the element which unites the material presence of the word with its meaning" (149). For Bakhtin/Medvedev, social evaluation is the primary dimension missing from the history of interpretation of literature and art. Since "[e]very concrete utterance is a social act" (120), "[s]ocial evaluation actualizes the utterance both from the standpoint of its factual presence and the standpoint of its semantic meaning" (121).

The philosophical grounding of the "special" Bakhtinian assertions about genre that Vines presents in his essay, therefore, is to be found in the presentation of literature as "a three-dimensional constructive whole" (1987:130). In *The Formal Method*, these dimensions are called "forms, means, and concrete conditions of communication" (152). In *Art and Answerability*, "forms" becomes "form," "means" becomes "content," and "concrete conditions of communication" becomes "material." Vines has chosen the singular terms *form*, *content*, and *material* rather than the plural terms *forms*, *means*, and *concrete conditions of communication.* This becomes very important as Vines moves to his emphasis on "meta-linguistic form," "architectonic form," "form-shaping ideology," "chronotope," "genre," and "essential unity," all of which are singular constructs. In highly important ways, Vines's essay leaves behind the plurality of Bakhtin's heteroglossia and dialogism to present "singular" concepts that guide the reader's understanding toward *the* chronotope that presents *the* essential unity of *the* genre of apocalyptic.

This means that the reader yearns to see more of Bakhtin's dialogism as Vines's essay unfolds (cf. Gowler). But the absence of a discussion of the dialogic nature of apocalyptic is not just an oversight. Vines thinks only modern writings are truly dialogical. In contrast, ancient works "remain essentially monologic, since the values of the author control the representation of the dialogic voices within the text and distort their perspective on life." The control about which Vines speaks is activated by the author in the context of an "external" ideological environment in which the author performs the ideological artistic act of constructing the literary work. The act of constructing the work produces a dynamic merger of form, content, and material (all singulars) that produce an essential unity.

Vines would have done well in his essay to use Bakhtin's distinction between primary and secondary genres (1986:62), which he explains very adroitly in his earlier work on Markan genre (Vines 2002:55). Apocalypse, in Bakhtin's system, seems quite clearly to be a secondary genre, at least when it began during the third and second centuries B.C.E. This means that apocalypse is derivative of one or more primary genres, "formed through the incorporation and modification of various types of speech genres for specific purposes" (Vines 2002:55). In the context of a secondary genre, each primary genre "serves a more complex ideological function than the one it once had in everyday speech. Within the secondary genre, it functions as an indirect indicator of condensed social evaluations" (55; cf. Bakhtin 1986:62).

Vines makes excellent observations about the relation of biblical prophecy to apocalypse. He observes that both types of literature are "clearly revelatory and concerned with bringing a divine perspective to bear on the human condition." Also, he observes that both include "the fantastic" in a context where temporal and spatial boundaries are permeable. Then he astutely observes three differences: (1) the prophetic hero is active; the apocalyptic hero is passive; (2) prophetic tests the faithfulness of the prophet to confront a hostile audience with the word of God, while apocalyptic tests the cosmos in the context of the witness and internalization of the revelation by the apocalyptic seer; and (3) prophetic alternates between fantastic and realistic, while apocalyptic is more firmly rooted in the fantastic and the supernatural. Does this mean that prophetic is "serving a more ideological function" in a "secondary" genre, namely, apocalyptic?

Vines should have supplemented his excellent comparison of prophetic and apocalyptic with a comparison of speculative wisdom and apocalyptic. Students of apocalyptic know that recent scholarship not only observes a relation of apocalyptic to prophetic but also to wisdom (Wright and Wills 2005). Speculative wisdom also is significantly revelatory and concerned to bring a divine perspective to bear on the human condition. Also, its spatial and temporal boundaries are significantly permeable. What is the relation of the speculative sapiential hero to the prophetic and apocalyptic hero? What is the nature of test in speculative wisdom? What is the nature of the fantastic in relation to the realistic in speculative wisdom?

Do prophetic and wisdom function as "primary genres" in the secondary genre of apocalypse? Or have prophetic and wisdom become secondary genres in the context of apocalypse as a primary genre? Perhaps this could improve Vines's discussion of what John Collins calls Type I apocalypses (mystical visions) and Type II apocalypses (heavenly journeys). Vines asserts that the differences between the two types "appears to be only formal" in a context where they share the same "chronotope." Therefore, they belong to the same genre: apocalypse. Could a broader approach to apocalyptic, which has an eye both on prophetic and wisdom in apocalyptic, help with this analysis? Could Type I apocalypse (mystical vision) be a blend of visions both by prophets and speculative sages? Do both prophetic and wisdom function as secondary genres in Type I apocalyptic, or is Type I apocalyptic a secondary genre in which primary prophetic and wisdom genres function more ideologically than they conventionally did in Israelite culture? Alternatively, does prophetic journeying function as a secondary genre in Type II apocalyptic, or is Type II apocalyptic a secondary genre in which prophetic journeying and speculative wisdom function more ideologically than they conventionally did in Israelite culture?

One of the questions here is if a primary genre is a genre that has become "culturally conventional." Once a genre has become "primary," namely, culturally conventional, is it available for a more ideological use in a new, "secondary" genre? When a secondary genre has existed for a century or more, can it become "culturally conventional," namely, a "primary" genre? This takes us back to Newsom's essay on genre and prototype theory. When Ezekiel, 1 Enoch, and Daniel were written, were they "secondary apocalyptic genre" that functioned as "atypical prophetic literature"? When the Revelation to John became culturally conventional (a "primary" genre) in Christianity, did this make Ezekiel, 1 Enoch, and Daniel "typical apocalyptic literature"? Does 1 Enoch at some point become a "primary" genre after the emergence of the Revelation to John? The point, so well made by most of the authors of this volume, is that genre is both a diachronic and synchronic interpretive category. This means that it is necessary to maintain a dialogic relation between diachronicity and synchronicity in our discussions of genre. Vines's essay gives new life in many ways to genre analysis of apocalypse. Maintaining more of Bahktin's dialogism through analysis of the ways in which speech genres function culturally and ideologically in apocalypses might help us to build on his initial steps in ways that enable us to explain more successfully the remarkably complex relationships among different kinds of literature in the environment of biblical studies. The issue, however, is how Bakhtin understood dialogism in relation to chronotopes, and this leads us to the next essay.

Christopher Fuller discusses chronotopes in relation to the genealogy in Matt 1:1–17. He begins with a clarification that, for Bakhtin, chronotopes are not dialogical internally in the represented world of the work (Bakhtin 1981:252). Their function as "organizing centers" for a narrative "materializes" time and space in "the represented world of the text" in a manner that is primarily monological. A chronotope functions dialogically in relation to worlds outside the text, namely, the world of the reader and the "creating world" that emerges "to readers within different contexts and different historical periods." Fuller's phrase "creating world" is shorthand for Bakhtin's "special *creative* chronotope inside which th[e] exchange between work and life occurs, and which constitutes the distinctive life of the work" (1981:254). One of the keys to Fuller's approach is the concept of a genre as "a form of thinking." Another is a concept from the work of Jay Ladin of "local chronotopes" (1999). Fuller's procedure is to analyze and interpret dialogical relationships between the Matthean genealogy as a local chronotope and other local chronotopes.

Fuller begins with analysis of the temporal nature of the Matthean genealogy, namely, its linear progression from Abraham to the Messiah of Israel. Since this feature is present in the internal wording of the genealogy, his interpretation, as he says, does not argue for anything "that is foreign to standard scholarship on Matthew's genealogy." When he proceeds to the chronotopic focus on space, which "Matthean scholars have ignored," he does not tell the reader that scholars have ignored the spaces to which he points because these spaces exist in worlds "external" to the words in the text he is interpreting. Only one of the spaces is internal to the wording of the Matthean genealogy: the deportation of Israel to Babylonia (Matt 1:11–12, 17). All the other spaces (the movement of Abraham to another land, the movement of Judah and his brothers to Egypt, the desert wanderings, entry into the Holy Land, settling in Bethlehem, and Jerusalem becoming the capital of the kingdom of Israel and the location for the First and Second

Temples) are external to its wording. Thus the spatial dimensions Fuller cites, except for the deportation to Babylon, are all "intertextual" rather than "intratextual," residing in potential "local chronotopes" either in the world of the reader or in the creating world that lies between the reader and the text. It would be interesting to hear a discussion of the possibility that the one spatial reference, namely, to the deportation, encourages the reader to engage in dialogical conceptuality of the other spaces Fuller evokes in his interpretation of the Matthean genealogy.

For Fuller, the possibility that the Matthean genealogy can function as a local chronotope that exists in a dialogical relation to other local chronotopes both in Matthew and outside it lies in the relationship of genres, chronotopes, and utterances to memory. For Bakhtin, Fuller asserts, genre is "a form of thinking." Genres are forms of thinking, chronotopes in genres are special ways of thinking about time and space, and utterances are the speech genres that create genres and chronotopes. This means that genres, chronotopes, and utterances bear "the memory of their prior use whenever they are employed in other contexts." Here it is important to notice the internal dialogue in the approach between the personification of genre, chronotope, and utterance and the depersonalization of authors as form-shaping ideologies. Underlying Bakhtin's approach is a dialogism between social evaluation that is so deeply embedded in words, works, and genres that there is no way justifiably to escape their "bodily conceptuality" (my terminology) and ideology that depersonalizes authors into form, content, and material.

The bodiness of genres, chronotopes, and utterances means, for Bakhtin, that they not only think, but they also bear memories of their prior use. Fuller uses this memory to argue for "eschatological satire" in the Matthean genealogy. The Matthean genealogy includes four women for the purpose of subverting primogeniture. This act of subversion is a way of inviting "the reader to reevaluate other matters alluded to in the genealogy such as the chronotopic relationships between salvation history, land and temple." Like Bakhtin's menippean satire (1984:147), "[s]candal, eccentricity, impropriety, and cultural contravention are all present in Matthew's genealogy when it is read 'like' Bakhtin." This satire does not produce laughter, however, but "an overturning of cultural and narrative expectations through the active participation of the reader." It is eschatological satire, akin in many ways to Bakhtin's concept of the carnivalesque.

In the end, Fuller's essay uses not only Bakhtin's works but interpretations of Bakhtin's work to introduce a number of additional terms or phrases into a Bakhtinian *lexicon dialogicae* for biblical study: local chronotope, creating world, form-shaping ideology, genre as a form of thinking, memory, and eschatological satire. One of the questions Fuller leaves unaddressed is the relation of the local chronotope in the Matthean genealogy to other local chronotopes in Matthew. On the one hand, Fuller implies that the eschatological satire present in the local chronotope in the genealogy echoes throughout the remainder of the First Gospel. This could mean that the genealogy is a microcosm of the chronotope that unifies the overall Gospel of Matthew. This view would cohere with Bakhtin's assertion that chronotopes are not dialogical in the represented world of the text. On the other hand, Fuller asserts that local chronotopes are present in "forms" like the genealogy. Since local chronotopes exist in dialogical relationships to one another, is it possible that other forms in Matthew contain alternative local chronotopes that introduce dialogism into the represented world in Matthew? If this is possible, it could mean that Jay Ladin's view of local chronotope introduces the possibility of types of chronotopic dialogism in the represented world of the text of a work that conflicts with Bakhtin's assertions about chronotopes. Bakhtin strongly asserts that, while chronotopes exist in dialogical relationships to one another, "this dialogue cannot enter into the world represented in the work, nor into any of the chronotopes represented in it; it is outside the world represented, although not outside the work as a whole. It [this dialogue] enters the world of the author, of the performer, and the world of the listeners and readers. And all these worlds are chronotopic as well" (1981:252). Where does this leave us with the concept of "local chronotope"? It is clear that biblical interpreters, who have been trained in source, form, and tradition criticism, may want "local chronotopes" that have dialogical relationships to one another within the represented world of a work. But this appears not to be what Bakhtin saw. Vines's assertion in the previous essay about Bakhtin's perception, that there is only one chronotope in the represented world of a work, appears to present Bakhtin's view correctly. What, then, is the relation of multiple "local chronotopes" to one another in the represented world of a work? Are all of them, with the memories they bear, submissive to the chronotope that unifies the work? It appears that evoking the "memories" of each local chronotope introduces both the world outside the text and the "creating world" of readers. It appears that, for Bakhtin, the represented world of a work contains "a chronotope," which would mean that all local chronotopes exist outside the world of the represented text. Are some modern interpreters questioning this conclusion by Bakhtin through a concept of "local chronotope"? Or do those who use the concept keep it thoroughly within Bakhtin's system? More extended use of the concept by interpreters will tell us if perhaps this is a post-Bakhtinian way to introduce dialogism into a chronotope in the represented world of a work, where Bakhtin did not think it was present.

Paul N. Anderson discusses aspects of Bakhtin's dialogism in the initial pages of his essay, refers to Bakhtin periodically in the sections on the rhetorical function and form of the Johannine misunderstanding dialogue that reveal seven crises in the Johannine community, and returns to a discussion of Bakhtin in the conclusion. The essay focuses on "ironic misunderstanding" that targets "privileged" or "authoritative" groups and characters, which Bakhtin discusses in Cervantes and Dostoevsky. To set the stage for his analysis, Anderson argues, appealing to C. K. Barrett for support, that Plato's presentation of Socrates with naïve students and noncomprehending audiences represents the "highly parallel" narrative presentation of importance for analysis of the Johannine misunderstanding dialogues. The effect of this argument is to make Socratic dialogue primary to Bakhtin's view of dialogism for interpreting the Johannine misunderstanding dialogues. In accord with this effect, the essay uses a limited number of concepts from Bakhtin's *lexicon dialogicae*. Rather than applying Bakhtinian terminology as a strategic driving force for the analysis and interpretation, the essay uses the conventional status of Plato's dialogues of Socrates to challenge well-known New Testament scholarship and refers to Bakhtin periodically as support for the way in which the analysis and interpretation proceeds in the essay.

Most of the discussion in the essay is well-known to readers who have followed analysis and interpretation of the Gospel of John during the last thirty-five years. One of the most promising moments emerges when Anderson refers to novels of the "First Stylistic Line," which approach heteroglossia from above, and the "Second Stylistic Line," which approach heteroglossia from below (Bakhtin 1981:399–422). Unfortunately, Anderson does not develop the differences between the two Stylistic Lines for the reader or use the concepts to drive the analysis from the beginning to the end of the essay. The essay could have made a truly substantive contribution to Bakhtinian interpretation of the Johannine misunderstanding dialogues if it had framed the overall discussion of the Johannine misunderstanding dialogues with Bakhtin's insights into First Stylistic Line and Second Stylistic Line novels. On the one hand, it is clear from Anderson's references to concepts such as parody, the "fool," incomprehension, and "ennobled" language that he at some time has worked carefully through the section on First and Second Stylistic Line novels in *The Dialogic Imagination* (1981:399–422). On the other hand, he does not tell the reader how the concepts he discusses work in each Stylistic Line novel and explain to the reader the remarkable mixture of First Stylistic Line and Second Stylistic Line aspects that are present in the misunderstanding dialogues in the Gospel of John. Rather than featuring Bakhtin's understanding of Stylistic Line in novels, the essay contains only one reference to each kind of Stylistic Line novel with some comments that support analysis and interpretation that is primarily informed by traditional New Testament scholarship.

In the end, the reader can express gratitude to Anderson for his energetic, perceptive work on the Johannine misunderstanding dialogues and encourage him to reconfigure his remarkable knowledge about Johannine scholarship for readers by employing multiple insights from Bakhtin about novels of the First Stylistic Line (the Sentimental novel, 1981:400) and the Second Stylistic Line (the picaresque adventure novel, 1981:406). Anderson's keen eye has located a very important "touch point" for analysis and interpretation of the Gospel of John in Bakhtin's contrast between these two "Stylistic Lines" of novel. Those of us interested in Bakhtinian readings of New Testament writings look forward, either from Anderson or someone else, to a programmatic reading of aspects of the Gospel of John that builds on the beginning points about Bakhtin's two alternative Stylistic Lines of novel that Anderson introduces in this study of the challenge to "privileged, authoritative" discourse in the Johannine misunderstanding dialogues.

Bula Maddison brings the volume to a conclusion with a stunning Bakhtinian analysis of Toni Morrison's *The Beloved*. Building on insights into double-voicedness, the inherent dialogism in the word (Bakhtin 1981:294), and heteroglossia, which she calls conversation between languages or language-worlds (291), she analyzes "dialogized heteroglossia," which occurs through "interanimation" (295–96). Bypassing debates about whether chronotopes can be dialogical within the represented world in the text, she points to Bakhtin's discussion of hybridization (305–15, 358–71) as a way to talk about four or more languages or belief systems that can be revised and shaped and reshaped in a novel as they contend with one another. By my count, she discusses six languages in *The Beloved*, which participate in two kinds of time—conventional time: (1) the Bible; (2) the African American slave narrative; and (3) the conventional love story; and cyclical African and African American time: (4) the spirit world of African cosmology; (5) the African American mythic origin story in the biblical exodus and conquest; and (6) the watery creation story. These six languages contend with one another over "the politics of fulfillment" (conventional time) and "the African chronotope of rememory" (cyclical time) in a dialogue between "liberation story" and "apocalypse."

In contrast to Josef Pesch's view of *The Beloved* as a postapocalyptic novel, Maddison views it as a hybrid in which two chronotopes contend in a context where the apocalypse happened before (eighteen years ago) and "the four horsemen might ride up again" any time. Her thesis is that "the spatialization of time" in the novel has many languages or language-worlds (heteroglossia: perhaps six) within two contending chronotopes. The force of her essay in this volume is to press the issue whether more than one chronotope exists in works in the New Testament, especially when so many of them not only contain allusions but also extensive quotations of entire lines from "scripture." In fact, the analysis might raise the specific question if some kind of cyclical time is at work in some of the "language-worlds" of the Bible. Perhaps, for example, the idea of a new Moses or a new Elijah is the result of two chronotopes, one of a "prophetic politics of fulfillment" and another of a "cyclical prophetic language," contending with one another in the context of multiple "biblical" and "extrabiblical" languages in the Mediterranean world. Perhaps earlier discussions in biblical interpretation about type and antitype were a way of talking about relationships among characters and events that exist in contending conceptualities of space and time, and in multiple languages and language-worlds. And perhaps references to "allegory" were yet another way. Is it the case, then, that only the modern novel and works contemporary with it contain pervasive dialogism and heteroglossia? Or is there pervasive dialogism and heteroglossia especially, perhaps, in deuterocanonical, pseudepigraphical, and New Testament literature during the Hellenistic-Roman period?

Whether biblical interpreters are able to answer these questions correctly or not, this volume of essays can help them to enrich their interpretational strategies and insights with the aid of insights from the works of Bakhtin. One of the major achievements is to help the reader to have a significant understanding of terms and phrases that are central to the Bakhtinian *lexicon dialogicae* beyond the well-known language of dialogism and heteroglossia. This includes, as they appear in alphabetical order in the glossary of *The Dialogical Imagination* (1981:423–34), the concepts of authoritative (privileged) discourse, belief system, canonization, centripetal-centrifugal, chronotope, completed (finalization), dialogue, ennobled discourse, everyday life, genre, hybrid, ideology, interanimation (interillumination), language, monoglossia, polyglossia, refraction, speech, utterance, voice, and zone. It also includes additional Bakhtinian concepts such as speech genres, double-voicedness, architectonic form, carnivalesque, primary and secondary genres, world represented in the work, world outside the work, memory, First and Second Stylized Line novels, and dialogized heteroglossia. Then there are terms and phrases interpreters have crafted to clarify and build upon Bakhtin's hermeneutical system, such as form-shaping ideology, creating world, and local chronotopes. To these, authors of the essays in this volume have added words and phrases they consider to be related to Bakhtin's way of interpreting literature, such as genology, prototype theory, bodily aesthetics, eschatological satire, rememory, and the politics of fulfillment. This makes more than forty terms for a person to learn as a way of giving new energy to their strategies and conceptualities of interpretation. Kenneth Burke, as we recall, used thirty-nine words and phrases to construct his chapter on a *lexicon rhetoricae* for his time, and Michael Holquist included forty major topics to exhibit the inner workings of Mikhail Bakhtin's approach in *The Dialogical Imagination*. Once readers complete the essays in this Semeia Studies volume, they still have much more to learn about Bakhtin. But the forty special words and phrases discussed in the volume, some central to Bakhtin's thought and some related to it, are a highly respectable way for biblical interpreters to develop deeper insights into Bakhtin's exciting and productive hermeneutical system that can contribute to even more dynamic ways of interpreting biblical literature and literature throughout the centuries that carries the heritage of biblical tradition out into the world at large.

WORKS CONSULTED

Aberbach, David. 1998. *Revolutionary Hebrew, Empire, and Crisis: Four Peaks in Hebrew Literature and Jewish Survival.* New York: New York University Press.

Ackroyd, Peter R. 1973. *I and II Chronicles, Ezra, Nehemiah.* Torch Bible Commentaries. London: SCM.

Agassiz, Louis. 1962. *Essay on Classification.* Edited by Edward Lurie. Cambridge: Harvard University Press.

Alter, Robert. 1981. *The Art of Biblical Narrative.* New York: Basic Books.

———.1999. *The David Story: A Translation with Commentary of 1 and 2 Samuel.* New York: Norton.

Anderson, Janice Capel. 1983. Matthew: Gender and Reading. *Semeia* 28:3–28.

Anderson, Paul N. 1991. Was the Fourth Evangelist a Quaker? *Quaker Religious Thought* 76:27–43.

———. 1996. *The Christology of the Fourth Gospel: Its Unity and Disunity in the Light of John 6.* WUNT 2/78. Tübingen: Mohr Siebeck; Valley Forge, Pa.: Trinity Press International.

———. 1997. The *Sitz im Leben* of the Johannine Bread of Life Discourse and Its Evolving Context. Pages 1–59 in *Critical Readings of John 6.* Edited by Alan Culpepper. BIS 22. Leiden: Brill.

———. 1999. The Having-Sent-Me Father—Aspects of Agency, Irony, and Encounter in the Johannine Father-Son Relationship. *Semeia* 85:33–57.

———. 2000. *Navigating the Living Waters of the Gospel of John: On Wading with Children and Swimming with Elephants.* Wallingford, Pa.: Pendle Hill Press.

———. 2001a. John and Mark—the Bi-Optic Gospels. Pages 175–88 in *Jesus in Johannine Tradition.* Edited by Robert Fortna and Tom Thatcher. Philadelphia: Westminster John Knox.

———. 2001b. Mark, John, and Answerability: Aspects of Interfluentiality between the Second and Fourth Gospels. Online: http://catholic-resources. org/John/SBL2001-Anderson.html.

———. 2002. Interfluential, Formative, and Dialectical—A Theory of John's Relation to the Synoptics. Pages 19–58 in *Für und wider die Priorität des Johannesevangeliums*. Edited by Peter Hofrichter. TTS 9. Hildesheimm: Olms.

———. 2004. The Cognitive Origins of John's Christological Unity and Disunity. Pages 127–48 in vol. 3 of *Psychology and the Bible: A New Way to Read the Scriptures*. Edited by J. Harold Ellens and Wayne Rollins. Westport, Conn.: Praeger.

———. 2006. *The Fourth Gospel and the Quest for Jesus: Modern Foundations Reconsidered*. JSNTSup 321. London: T&T Clark.

Anderson, Paul N., J. Harold Ellens, and James W. Fowler. 2004. Cognitive-Critical Analysis—A Way Forward in the Scientific Investigation of Gospel Traditions. Pages 247–76 in vol. 4 of *Psychology and the Bible: A New Way to Read the Scriptures*. Edited by J. Harold Ellens and Wayne Rollins. Westport, Conn.: Praeger.

Aquinas, Thomas. 1926. *Summa Theologica*. Translated by Fathers of the English Dominican Province. 2nd. ed. Vols. III QQ XXVII–LIX. London: Burns, Oates & Washbourne.

Arnold, Bill T. 1993. Wordplay and Narrative Techniques in Daniel 5 and 6. *JBL* 112:479–85.

———. 1996. The Use of Aramaic in the Hebrew Bible: Another Look at Bilingualism in Ezra and Daniel. *JNSL* 22:1–16.

———. 2000. Word Play and Characterization in Daniel 1. Pages 231–50 in *Puns and Pundits: Word Play in the Hebrew Bible and Ancient Near Eastern Literature*. Edited by Scott B. Noegel. Bethesda, Md.: CDL.

Aune, David E. 1987. *The New Testament in Its Literary Environment*. LEC 8. Philadelphia: Westminster.

Avalos, Hector I. 1991. The Comedic Function of the Enumerations of Officials and Instruments in Daniel 3. *CBQ* 53:580–88.

Bach, Alice. 1998. Whatever Happened to Dionysus? Pages 91–116 in *Biblical Studies/Cultural Studies*. Edited by J. Cheryl Exum and Stephen D. Moore. JSNTSup 266. Sheffield: Sheffield Academic Press.

Bakhtin, Mikhail M. 1981. *The Dialogic Imagination*. Translated by Caryl Emerson and Michael Holquist. Austin: University of Texas Press.

———. 1984a. *Problems of Dostoevsky's Poetics*. Edited and translated by Caryl Emerson. Theory and History of Literature 8. Minneapolis: University of Minnesota Press.

———. 1984b. *Rabelais and His World*. Translated by Helene Iswolsky. Bloomington: Indiana University Press.

———. 1986. *Speech Genres and Other Late Essays*. Translated by Vern W. McGee. Edited by Caryl Emerson and Michael Holquist. Austin: University of Texas Press.

———. 1990. *Art and Answerability: Early Philosophical Essays by M. M. Bakhtin.* Translated by Vadim Liapunov and Kenneth Brostrom. Edited by Michael Holquist and Vadim Liapunov. Austin: University of Texas Press.

———. 1993. *Toward a Philosophy of the Act.* Translated by Vadim Liapunov. Edited by Vadim Liapunov and Michael Holquist. Austin: University of Texas Press.

Bakhtin, Mikhail M., and P. N. Medvedev. 1978. *The Formal Method in Literary Scholarship: A Critical Introduction to Sociological Poetics.* Translated by Albert J. Wehrle. Baltimore: Johns Hopkins University Press.

Barnet, John A. 2003. *Not the Righteous but Sinners: M. M. Bakhtin's Theory of Aesthetics and the Problem of Reader-Character Interaction in Matthew's Gospel.* JSNTSup 246. London: T&T Clark.

Barr, James. 1968. *Comparative Philology and the Text of the Old Testament.* Oxford: Clarendon.

Barrett, C. K. 1972. *New Testament Essays.* London: SPCK.

Bauckham, Richard. 1998. John for Readers of Mark. Pages 147–71 in *The Gospels for all Christians: Rethinking the Gospel Audiences.* Edited by Richard Bauckham. Grand Rapids: Eerdmans.

Baumann, Gerlinde. 2003. *Love and Violence: Marriage as Metaphor for the Relationship between YHWH and Israel in the Prophetic Books.* Collegeville, Minn.: Liturgical Press.

Bauer, David R. 1996. The Literary and Theological Function of the Genealogy in Matthew's Gospel. Pages 129–60 in *Treasures New and Old: Recent Contributions to Matthean Studies.* Edited by David R. Bauer and Mark Allan Powell. SBLSymS 1. Atlanta: Scholars Press.

Beebee, Thomas. 1994. *The Ideology of Genre: A Comparative Study of Generic Instability.* University Park: Pennsylvania State University Press.

Beer, Dan. 2002. *Michel Foucault: Form and Power.* Oxford: Legenda/European Humanities Research Centre.

Benardete, Seth, trans. 2001. *Plato's Symposium.* Chicago: University of Chicago Press.

Ben-Porat, Ziva. 1976. The Poetics of Literary Allusion. *PTL: A Journal for Descriptive Poetics and Theory of Literature* 1:105–28.

Ben Zvi, Ehud. 1998. Looking at the Primary (Hi)story and the Prophetic Books as Literary/Theological Units within the Frame of the Early Second Temple: Some Considerations. *SJOT* 12:26–43.

Bergen, David A. 1999. Bakhtin Revisits Deuteronomy: Narrative Theory and the Dialogical Event of Deut 31:2 and 34:7. *Journal of Hebrew Scriptures* 2. Online: www.arts.ualberta.ca/JHS/Articles/article_10.htm.

Berlin, Adele. 2002. *Lamentations.* OTL. Louisville: Westminster John Knox.

Bizzell, Patricia, and Bruce Herzberg. 1990. *The Rhetorical Tradition: Readings from Classical Times to the Present*. Boston: St. Martin's.

Blenkinsopp, Joseph. 2000. *Isaiah 1–39: A New Translation with Introduction and Commentary*. AB 19A. New York: Doubleday.

Bloch, Maurice. 1974. Symbols, Song, Dance and features of Articulation. *Archives Europeenes de Sociologie* 15:55–81.

Borgen, Peder. 1965. *Bread from Heaven: An Exegetical Study of the Concept of Manna in the Gospel of John and the Writings of Philo*. NovTSup 11. Leiden: Brill.

Branham, R. Bracht. 1995. Inventing the Novel. Pages 79–87 in *Bakhtin in Contexts: Across the Disciplines*. Edited by Amy Mandelker. Evanston, Ill.: Northwestern University Press.

———. 2002. A Truer Story of the Novel? Pages 161–86 in *Bakhtin and the Classics*. Edited by R.Bracht Branham. Evanston, Ill.: Northwestern University Press.

Brenner, Athalya. 1994. Who's Afraid of Feminist Criticism? Who's Afraid of Biblical Humour? The Case of the Obtuse Foreign Ruler in the Hebrew Bible. *JSOT* 63:38–55.

Brown, Raymond E. 1993. *The Birth of the Messiah: A Commentary on the Infancy Narratives in the Gospels of Matthew and Luke*. 2nd ed. ABRL. New York: Doubleday.

———. 2003. *An Introduction to the Gospel of John*. Edited by Francis Moloney. New York: Doubleday.

Bruce, Gregory C. 1990. Rethinking Bakhtin: Extensions and Challenges. *Literature and Theology* 4:347–51.

Brueggemann, Walter. 1982. *Genesis*. IBC. Atlanta: John Knox.

Bucholtz, Mary, ed. 2004. *Language and Woman's Place: Text and Commentaries*. New York: Oxford University Press.

Bultmann, Rudolf. 1971. *The Gospel of John: A Commentary*. Translated by G. R. Beasley-Murray, W. R. N. Hoare, and J. K. Riches. Oxford: Blackwell.

Burke, Kenneth. 1968. *Counter-Statement*. Berkeley and Los Angeles: University of California Press.

Burridge, Richard A. *What Are the Gospels? A Comparison with Graeco-Roman Biography*. Cambridge: Cambridge University Press, 1992.

Buss, Martin J. 1969. *The Prophetic Word of Hosea: A Morphogical Study*. BZAW 111. Berlin: Töpelmann.

———. 1974. "The Study of Forms." Pages 1–56 in *Old Testament Form Criticism*. Edited by John H. Hayes. San Antonio: Trinity University Press.

———. 1977. The Distinction between Civil and Criminal Law in Ancient Israel. Pages 51–62 in vol. 1 of *Proceedings of the Sixth World Congress of Jewish Studies*. Jerusalem: Academic Press.

————. 1996. "Hosea as a Canonical Problem." Pages 79–93 in *Prophets and Paradigms: Essays in Honor of Gene M. Tucker*. Edited by Stephen Breck Reid. JSOTSup 229. Sheffield: Sheffield Academic Press:.

————. 1999. *Biblical Form Criticism in Its Context*. JSOTSup 274. Sheffield: Sheffield Academic Press.

Campbell, Antony F. 2003. *1 Samuel*. FOTL 7. Grand Rapids: Eerdmans.

Caplice, Richard I. 1992. Languages (Akkadian). *ABD* 4:170–73.

Carter, Warren. 1996. *Matthew: Storyteller, Interpreter, Evangelist*. Peabody, Mass.: Hendrickson.

————. 2000. *Matthew and the Margins: A Sociopolitical and Religious Reading*. The Bible and Liberation. Maryknoll, N.Y.: Orbis.

Cartwright, Michael G. 1992. The Uses of Scripture in Christian Ethics: After Bakhtin. *Annual of the Society of Christian Ethics* 1992:263–76.

Cassidy, Richard J. 1991. *John's Gospel in New Perspective*. Maryknoll, N.Y.: Orbis.

Chia, Philip P. 1997. On Naming the Subject: Postcolonial Reading of Daniel 1. *Jian Dao* 7:17–36.

Childs, Brevard. 1967. *Isaiah and the Assyrian Crisis*. SBT 3. London: SCM.

Christian, Barbara. 1994. Literature as a Source of Theological Reflection. Videocassette. T. V. Moore Lectures. San Anselmo, Calif.: San Francisco Theological Seminary.

————. 1997a. Beloved, She's Ours. *Narrative* 5:36–49.

————. 1997b. Fixing Methodologies: *Beloved*. Pages 363–70 in *Female Subjects in Black and White: Race, Psychoanalysis, Feminism*. Edited by Elizabeth Abel, Barbara Christian, and Helene Moglen. Berkeley and Los Angeles: University of California Press.

Clark, Katerina, and Michael Holquist, eds. 1984. *Mikhail Bakhtin*. Cambridge: Harvard University Press.

Classens, L. Juliana M. 2003. Biblical Theology as Dialogue: Continuing the Conversation on Mikhail Bakhtin and Biblical Theology. *JBL* 122:127–44.

Coates, Ruth. 1998. *Christianity in Bakhtin: God and the Exiled Author*. Cambridge Studies in Russian Literature. Cambridge: Cambridge University Press.

Cobley, Evelyn. 1988. Mikhail Bakhtin's Place in Genre Theory. *Genre* 21:321–38.

Cogan, Mordecai, and Hayim Tadmor. 1988. *II Kings: A New Translation with Introduction and Commentary*. AB 11. New York: Doubleday.

Cohen, Ralph. 1986. History and Genre. *New Literary History* 17:203–18.

————. 2003. Introduction. *New Literary History* 34:v–xv.

Collins, Adela Yarbro. 1995. Genre and the Gospels. *JR* 75:239–46.

Collins, John J. 1979a. Introduction: Toward the Morphology of a Genre. *Semeia* 14:1–20.

———. 1979b. The Jewish Apocalypses. *Semeia* 14:21–59.

———, ed. 1979c. *Apocalypse: The Morphology of a Genre. Semeia* 14. Missoula, Mont.: Society of Biblical Literature.

———. 1993. *Daniel: A Commentary on the Book of Daniel.* Hermeneia. Minneapolis: Fortress.

———. 1997. *Apocalypticism in the Dead Sea Scrolls.* London: Routledge.

Cooper, Jerrold S. 1992. Sumer, Sumerians. *ABD* 6:231–34.

Coxon, Peter W. 1986. The "List" Genre and Narrative Style in the Court Tales of Daniel. *JSOT* 35:95–121.

Craig, Kenneth M. 1995. *Reading Esther: A Case for the Literary Carnivalesque.* Louisville: Westminster John Knox.

Culler, Jonathan. 1975. *Structuralist Poetics: Structuralism, Linguistics, and the Study of Literature.* Ithaca, N.Y.: Cornell University Press.

Culpepper, R. Alan. 1983. *Anatomy of the Fourth Gospel: A Study in Literary Design.* Philadelphia: Fortress.

Davies, William D. 1964. *The Setting of the Sermon on the Mount.* Cambridge: Cambridge University Press.

Davies, William D., and Dale C. Allison. 1988. *The Gospel according to Saint Matthew.* ICC 1. Edinburgh: T&T Clark.

Deist, Ferdinand. 1997. Boundaries and Humour: A Case Study from the Ancient Near East. *Scriptura* 63:415–24.

Deleuze, Gilles. 1997. Desire and Pleasure. Translated by Daniel W. Smith. Pages 183–92 in *Foucault and His Interlocutors.* Edited by Arnold I. Davidson. Chicago: University of Chicago Press.

Derrida, Jacques. 2000. The Law of Genre. Pages 219–31 in *Modern Genre Theory.* Edited by David Duff. Harlow, U.K.: Longman.

Di Lella, Alexander A. 1981. Daniel 4:7–14: Poetic Analysis and Biblical Background. Pages 247–58 in *Melanges bibliques et orientaux en l'honneur de M. Henri Cazelles.* Edited by A. Caquot and M. Delcor. AOAT 212. Kevelaer: Butzon & Bercker.

Dobbs-Allsopp, F. W. 1993. *Weep O Daughter of Zion: A Study of the City-Lament Genre in the Hebrew Bible.* BibOr 44. Rome: Editrice Pontifico Istituto Biblico.

———. 2002. *Lamentations.* Louisville: Westminster John Knox.

Duff, David. 2000. Introduction. Pages 1–22 in *Modern Genre Theory.* Edited by David Duff. Harlow, U.K.: Longman.

Duke, Rodney K. 1990. *The Persuasive Appeal of the Chronicler: A Rhetorical Analysis.* JSOTSup 88. Sheffield: Almond.

Dunn, Francis. 2002. Rethinking Time: From Bakhtin to Antiphon. Pages

187–219 in *Bakhtin and the Classics*. Edited by R. Bracht Branham. Evanston, Ill.: Northwestern University Press.

Durey, Jill Felicity. 1991. The State of Play and Interplay in Intertextuality. *Style* 25:616–35.

Edelman, Diana Vikander. 1991. *King Saul in the Historiography of Judah.* JSOTSup 121. Sheffield: Sheffield Academic Press.

Fauconnier, Gilles, and Mark Turner. 2002. *The Way We Think: Conceptual Blending and the Mind's Hidden Complexities.* New York: Basic Books.

Fewell, Danna Nolan. 1991. *Circle of Sovereignty: Plotting Politics in the Book of Daniel.* 2nd ed. Nashville: Abingdon.

Finkel, Irving L. 1980. Bilingual Chronicle Fragments. *JCS* 32:65–80.

Fischer, Alexander A. 1977. *Skepsis oder Furcht Gottes?* BZAW 247. Berlin: de Gruyter.

Fishelov, David. 1993. *Metaphors of Genre: The Role of Analogies in Genre Theory.* University Park: Pennsylvania State University Press.

Fokkelman, Jan P. 1986. *The Crossing Fates.* Vol. 2 of *Narrative Art and Poetry in the Books of Samuel.* Assen: Van Gorcum.

Foucault, Michel. 1978. *An Introduction.* Vol. 1 of *The History of Sexuality.* Translated by Robert Hurley. New York: Random House.

———. 1983. Afterword: The Subject and Power. Pages 208–26 in *Michel Foucault: Beyond Structuralism and Hermeneutics.* Edited by Hubert L. Dreyfus and Paul Rabinow. 2nd. ed. Chicago: University of Chicago Press.

Fowler, Alastair. 1982. *Kinds of Literature: An Introduction to the Theory of Genres and Modes.* Cambridge: Harvard University Press.

Fox, Michael V. 1989. *Qohelet and his Contradictions.* JSOTSup 71. Sheffield: Almond.

Frye, Northrop. 1957. *Anatomy of Criticism: Four Essays.* Princeton: Princeton University Press.

Fuller, Christopher C. 2004. "Udiste Che Fu Detto…, Ma Io Dico Che…": Pasolini as Interpreter of the Gospel of Matthew. Ph. D. diss., Graduate Theological Union.

Garland, David E. 1993. *Reading Matthew: A Literary and Theological Commentary on the First Gospel.* New York: Crossroad.

Gilroy, Paul. 1993. *The Black Atlantic: Modernity and Double Consciousness.* London: Verso.

Goldingay, John. 1989. *Daniel.* WBC 30. Dallas: Word Books.

Goodchild, Philip. 1996. *Deleuze and Guattari: An Introduction to the Politics of Desire.* London: Sage.

Gowler, David B. 2000. Heteroglossic Trends in Biblical Studies: Polyphonic Dialogues or Clanging Cymbals? *RevExp* 97:443–66

Green, Barbara. 2000. *Mikhail Bakhtin and Biblical Scholarship: An Introduction.* SemeiaSt 38. Atlanta: Society of Biblical Literature.

———. 2003a. The Engaging Nuances of Genre: Reading Saul and Michal Afresh. Pages 141–59 in *Relating to the Text.* Edited by Timothy Sandoval and Carleen Mandolfo. London: T&T Clark.

———. 2003b. *How Are the Mighty Fallen? A Dialogical Study of King Saul in 1 Samuel.* JSOTSup 365. Sheffield: Sheffield Academic Press.

Gundry, Robert H. 1994. *Matthew: A Commentary on His Handbook for a Mixed Church under Persecution.* Grand Rapids: Eerdmans.

Gunkel, Hermann, and Joachim Begrich. 1966. *Einleitung in die Psalmen.* Göttingen: Vandenhoeck & Ruprecht.

Gunn, David, and Danna Nolan Fewell. 1993. *Narrative in the Hebrew Bible.* Oxford Bible Series. New York: Oxford University Press.

Hagner, Donald A. 1993. *Matthew.* WBC 33. Dallas: Word.

Harrington, Daniel J. 1991. *The Gospel of Matthew.* SP 1. Collegeville, Minn.: Liturgical Press.

Harris, Trudier. 1993. Escaping Slavery but Not Its Images. Pages 330–41 in *Toni Morrison: Critical Perspectives Past and Present.* Edited by Henry Louis Gates Jr. and K. A. Appiah. New York: Amistad.

Heil, John Paul. 1991. The Narrative Roles of the Women in Matthew's Genealogy. *Bib* 72:538–45.

Henze, Matthias. 1999. *The Madness of King Nebuchadnezzar.* JSJSup 61. Leiden: Brill.

Higgins, Therese E. 2001. *Religiosity, Cosmology, and Folklore: The African Influence in the Novels of Toni Morrison.* New York: Routledge.

Hillers, Delbert. 1972. *Lamentations: Introduction, Translation, and Notes.* AB 7A. Garden City, N.Y.: Doubleday.

Hirsch, E. D., Jr. 1967. *Validity in Interpretation.* New Haven: Yale University Press.

Hirschkop, Ken. 1999. *Mikhail Bakhtin: An Aesthetic for Democracy.* Oxford: Oxford University Press.

Holm, Tawny. 2005. Daniel 1–6: A Biblical Story Collection. Pages 149–66 in *Ancient Fiction: The Matrix of Early Christian and Jewish Narrative.* Edited by Jo-Ann A. Brant, Charles W. Hedrick, and Chris Shea. SBLSymS 32. Atlanta: Society of Biblical Literature.

Holquist, Michael. 1990. *Dialogism; Bakhtin and His World.* London: Routledge.

———. 2002. *Dialogism: Bakhtin and His World.* 2nd ed. London: Routledge.

Hove, Thomas B. 2002. Toni Morrison. Pages 254–60 in *Postmodernism: The Key Figures.* Edited by Hans Bertens and Joseph Natoli. Malden, Mass.: Blackwell.

Huehnergard, John. 1992. Languages: Introductory. *ABD* 4:155–70.

Iser, Wolfgang. 1978. *The Act of Reading: A Theory of Aesthetic Response*. Baltimore: Johns Hopkins University Press.

Jackson, Richard. 1987. The Dialogic Self. *Georgia Review* 41:415–20.

Jaffee, Martin S. 1997. *Early Judaism*. Upper Saddle River, N.J.: Prentice Hall.

Japhet, Sara. 1993. *I and II Chronicles: A Commentary*. OTL. Louisville: Westminster John Knox.

Jauss, Hans Robert. 1982. *Toward an Aesthetic of Reception*. Translated by Timothy Bahti. Theory and History of Literature 2. Minneapolis: University of Minnesota Press.

Jeansonne, Sharon Pace. 1990. *The Women of Genesis: From Sarah to Potiphar's Wife*. Minneapolis: Fortress.

Jerome. 1959. *Commenarium in Metheum*. CCSL 77. Turnholt: Brepols.

Jobling, David. 1998. *1 Samuel*. Collegeville, Minn.: Liturgical Press.

Johnson, M. D. 1969. *The Purpose of the Biblical Genealogies with Special Reference to the Settings of the Gospel of Jesus*. SNTSMS 8. Cambridge: Cambridge University Press.

Johnson, Mark. 1987. *The Body in the Mind: The Bodily Basis of Meaning, Imagination, and Reason*. Chicago: University of Chicago Press.

Käsemann, Ernst. 1968. *The Testament of Jesus according to John 17*. Translated by Gerhard Krodel. Philadelphia: Fortress.

Kaufman, Steven A. 1992. Languages (Aramaic). *ABD* 4:173–78.

Keener, Craig S. 1999. *A Commentary on the Gospel of Matthew*. Grand Rapids: Eerdmans.

Knoppers, Gary N. 2004. *I Chronicles 1–9: A New Translation with Introduction and Commentary*. AB 12. New York: Doubleday.

Knowles, Michael P. 2004. What Was the Victim Wearing? Literary, Economic, and Social Contexts for the Parable of the Good Samaritan. *BibInt* 12:145–74.

Krumholz, Linda. 1999. The Ghosts of Slavery: Historical Recovery in Toni Morrison's *Beloved*. Pages 107–25 in *Toni Morrison's Beloved: A Casebook*. Edited by William L. Andrews and Mellie Y. McKay. New York: Oxford University Press.

Ladin, Jay. 1999. Fleshing Out the Chronotope. Pages 212–26 in *Critical Essays on Mikhail Bakhtin*. Edited by Caryl Emerson. Critical Essays on World Literature. New York: Hall.

Lakoff, George. 1987. *Women, Fire, and Dangerous Things: What Categories Reveal about the Mind*. Chicago: University of Chicago Press.

Lakoff, George, and Mark Johnson. 2003. *Metaphors We Live By*. Chicago: University of Chicago Press.

Lakoff, Robin. 2004. *Language and Woman's Place: Text and Commentaries*. 2nd ed. Edited by Mary Bucholtz. New York: Oxford University Press.

Levenson, Jon. 1978. 1 Samuel 25 as Literature and History. *CBQ* 40:11–28.

Levine, Amy-Jill. 1998. Matthew. Pages 339–49 in *Women's Bible Commentary*. Edited by Carol A. Newsom and Sharon H. Ringe. Louisville: Westminster John Knox.

Levine, Herbert. 1992. The Dialogic Discourse of Psalms. Pages 145–61 in *Hermeneutics, the Bible and Literary Criticism*. Edited by Ann Loades and Michael McLain. New York: St Martin's.

Lindars, Barnabas. 1971. *Behind the Fourth Gospel*. London: SPCK.

———. 1981. *The Gospel of John*. Grand Rapids: Eerdmans.

Lotman, Yuri. 1993. The Text within the Text. Translated by Jerry Leo and Amy Mandelker. *PMLA* 109:377–84.

Ludwig, Paul. 2002. *Eros and Polis: Desire and Community in Greek Political Theory*. Cambridge: Cambridge University Press.

Luz, Ulrich. 1989. *Matthew 1–7*. Translated by Wilhelm C. Linss. Minneapolis: Augsburg Fortress.

Maddison, Bula. 2005. *The Word in Dialogue: Biblical Allusion and Bakhtin's Theory of the Novel*. Ph.D. diss., Graduate Theological Union.

Malbon, Elizabeth S. 1993. Characterization in Biblical Literature. *Semeia* 63:3–227.

Malina, Bruce J. 1981. *The New Testament World: Insights from Cultural Anthropology*. Louisville: Westminster John Knox.

Mandolfo, Carleen. 2002a. Finding Their Voices: Sanctioned Subversion in Psalms of Lament. *HBT* 24.2:27–52.

———. 2002b. *God in the Dock*. Sheffield: Sheffield Academic Press.

———. 2007. *Daughter Zion Talks Back to the Prophets*. SemeiaSt 58. Atlanta: Society of Biblical Literature.

Martyn, J. Louis. 2003. *History and Theology in the Fourth Gospel*. 3rd ed. Louisville: Westminster John Knox.

McCracken, David. 1993. Character in the Boundary: Bakhtin's Interdividuality in Biblical Narratives. *Semeia* 63:29–42.

Meadowcroft, T. J. 1995. *Aramaic Daniel and Greek Daniel: A Literary Comparison*. JSOTSup 198. Sheffield: Sheffield Academic Press.

Medvedev, Pavel. 1978. *The Formal Method in Literary Scholarship: A Critical Introduction to Sociological Poetics*. Translated by A. Wehrle. Baltimore: Johns Hopkins University Press.

Meeks, Wayne A. 1967. *The Prophet King: Moses Traditions and the Johannine Christology*. NovTSup 14. Leiden: Brill.

———. 1986. The Man from Heaven in Johannine Sectarianism. Pages 141–73 in *Interpreting the Fourth Gospel*. Edited by John Ashton. London: SPCK.

Mendels, Doron. 1992. *The Rise and Fall of Jewish Nationalism*. ABRL. New York: Doubleday.

Michalowski, Piotr. 1989. *The Lamentations over the Destruction of Sumer and Ur*. Winona Lake, Ind.: Eisenbrauns.

Miles, Jack. 2001. *Christ: A Crisis in the Life of God*. New York: Vintage Books.

Miller, Charles W. 2001. Reading Voices: Personification, Dialogism, and the Reader of Lamentations 1. *BibInt* 9:393–408.

Mills, Mary E. 2003. *Reading Ecclesiastes*. Aldershot: Ashgate.

Moore, Stephen D. 1997. History after Theory? Biblical Studies and the New Historicism. *BibInt* 5:289–99.

Morrison, Toni. 1987. *Beloved*. New York: Knopf.

Morson, Gary Saul. 2003. The Aphorism: Fragments from the Breakdown of Reason. *New Literary History* 34:409–29.

Morson, Gary Saul, and Caryl Emerson. 1990. *Mikhail Bakhtin: Creation of a Prosaics*. Stanford, Calif.: Stanford University Press.

———. 1997. Extracts from a *Heteroglossary*. Pages 256–72 in *Dialogue and Critical Discourse: Language, Culture, Critical Theory*. Edited by Michael Mascovi. New York: Oxford University Press.

Mowinckel, Sigmund. 1962. *Israel's Worship*. Vol. 2. New York: Abingdon.

Mussies, Gerard. 1992. Languages (Greek). *ABD* 4:195–203.

Myers, Jacob M. 1965. *II Chronicles*. AB 13. New York: Doubleday.

Newsom, Carol A. 1996. Bakhtin, the Bible, and Dialogic Truth. *JR* 76:290–306.

———. 2000. Bakhtin. Pages 20–27 in *Handbook of Postmodern Biblical Interpretation*. Edited by A. K. M. Adam. St. Louis: Chalice.

———. 2003. *The Book of Job*. Oxford: Oxford University Press.

———. 2005. Spying Out the Land: A Report ftom Genology. Pages 437–50 in *Seeking Out the Wisdom of the Ancients: Essays Offered to Honor Michael V. Fox on the Occasion of His Sixty-Fifth Birthday*. Edited by Ronald L. Troxel, Kelvin G. Friebel, and Dennis R. Magary. Winona Lake, Ind.: Eisenbrauns.

Olson, Dennis T. 1998. Biblical Theology as Provisional Monologization: A Dialogue with Childs, Brueggemann and Bakhtin. *BibInt* 6:162–80.

Patte, Daniel. 1987. *The Gospel according to Matthew: A Structural Commentary on Matthew's Gospel*. Valley Forge, Pa.: Trinity Press International.

Patterson, David. 1985. *Journal of Aesthetics and Art Criticism* 44:131–39.

Paul, Andre. 1984. *L'évangile de l'énfance selon Saint Matthieu*. Rev. ed. Lire la Bible 17. Paris: Cerf.

Paul, Shalom. 1992. Decoding a "Joint" Expression in Daniel 5:6,16. *JANESCU* 22:121–27.

Peach, Linden. 2000. *Toni Morrison*. New York: St. Martin's.

Pearce, Lynne. 1994. *Reading Dialogics*. London: Edward Arnold.

Petrotta, Anthony J. 1991. *Lexis Ludens: Wordplay and the Book of Micah*. New York: Lang.

Pham, Xuan Huong Thi. 1999. *Mourning in the Ancient Near East and the Hebrew Bible*. JSOTSup 302. Sheffield: Sheffield Academic Press.

Pleins, J. David. 1992. Son-Slayers and Their Sons. *CBQ* 54:29–38.

Polzin, Robert. 1980. *Deuteronomy, Joshua, Judges.* Part 1 of *Moses and the Deuteronomist: A Literary Study of the Deuteronomic History.* New York: Seabury.

Polzin, Robert M. 1989. *1 Samuel.* Part 2 of *Samuel and the Deuteronomist: A Literary Study of the Deuteronomic History.* San Francisco: Harper & Row.

Rad, Gerhard von. 1961. *Genesis.* OTL. Philadelphia: Westminster.

———. 1962. Deuteronomy. *IDB* 1:831–38.

Radin, Paul. 1927. *Primitive Man as Philosopher.* New York: Appleton.

Ramey, Lauri. 2002. The Theology of the Lyric Tradition in African American Spirituals. *JAAR* 70:347–63.

Redditt, Paul L. 1999. *Daniel.* NCB. Sheffield: Sheffield Academic Press.

Reed, Walter L. 1993. *Dialogues of the Word: The Bible as Literature according to Bakhtin.* New York: Oxford University Press.

Rensberger, David. 1988. *Johannine Faith and Liberating Community.* Philadelphia: Westminster.

Riffaterre, Michel. 1997. The Interpretant. Pages 173–84 in *Reading Eco: An Anthology.* Edited by R. Capozzi. Bloomington: Indiana University Press.

Robbins, Vernon K. 1990. *Ancient Quotes and Anecdotes: From Crib to Crypt.* Sonoma, Calif.: Polebridge.

———. 1996. *Exploring the Texture of Texts: A Guide to Socio-rhetorical Interpretation.* Harrisburg, Pa.: Trinity Press International.

Rosch, Eleanor. 1975. Cognitive Representations of Semantic Categories. *Journal of Experimental Psychology (General)* 104:192–233.

———. 1978. Principles of Categorization. Pages 27–48 in *Cognition and Categorization.* Edited by E. Rosch and B. Lloyd. Hillsdale, N.J.: Erlbaum.

Rosmarin, Adena. 1985. *The Power of Genre.* Minneapolis: University of Minnesota Press.

Rouillard-Bonraisin, Hedwige. 1996. Problemes du bilinguisme en Daniel. Pages 145–70 in *Mosaïque de langues, mosaïque culturelle: Le bilinguisme dans le Proche-Orient ancient.* Edited by Francoise Briquel-Chatonnet. Paris: Maisonneuve.

Rumble, Patrick. 1996. *Allegories of Contamination: Pier Paolo Pasolini's Trilogy of Life.* Toronto: University of Toronto Press.

Ryan, Marie-Laurie. 1981. Introduction: On the Why, What, and How of Generic Taxonomy. *Poetics* 19:109–26.

Schaberg, Jane. 1995. *The Illegitimacy of Jesus: A Feminist Theological Interpretation of the Infancy Narratives.* Biblical Seminar 28. Sheffield: Sheffield Academic Press.

Schellenberg, Annette. 2002. *Erkenntnis als Problem: Qohelet und die alttestamentliche Discussion um das menschliche Erkennen.* OBO 188. Fribourg: Universitätsverlag.

Schnackenburg, Rudolf. 2002. *The Gospel of Matthew*. Translated by Robert R. Barr. Grand Rapids: Eerdmans.

Schneiders, Sandra. 1982. Women in the Fourth Gospel and the Role of Women in the Contemporary Church. *BTB* 12:35–45.

Schnelle, Udo. 1992. *Antidocetic Christology in the Gospel of John*. Translated by Linda Maloney. Minneapolis: Fortress.

Scott, James C. 1990. *Domination and the Arts of Resistance: Hidden Transcripts*. New Haven: Yale University Press.

Senior, Donald. 1998. *Matthew*. ANTC. Nashville: Abingdon.

Seow, C. L. 1997. *Ecclesiastes: A New Translation with Introduction and Commentary*. AB 18C. New York: Doubleday.

Sérandour, Arnaud. 2000. Hebreu et Araméen dans la Bible. *REJ* 159:345–55.

Shestova, Maria. 1992. Dialogism in the Novel and Bakhtin's Theory of Culture. *New Literary History* 23:747–63.

Shklovsky, Viktor. 1990. *Theories of Prose*. Translated by Benjamin Sher. Elmwood Park, Ill.: Dalkey Archive.

Sinding, Michael. 2002. After Definitions: Genre, Categories, and Cognitive Science. *Genre* 35:181–220.

———. 2004. Conceptual Blending and the Origins of Genres. Paper presented at the Cognitive Approaches to Literature Session of the Modern Language Association Convention. Philadelphia, 28 December 2004.

Singer, Alan. 1988. The Voice of History/The Subject of the Novel. *Novel* 21:173–79.

Smith-Christopher, Daniel. 1996. Daniel. *NIB* 7:17–152.

———. 2002. *A Biblical Theology of Exile*. OBT. Minneapolis: Fortress.

Snell, Daniel C. 1980. Why Is There Aramaic In The Bible? *JSOT* 18:32–51.

Snyder, John. 1991. *Prospects of Power: Tragedy, Satire, the Essay, and the Theory of Genre*. Lexington: University of Kentucky Press.

Speiser, E. A. 1981. *Genesis*. AB 1. Garden City, N.Y.: Doubleday.

Stansell, Gary. 1996. Honor and Shame in the David Narratives. *Semeia* 68:55–79.

Stendahl, Krister. 1960. Quis et Unde? An Analysis of Matthew 1–2. Pages 94–105 in *Judentum Urchristentum Kirche*. Edited by W. Eltester. 2nd. ed. BZNW 26. Berlin: Töpelmann.

Streete, Gail Corrington. 1997. *The Strange Woman: Power and Sex in the Bible*. Louisville: Westminster John Knox.

Swales, John M. 1990. *Genre Analysis: English in Academic and Research Settings*. Cambridge: Cambridge University Press.

Sweeney, Marvin, and Ehud Ben Zvi, eds. 2003. *The Changing Face of Form Criticism for the Twenty-First Century*. Grand Rapids: Eerdmans.

Talbert, Charles H. 1977. *What Is a Gospel? The Genre of the Canonical Gospels*. Philadelphia: Fortress.

Thomson, Clive. 1984. Bakhtin's "Theory" of Genre. *Studies in Twentieth Century Literature* 9:29–40.

Todorov, Tzvetan. 1984. *Mikhail Bakhtin: The Dialogical Principle.* Translated by Wlad Godzich. Minneapolis: University of Minnesota Press.

Tolbert, Mary Ann. 1989. *Sowing the Gospel: Mark's World in Literary-Historical Perspective.* Minneapolis: Fortress.

Tull, Patricia K. 1997. *Remember the Former Things: The Recollection of Previous Texts in Second Isaiah.* SBLDS 161. Atlanta: Scholars Press.

———. 2003. Rhetorical Criticism and Beyond in Second Isaiah. Pages 326–34 in Sweeney and Ben Zvi 2003.

———. 2005. Bakhtin's Confessional Self-Accounting and Psalms of Lament. *BibInt* 1:41–55.

Tynyanov, Yuri. 2000. The Literary Fact. Pages 29–49 in *Modern Genre Theory.* Edited by David Duff. Harlow, U.K.: Longman.

Valeta, David M. 2005. Court or Jester Tales? Resistance and Social Reality in Daniel 1–6. *PRSt* 32:309–24.

———. 2007. *Lions and Ovens and Visions: A Satirical Analysis of Daniel 1–6.* Sheffield: Sheffield Phoenix Press.

Van Deventer, H. J. M. 1999. Would the Actually "Powerful" Please Stand? The Role of the Queen (Mother) in Daniel 5. *Scriptura* 70:241–51.

Van Leeuwen, Raymond C. 2003. Form Criticism, Wisdom, and Psalms 111–112. Pages 65–84 in Sweeney and Ben Zvi 2003.

Vice, Sue. 1997. *Introducing Bakhtin.* Manchester: Manchester University Press.

Vines, Michael E. 2002. *The Problem of Markan Genre: The Gospel of Mark and the Jewish Novel.* SBLAcBib 3. Atlanta: Society of Biblical Literature.

Voloshinov, V. N. 2006. *Marxism and the Philosophy of Language.* Translated by Ladislav Matejka and I. R. Titunik. Cambrdige: Harvard University Press.

Voloshinov, V. N. (Mikhail Bakhtin et al.) 1983. *Bakhtin School Papers.* Translated by N. Owens. Edited by Ann Shukman. Russian Poetics in Translation 10. Oxford: Oxon.

Waetjen, Herman C. 1976. The Genealogy as the Key to the Gospel according to Matthew. *JBL* 95:205–30.

Wahlde, Urban C. von. 1990. *The Johannine Commandments: 1 John and the Struggle for the Johannine Tradition.* New York: Paulist.

Wainwright, Elaine. 1991. *Towards a Feminist Critical Reading of the Gospel According to Matthew.* BZNW 60. Berlin: de Gruyter.

Waltke, Bruce K., and M. O'Connor. 1990. *An Introduction to Biblical Hebrew Syntax.* Winona Lake, Ind.: Eisenbrauns.

Ward, Frances. 1997. Writing the Body of Christ. *Theology* 100:163–70.

Wenzel, Siegfried. 1994. *Macaronic Sermons: Bilingualism and Preaching in Late-Medieval England*. Recentiores: Later Latin Texts and Contexts. Ann Arbor: University of Michigan Press.

Wesselius, Jan-Wim. 2005. The Literary Nature of the Book of Daniel and the Linguistic Character of Its Aramaic. *AS* 3:241–83.

Williamson, H.G.M. 1982. *1 and 2 Chronicles*. NCB. Grand Rapids: Eerdmans.

Wittgenstein, Ludwig. 1958. *Philosophical Investigations*. Oxford: Blackwell.

Wolters, Al. 1991a. The Riddle of the Scales in Daniel 5. *HUCA* 62:155–77.

———. 1991b. Untying the King's Knots: Physiology and Word Play in Daniel 5. *JBL* 110:117–22.

Wright, Benjamin G., III, and Lawrence M. Wills. 2005. *Conflicted Boundaries in Wisdom and Apocalypticism*. SBLSymS 35. Atlanta: Society of Biblical Literature.

Yamasaki, Gary. 1998. *John the Baptist in Life and Death: Audience-Oriented Criticism of Matthew's Narrative*. JSNTSup 167. Sheffield: Sheffield Academic Press.

Yee, Gale. 2003. *Poor Banished Children of Eve: Women as Evil in the Hebrew Bible*. Minneapolis: Fortress.

Contributors

Paul N. Anderson is Professor of Biblical and Quaker Studies at George Fox University, where he serves as chair of the Department of Religious Studies. His *Christology of the Fourth Gospel* (1996) introduced cognitive-critical analysis to the study of Gospel traditions and Bakhtinian dialogism to the rhetorical study of John. His *The Fourth Gospel and the Quest for Jesus* (2006) poses a new theory of Johannine-Synoptic relations and invites a nuanced approach to the quest for Jesus with the Fourth Gospel at the table. He is co-chair of the John, Jesus, and History Project and has co-edited the first of its three volumes (2007). He is editor of *Quaker Religious Thought* and is the recipient of a Lilly grant on congregational discernment.

Keith Bodner is Professor of Religious Studies at Atlantic Baptist University in Moncton, New Brunswick, Canada. His recent books include *David Observed* (2005) and a commentary on 1 Samuel (2003). His long-term goal is to write a exhausting commentary on Chronicles, but three young children are proving to be serious impediments to the study of genealogies.

Roland Boer is Reader in Comparative Literature and Cultural Studies at Monash University, Melbourne. When he is not cycling or making bookshelves, he writes in the areas of biblical studies, political thought, and religion. He has written ten books of criticism, one of fiction and over one hundred scholarly articles. His most recent book is *Criticism of Heaven* (2007), and his works have been and are being translated into Bulgarian, Danish, German, Serbian, and Chinese. He has been an invited lecturer in the United States, Denmark, Taiwan, The Netherlands, Bulgaria, Serbia, England, Greenland, and Australia.

Martin J. Buss is a freshly minted professor emeritus in the Department of Religion at Emory University. Relevant publications that demonstrate or discuss genre theory include *The Prophetic Word of Hosea* (1969), "Understanding Communication," in *Encounter with the Text* (ed. Buss, 1979); and

Biblical Form Criticism in Its Context (1999). A work describing relational, including dialogical, theory is about to be published.

Judy Fentress-Williams is Associate Professor of Old Testament at Virginia Theological Seminary in Alexandria, Virginia. Judy is particularly interested in the role of dialogue in biblical narrative and the dialogues that exist between texts. Her essay, "The Bible and Dialogue," appears in *September 11: Religious Perspectives on the Causes and the Consequences* (2002). She is currently working on a commentary on the book of Ruth.

Christopher Fuller is an assistant professor of theology at Carroll College in Helena, Montana. His research interests include theological biblical interpretation, theology and film, and Italian cinema. His essay "Two Thousand Years of Storytelling about Jesus: How Faithful is Pasolini's *Gospel* to Matthew's Gospel?" will be published in *The Passion Story: From Visual Representation to Social Drama* (forthcoming). He is currently seeking a publisher for his dissertation, " '*Udiste che fu ditto…, ma io dico che…*': Pasolini as Interpreter of the Gospel of Matthew." If he was not a theologian, he would be making even less money as a photographer

Barbara Green is Professor of Biblical Studies at the Dominican School of Philosophy and Theology, Graduate Theological Union, Berkeley, California. She has written on various biblical characters (Ruth, Joseph, Saul, Jonah) and on theory (*Mikhail Bakhtin and Biblical Scholarship: An Introduction* [2000]; *How Are the Mighty Fallen: A Dialogical Study of King Saul in 1 Samuel* [2003]). She is currently working on the book of Deuteronomy and on Bible-based fiction. She is a Dominican Sister.

Bula Maddison is Visiting Assistant Professor of English at Mills College, Oakland, California, and Adjunct Instructor in Religious Studies at Saint Mary's College, Moraga, California. She is interested in Bible, Bible and modern literature, and Bible and culture. Among her recent publications is "A Bakhtinian Reading of Biblical Allusion in Dostoevsky's *Crime and Punishment*," in *Perspectives in Religious Studies* 32.3 (2005). Other recent work on Bakhtin and the Bible and modern literature can be seen at http://home. nwciowa.edu/wacome/bakhtinsbl.html, a site for participants in the SBL group on Bakhtin and the Biblical Imagination.

Carleen Mandolfo is Associate Professor of Religious Studies at Colby College in Waterville, Maine. Her work concentrates on lament psalms and Lamentations, as well as what these genres contribute to our understanding of biblical theology. She is the author of *God in the Dock: Dialogic Tension in Psalms of Lament* and *Daughter Zion Talks Back to the Prophets: A Dialogic Theology of the Book of Lamentations* (forthcoming). She is currently working on a book about cinematic representations of biblical stories and themes.

Christine Mitchell is Professor (without rank) of Hebrew Scriptures at St. Andrew's College in Saskatoon, Saskatchewan, Canada. She has been working with the Bakhtin corpus since the first day of graduate school and now cannot remember how to think in any other way. She has written articles on Chronicles, Haggai, and Xenophon. Her current project is a comparative postcolonial reading of Haggai, Zechariah, Malachi, and Persian imperial inscriptions.

Carol A. Newsom is Charles Howard Candler Professor of Old Testament at the Candler School of Theology, Emory University. Her most recent books include *The Book of Job: A Contest of Moral Imaginations* and *The Self as Symbolic Space: Constructing Identity and Community at Qumran*. She is currently working on a translation of the Qumran *Hodayot* and on a commentary on the book of Daniel for the Old Testament Library series.

Vernon K. Robbins is Professor of New Testament and Comparative Sacred Texts in the Department and Graduate Division of Religion at Emory University in Atlanta, Georgia. He was appointed Winship Distinguished Research Professor in 2001 and Professor Extraordinary at the University of Stellenbosch School of Theology, South Africa, 2006. His *Jesus the Teacher* (1984) launched sociorhetorical criticism in New Testament studies. *The Tapestry of Early Christian Discourse* (1996) and *Exploring the Texture of Texts* (1996) present programmatic strategies for the approach. A Festschrift in his honor, *Fabrics of Discourse* (2004), contains essays displaying sociorhetorical interpretation. Volume 1 of *The Invention of Christian Discourse: Wisdom, Prophecy and Apocalyptic* will appear in 2008. He is General Editor of Emory Studies in Early Christianity.

David M. Valeta (Ph.D. in Biblical Interpretation, University of Denver/Iliff School of Theology) is an Instructor in Religious Studies at the University of Colorado, Boulder.

Michael E. Vines is Chair of the Division of Humanities and Associate Professor of Religious Studies at Lees-McRae College in Banner Elk, North Carolina. The author of *The Problem of Markan Genre: The Gospel of Mark and the Jewish Novel* (2002), he continues to be interested in the theoreti-

cal problems surrounding literary genre and the usefulness of the theories of
Mikhail Bakhtin for biblical interpretation.

INDEX OF ANCIENT SOURCES

HEBREW BIBLE

New Testament

EXTRABIBLICAL LITERATURE

INDEX OF AUTHORS